D0369094

Beat The
Curve

Published by CelebrityPress®, Orlando, FL

CelebrityPress® is a registered trademark.

Printed in the United States of America.

ISBN: 978-0-9966887-1-0
LCCN: 2015949896

Most CelebrityPress® titles are available at special quantity discounts for bulk purchases for sales promotions, premiums, fundraising, and educational use. Special versions or book excerpts can also be created to fit specific needs.

For more information, please write:
CelebrityPress®
520 N. Orlando Ave, #2
Winter Park, FL 32789
or call 1.877.261.4930

Visit us online at: www.CelebrityPressPublishing.com

The World's Leading Entrepreneurs & Professionals

Reveal Their Secrets to **_Outperforming the Status Quo_** in

Health, Wealth & Success

Beat The
Curve

CELEBRITYPRESS®
Winter Park, Florida

CONTENTS

CHAPTER 1

THE KEY TO HAPPINESS

BY BRIAN TRACY

One of the most important discoveries of my young life was: "Your happiness should be your chief goal in life." When I realized the sweeping truth of this observation, the root of all religion, philosophy and great thought, I was never the same.

Whether or not something makes you happy should be the primary organizing principle of everything you do. It should be the standard by which you measure every choice and decision. Your ability to achieve your true happiness is the measure of how well you are really doing as a human being. Everything else should be subordinated to this key objective.

THE KEY TO HAPPINESS

The key to happiness is both simple and complex. It is the sum total result of more than 2000 years of philosophy, psychology, speculation and discussion about the meanings and sources of happiness, and how it might best be accomplished. From Aristotle in 340 BC through to the modern thinkers, speakers, and writers of today, the definition of happiness has hardly changed at all. It is the same for almost all men and women, in all countries and situations and in all walks of life.

The key to happiness is this: Dedicate yourself to the development of your natural talents and abilities by doing what you love to do, and doing it better and better, in the service of a cause that is greater than yourself.

This is a big statement and a big commitment. Being happy requires that you define your life in your own terms and then throw your whole heart into living your life to the fullest. In a way, happiness requires that you be perfectly selfish with yourself in the beginning so that you can be unselfish with others throughout your life.

PLEASE AT LEAST YOURSELF

In Edmund Rostand's play, *Cyrano de Bergerac*, the key figure Cyrano is asked why it is that he is so intensely individualistic and unconcerned with the opinions or judgments of others. He replies with these wonderful words, "I am what I am because early in life I decided that what I did or didn't do might please or displease others. Therefore, I would assure that, no matter what I did, one person would be happy. I resolved from that point forward that I would please at least myself in all things."

Your happiness likewise depends upon your ability to please at least yourself in all things as well. You can only be happy when you are living your life in the very best way possible. No one can define happiness for you. Only you know what makes you happy. Only you can do the things that make you happy. Just as you cannot make someone else happy, no one else can make you happy either. Happiness is an inside job.

NO SELFISHNESS INVOLVED

As it happens, there is a good deal of confusion on the subject of happiness. When I was growing up, I was told by older relatives that my own happiness was not important. I was reminded again and again that it was selfish for me to set my own happiness as a goal and to strive toward it. I was told that I was here on earth to make other people happy and that if I got a little happiness on the way through, I should consider myself lucky.

Many people fool themselves into thinking that they will give up their own personal happiness in order to make someone else happy, usually members of their family. But this way of thinking is completely confused. You can't give away something that you don't have. You can't reap where you haven't sown. Just as you cannot make someone else healthy by being sick, you cannot make someone else happy by being unhappy. People who allow themselves to think that they are being unhappy so that others can be happy are deluding themselves. They are rationalizing their own dissatisfaction by somehow pretending that it is noble to be miserable.

Study after study shows that the best thing that you can do for the people around you, especially the members of your family, is to be a happy person. If you want to raise happy children, be a happy parent. If you want to have a happy spouse, be a happy husband or wife. You can't get it out if you don't put it in. Only happy people can make other people happy.

YOU DESERVE TO BE HAPPY

A key question in the quest for happiness is whether or not you feel that you "deserve" to be happy. The question of deservingness is one of the most fundamental and disturbing questions that we have to deal with throughout life. Most of us have been brought up with feelings of guilt and unworthiness. Deep down inside, we often don't feel that we deserve to be truly happy. Later in life, these feelings of guilt and inferiority can lead us to sabotage our own happiness when we finally do achieve it.

The starting point of becoming a truly happy person is for you to accept that you deserve all the happiness you can honestly attain through your own efforts and the application of your special talents and abilities. And wonderfully enough, the more you like and respect yourself, the more deserving you will feel of the good things in life. The more deserving you feel, the more likely it will be that you will attain and hold on to the happiness you are working toward.

YOU ARE A PURPOSEFUL PERSON

In his Nicomachean Ethics, the philosopher Aristotle wrote about happiness and the human condition with such clarity and force that his works have been studied for more than 2000 years by students wanting to understanding the human condition in greater depth. Aristotle wrote that all human action is *teleological.* That is, it has an aim or goal. In other words, everything you do, you do for a reason. You act because you want to accomplish something. You want to get from where you are to where you want to be. Every action therefore has a cause and the cause is the effect that you expect to enjoy as the result of acting versus not acting.

Aristotle then went on to distinguish means and ends. He concluded that all action ultimately aims at a particular end, the end of all action. Everything prior to that final end or goal is a means toward it. And the final end or goal of all human behavior is the condition of happiness. Everyone wants to be happy. Everyone strives toward happiness in his or her own way in everything they do, every single day.

A BASIS FOR COMPARISON

When happiness becomes the organizing principle of your life, you can then compare every possible action, choice and decision against the standard of happiness to see whether it would make you happier or less happy. By using this standard, you will find that almost all of the problems of your life come from choices that you have made, or are currently making, that do not contribute to your happiness. When you develop sufficient courage and willpower to set your happiness as your highest standard, you will probably never make another mistake.

Of course, there are countless times where you will have to do little things that don't make you happy in the short term so that you can enjoy greater things in the long term that will make you very happy indeed. We call this "paying the price of success in advance."

You must pay your dues. If you want to enjoy the good life of success, prestige, respect and inner satisfaction that comes from successful selling, you must often get up early, make cold calls, prospect on rude or indifferent people to find business, and stay later at work than anyone else. Sometimes these interim steps or means to the success and happiness you desire don't make you happy immediately, but the happiness you achieve from attaining your goals is so great that it overwhelms and washes away the temporary inconveniences and dissatisfactions you had to endure in order to get there.

ACHIEVING YOUR GOALS

Earl Nightingale once said that, "Happiness is the progressive realization of a worthy ideal." You only feel really happy when you are moving, step-by-step, toward the accomplishment or attainment of something that is important and valuable to you. Since you are a goal-seeking organism, you are only really happy when you are moving toward clearly defined goals that you feel will enhance the quality of your life.

Since you can't be happy, truly happy, until you are clear about your amazing potential, it's very important that you take some time on a regular basis to analyze yourself and identify your strengths and weaknesses. There is an old saying that, "Success leaves tracks." You can often look back into your life, and look around you today, to identify who you really are and what you should really be doing with your life. Here are some ways to do this, and some questions to ask.

ASKING YOURSELF QUESTIONS

My favorite question is: "What one great thing would you **dare** to dream if you knew you could not fail?'

Imagine that you were absolutely guaranteed success in anything that you could set as a goal, big or small, short term or long term. Imagine that you had all the money, all the time, all the education, all the contacts, all the resources and everything else that you could possibly need to achieve any one big goal in life. What goal would have the greatest positive impact on your life?

This is an important question because when you think about what you would do if you had no limitations whatsoever, you often get a very clear idea of exactly what it is you should be doing with your life. All successful men and women are big dreamers. They imagine what their future would look like, perfect in every respect, and then they work every day toward that distant vision, that goal, or purpose. The step-by-step realization of their ideal makes them genuinely happy.

WHAT IS REALLY IMPORTANT?

You can also ask yourself, "What would I do, how would I spend my life if I learned today that I only had six months to live?" If you could only do a few things before your time on earth was over, what would they be? Where would you go? Who would you spend your time with? What would you want to complete before you crossed the great divide?

Often when you think about only having a short time left, you become very clear about exactly what it is that you should be doing with your life.

Both of these questions, "What one great thing would you dare to dream?" and "How would you spend your last six months?" are value questions. They go right to the very heart of the person you really are.

They often give you indications of what is really important to you. Mark Twain wrote that "The two most important days of your life are the day you are born, and the day you figure out why."

Look back over your life. What has been responsible for your greatest success so far? What had you done in the past that gave you a tremendous feeling of inner satisfaction? What have been your "peak experiences" in life? Look back over the months and years and identify your high points, your moments of greatest happiness and joy. What do these moments or experiences have in common? What are the sort of things that you have been doing, and who have you been doing them with, when you felt the very best about yourself and life?

YOUR HEART'S DESIRE

The wonderful thing about finding your heart's desire, the key to your happiness in life, is that you get indications of it throughout your life. The things that you were doing with the greatest joy and happiness between the ages of seven and fourteen often contain the seeds of what you should be doing as an adult if you want to fulfill your full potential and become everything you are capable of becoming.

Think back to when you were fourteen years old. What did you most enjoy doing? What results did you most enjoy getting? What kind of people did you most enjoy associating with? What sort of things did you most enjoy learning about? What sort of activities did you most enjoy engaging in?

YOUR SEARCH FOR MEANING

Dr. Victor Frankl, in his book, *Man's Search for Meaning*, said that you can divide the work you do in life into four potential categories. The first category consists of the things that are hard to learn and hard to do. For example, mathematics. You may have struggled with math in school, and you struggle with bookkeeping, accounting, financial statements and tax returns as an adult. You find mathematics hard to learn and hard to do. This is the sort of activity for which you are clearly not suited. No matter how much of it you do, or how well you get at it, you will never achieve any lasting satisfaction or happiness from it.

The next category consists of things that are hard to learn but easy to do. Tying your shoes is an example. Typing might be another. Riding a bicycle and driving a car are hard to learn but easy to do afterwards. These are seldom the sort of activities where you will feel terrific about yourself when you engage in them. They do not demand your very best.

EASY TO LEARN, HARD TO DO

The third type of activity consists of things that are easy to learn but hard to do. Physical labor falls into this category. Digging a ditch with a shovel or chopping wood with an ax are easy to learn but they are hard to do. And they never get any easier. There is no future in these activities either.

The fourth category is the key. These are things that are easy to do, and you don't even remember learning how to do them. You seem to have a natural talent for them. You picked these skills up almost automatically and did them with ease. When you are engaged in this sort of activity, time flies. They give you energy and you can hardly wait to get back to them.

The things that are easy to learn and are easy to do for you are the sort of things that you should be doing with your life. They indicate where your natural talents and abilities lie. It is in engaging in these activities with your whole heart, and committing yourself to becoming better and better at them, that will give you all the joy, satisfaction and happiness you could want in life.

YOUR AREA OF EXCELLENCE

Everyone has an area of excellence. Everyone has something that he or she can do, or has the potential to do, in an outstanding fashion. It may take weeks, months and even years for you to develop yourself in that area so that you can really perform at an extraordinary level, but the indications will be there. You will be strongly attracted to that sort of activity.

You like to read about it and talk about it and think about it. You admire people who are outstanding in that area. You look longingly at that field and wonder what it would be like to be in it and to be successful at it. This is very often your heart's desire. That area of activity, the area where you can become excellent, is probably what you were put on this earth to do.

Your area of excellence, your area of natural talent and ability, your heart's desire, will always involve doing something that somehow uplifts and enhances the life or work of other people. You can never be really happy until you know that what you are doing makes a difference in the world. The key to happiness is to know in your heart that you are making a contribution to the lives of other people.

THE SEVEN STEP FORMULA

There are seven steps in the formula for happiness, seven steps to turn the key in the lock that leads to life-long fulfillment, satisfaction and full self-expression.

Step number one is to "dream big dreams." Imagine that you could do, be, or have anything that you want in life. Mentally project yourself five or ten years into the future and think about what your life would be if every part of it was exactly as you would want it to be, and you were perfectly happy. What would you be doing? Who would be there? What would it look like? Don't hold back. Allowing yourself to dream is the first step.

The second step to happiness is to identify your unique talents and abilities. What makes you special, and different from anyone else? What is it that you do easily and well that seems to be difficult for most other people? What has been most responsible for your success in life to date? What do you most enjoy doing? As an exercise, ask your family members and close friends what they think you should be doing with your life. You will be amazed at how accurate and insightful the people around you can be. Often they will see talents and abilities in you that you might not have recognized or been willing to accept.

DO WHAT YOU LOVE

Step number three is to resolve to do what you love to do and to commit to becoming excellent at it. It is only when you are using your natural talents and abilities to fulfill your dreams and you are becoming better and better, and loving every minute of it, that you are really happy and excited about life.

There is a direct correlation between the feeling of growth and a feeling of motivation or personal power. It is when you feel that you are growing continually, becoming better and better at something that is important to you, that you really feel alive and in touch with your world. And remember, excellence is not a destination; it is a life-long journey.

Step number four is for you to accept 100 percent responsibility for yourself, your life and for everything that happens to you. Accept that you are where you are and what you are because of yourself, because you have chosen to be there. You are where you are and what you are as the direct consequences of your own decisions, your own actions and your own behaviors. If you want to change the future, you must change what you are doing in the present. True maturity begins when you finally realize that no one is coming to the rescue.

BE HONEST WITH YOURSELF

Step number five is to be absolutely honest with yourself. Refuse to engage in self-delusion. Refuse to pray for miracles or trust to luck. Refuse to engage in the fantasy that the Laws of Cause and Effect will somehow be suspended for you.

You know that everything that you get out will be a result of something that you have put in. You only gain success by paying the price of success, in full, in advance. The biggest mistake that some people make is that they are trying to get something for nothing.

Step number six is for you to set clear, specific written goals for everything you want in life. Less than three percent of adults have written goals, and everybody else works for them. You can actually tell how serious you are about achieving your goals by how disciplined you are to write them out in complete detail. The more you write and rewrite your goals, the more you come to believe that they are attainable. They more you believe that they are attainable, the more motivated you will be to overcome the inevitable obstacles and difficulties you will experience in achieving them. The very act of writing your goals down on paper will clarify your thinking, crystallize your objectives and concentrate your energies on doing the things that make you truly happy.

The seventh and final step on the road to happiness is to resolve to persist until you succeed. Just as the first part of courage is the courage to launch in faith toward your objectives, the second part of courage is your willingness to endure in the face of the inevitable disappointments and setbacks along the road.

PERSISTENCE IS THE KEY

Persistence is self-discipline in action. Your persistence is your measure of your belief in yourself and your ability to succeed. And the more you persist, the more you believe in yourself. The more you believe in yourself, the higher will be your self-esteem, self-respect and personal pride. And you learn to become a persistent person by practicing persistence at every opportunity. Eventually you will develop yourself to the point where you will become unstoppable in the pursuit of your goals and your objectives. You will move from positive thinking to positive *knowing*. You will develop a deep, inner conviction that there is nothing that you cannot accomplish if you stay at it long enough.

The ultimate goal of all human behavior is the achievement of happiness. But happiness is not an accident. Happy people are those who deliberately do the things that inevitably lead to happiness. Happy people are those who know what they want and who then throw their whole hearts into using their unique talents and abilities to the full to make a contribution to the world in the achievement of their goals.

You have the capacity to live a life filled with greater joy, satisfaction and happiness than you have ever imagined. There are no limitations except the ones that you put on yourself by your own thinking. You are put on this earth with a special purpose, programmed with unique talents and abilities that have not yet been fully tapped and utilized. When you set happiness as your highest goal and focus all of your energies on becoming the very best person you can possibly be in service to others, you unlock your potential, you open the door to happiness and your future becomes unlimited.

About Brian

Brian Tracy is Chairman and CEO of Brian Tracy International, a company specializing in the training and development of individuals and organizations. Brian's goal is to help people achieve their personal and business goals faster and easier than they ever imagined.

Brian Tracy has consulted for more than 1,000 companies and addressed more than 5,000,000 people in 5,000 talks and seminars throughout the US, Canada and 55 other countries worldwide. As a Keynote speaker and seminar leader, he addresses more than 250,000 people each year.

For more information on Brian Tracy programs, go to: www.briantracy.com

CHAPTER 2

MAKE YOUR BUSINESS MISSION-DRIVEN! THE THREE-STAGE PROCESS TO BEAT THE CURVE

BY NICK NANTON & JW DICKS

The brand was at a standstill.

Dove Soap, a product created in 1953 by Lever Brothers, had been a steady seller since its inception. Its innovative "beauty bar," a soap that was composed of one-quarter cleansing cream, was sold on the basis of straightforward marketing messages touting its uniqueness. Taglines such as "Dove Won't Dry Your Skin Like Soap Can" and "Dove is Good for Your Skin" had a built-in appeal to its female target audience, and, by the 1990's, it was a $200 million brand.

By the early 2000's, however, Dove had seemingly flown as high as it could with its traditional marketing approach. Up until then, the beauty brand, like its competition, had always used attractive models to demonstrate its product – but more and more, those attractive models seemed like an alien species to the majority of women. Result? Dove seemed like a dated commodity that was quickly losing its luster.

So - how could the 1950's beauty bar be made relevant in the 21st Century?

Unilever, which had absorbed Lever Brothers a decade earlier, decided rather than simply introduce a new glitzy marketing campaign, it was time to dig deeper – and actually reexamine what exactly beauty meant to women in this day and age. That was the kind of undertaking that would require a great deal of time, effort and money; the multinational corporation was willing to commit to a heavy investment in all three.

Unilever commissioned a global study on the uneasy relationship between women and their appearance. And this study was the real deal, based on quantitative data collected from a global study of 3,200 women, aged 18 to 64. StrategyOne, an applied research firm based in New York, managed the study in collaboration with Harvard University and the London School of Economics. Interviews were conducted across ten countries: the U.S., Canada, Great Britain, Italy, France, Portugal, Netherlands, Brazil, Argentina and Japan. And never once was the Dove brand mentioned or alluded to in any of these interviews.

In other words, this was not brand research – this was *human* research.

And the results were fairly shocking. Only 2% of the women respondents felt comfortable describing themselves as "beautiful." 40% of women "strongly disagreed" that they were beautiful.[1] The conclusion of the study came down to this: "The definition of beauty had become limiting and unattainable."[2] That meant Dove had to figure out how to sell a beauty product to women who didn't think of themselves as beautiful.

The company's solution? Expand the definition of beauty.

That effort began with a revolutionary photo exhibit, "Beyond Compare: Women Photographers on Real Beauty," a show organized by Dove and Ogilvy & Mather. The showing featured work from world-famous female photographers showcasing so-called "ordinary women," photographed like models. In 2005, this concept expanded into a print campaign also centered on portraying real women with real bodies, but treating them as though they were professional models in print ads and photos.

This attention-getting approach generated such huge media conversations both in social media and on television talk shows that

1. "The Real Truth about Beauty: A Global Report" - Findings of the Global Study on Women, Beauty and Well-Being, September 2004, available at http://www.clubofamsterdam.com/contentarticles/52%20 Beauty/dove_white_paper_final.pdf
2. http://www.dove.us/Social-Mission/campaign-for-real-beauty.aspx

Dove's ad agency estimated it got 30 times the marketing value from the ad space it purchased. That success prompted a continuation and expansion of the campaign. In 2006, Dove produced several compelling videos chronicling the world's unrealistic expectations of female beauty – all of which went viral. One of them, "Evolution," alone garnered over 18 million views on YouTube.[3] Dove further cemented its commitment to this social issue by aligning itself with the Girl Scouts, the Boys and Girls Clubs of America and Girls Inc. to promote self-esteem in girls about their looks.

Dove's Real Beauty campaign continues to this day, attracting enormous media attention and creating heated controversy. Their Facebook page alone has 19 million "likes." According to Sharon MacLeod, vice president of Unilever North America Personal Care, "The conversation is as relevant and fresh today as it was 10 years ago, I believe we'll be doing this campaign 10 years from now."[4]

Why is she so sure about that? Perhaps because the former $200-million-dollar-a-year brand is now worth about $4 *billion* – purely as a result of the company transforming itself from an everyday soap seller into a Mission-Driven Brand.

If you've never understood what the power of a mission can do for a nuts-and-bolts business, the preceding Dove story illustrates what a difference it can make. If a fifty-year-old fading soap company can completely reinvigorate its image and become one of the most talked-about brands of our times – simply by taking on a mission that's more about society than marketing - it's hard to see why any other kind of business would be unable to do the same, no matter how old or seemingly set in its ways it happens to be.

Does that include *your* business?

Think about it. What if you were to become a Mission-Driven business? How might a mission transform both your brand and your business results? How might it attract a whole new base of customers and clients – as well as boost your profile and your prestige?

---

3. https://www.youtube.com/watch?v=iYhCn0jf46U

4. Bahadur, Nina. "Dove 'Real Beauty' Campaign Turns 10: How A Brand Tried To Change The Conversation About Female Beauty," *The Huffington Post*, January 21, 2014 http://www.huffingtonpost.com/2014/01/21/dove-real-beauty-campaign-turns-10_n_4575940.html

If you really want to beat the curve, becoming Mission-Driven can make that crucial difference and lift you above your competition. In this chapter, we're going to help you explore your Mission-Driven possibilities by revealing the three stages you must work through in order to put your specific mission into action. And remember, even if you *already* run a business, you can easily adapt it to a Mission-Driven one (in the same way Dove Soap did in the story that opened this chapter).

We uncovered these three stages through our work with more than 2000 clients at our agency. Our interest is always in helping them develop the potential of their businesses to the fullest. That's of course not an entirely altruistic impulse on our part – because, frankly, if our clients don't succeed, we don't succeed.

One of the easiest ways for us to set the foundation for our process is to relate it to a concept you may have already heard of. That concept is entitled "The Golden Circle," articulated in a world-famous TED talk given by ex-advertising executive Simon Sinek[5]. The basis of the Golden Circle is Sinek's analysis of the reason many of the world's most effective individuals and companies find such high levels of success. His research demonstrated that success is a result of "Inside-Out" thinking – a progression from "Why" to "How" to, finally, "What."

Here's Sinek's graphic representation of this progression:

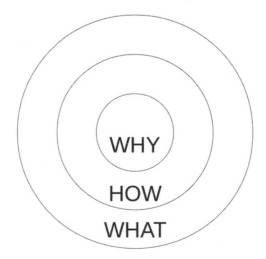

WHY

HOW

WHAT

5. For more on the Golden Circle, Sinek's TED talk can be viewed at this link: http://www.ted.com/talks/
simon_sinek_how_great_leaders_inspire_action?language=en

The successful people and companies Sinek profiles always start with the "Why"; in other words, before they started out towards a major accomplishment, they keyed into their inner passions and what mattered to them most. Their next step was to figure out "How" they were going to line up their life direction with those passions – and then, finally, they would take a look at "What" they were going to do to bring all that to fruition.

How is that different from most people's approaches? According to Sinek, too many individuals instead start with their "What," leading them into lives with which they don't feel a real connection. These are the kinds of people that take a job simply to have a job and don't make enough of an effort to explore what they *really* want to do. Granted, we all have to do things to support ourselves, but when that short-term need dominates our long-term lives, we often dull the real individual power that comes from our intuition and true inner motivations.

What appeals to us about Sinek's model is it provides the perfect path for taking a personal mission from the theoretical to the practical. An idea isn't really worth a lot until you find a way to actually put it to work in the real world – and we've developed a process designed to do just that, and as you'll see, it aligns very well with Sinek's "Why," "How" and "What" progression.

Now, let's go more into detail about the 3 stages of our Action Process.

STAGE ONE: YOUR "WHY"
- DISCOVERING YOUR LIFE MISSION

This is where it all begins.

Your Life Mission lays the foundation of your Mission-Driven organization. It represents one or more aspects of what you care about the most – your deepest passion, your greatest talent and/or your biggest social concern. Your Life Mission is your greatest motivator to both dream and achieve.

Here are three historic figures who have readily identifiable Life Missions that you're almost certainly already aware of:

- **Mother Theresa:** To continually help the poor and needy.
- **Mahatma Gandhi:** To fight for justice, freedom and dignity for all.

- **Steve Jobs:** A relentless drive to create and innovate with technology.

In the case of all three of the above individuals, most people immediately think of their Life Mission when they hear their names. It defined them more than anything else about them.

The right Life Mission will do the same for you. It will make you identifiable and memorable – as well as shape others' opinions of you. It will also draw supporters to your side and create a directed energy that helps you clear a strong and specific path. But your Life Mission will only succeed at all that if comes from something strong and authentic within you.

The bottom line of your Life Mission is your "Why." It ties directly into your life motivations as well as your greatest enthusiasms in your day-to-day life.

It's what gives you *purpose*.

STAGE TWO: YOUR "HOW"
– FINDING THE VEHICLE TO ACTIVATE
YOUR LIFE MISSION

If your Life Mission represents the idealistic "Why" that motivates you, then your company or non-profit represents the practical *Vehicle* that becomes "How" – the way you work towards your Life Mission in the real world.

For example, you might be someone who in general loves gourmet food – that's your Life Mission. But what do you do with that love – how do you fulfill your Life Mission? Do you open a restaurant? Become a chef? Or a food critic? The choice of Vehicle for your Life Mission will most likely be made based on your other talents, interests, resources and opportunities.

More on that later. For now, let's take the three individuals whose Life Missions we just described – and talk about the Vehicles they used to realize them.

- Mother Theresa decided her Life Mission to help the needy needed as its Vehicle an infrastructure to enable her to help the impoverished on a global level. With that in mind, she founded the Missionaries of Charity, a Roman Catholic religious congregation, which currently consists of over 4,500 sisters and operates health clinics and programs for the disadvantaged in over 130 countries.

- Gandhi's Life Mission of justice and freedom drove him to lead India to gain independence from British rule. He used as his Vehicle political power by working with the Indian Congress to build his national influence, and then, in turn, inspiring his countrymen to participate in mass protests demanding self-governance for India.

- Steve Jobs' Life Mission to innovate found its Vehicle through the founding and running Apple, and leading that corporation to release a steady stream of groundbreaking and ridiculously successful products.

In each case, an authentic Life Mission manifested itself in a Vehicle that allowed the accomplishment of the mission. Your Vehicle therefore, is your "How" – it's how your Life Mission gets out of your brain and into the world.

STAGE THREE: YOUR "WHAT"
– DETERMINING YOUR ANNUAL CAMPAIGN

Rome wasn't built in a day. And you certainly can't accomplish a true Life Mission in 24 hours or less either. That's why you need to figure out "What" to do with your Vehicle to move towards your Life Mission in a thought-out step-by-step process.

Many people get caught up in the fact that they aren't able to visualize what their life or business will look like in 5, 10, 15, or even 20 years. While we absolutely think it's important to have long-term goals, we also don't want your inability to see the future (believe us, we can't either!) to keep you from getting started. Creating a succession of short-term plans designed to take you closer to your ultimate ambitions also enables you to change up things more easily when the unexpected throws you for a loop. Because, as former boxer Mike Tyson once said, "Everybody has a plan until they get punched in the mouth." In life and business, we often get some blows we didn't expect, which is why we believe employing *Annual Campaigns* is the best ongoing strategy.

In our mind, every single calendar year a new Annual Campaign should be put into place that will enable a company or nonprofit to reach some significant benchmark in the effort to reach its Life Mission. This is where the rubber meets the road; practicality is the order of the day and a nuts-and-bolts approach must be found that everyone you work with can understand and get on board with.

If you've read or seen any of the numerous Steve Jobs' biographies, you know that this man rode herd on Apple execs and employees to deliver what he knew he wanted. From the iMac to iTunes to the iPod and the iPhone, he constantly provided an updated Annual Campaign to take the company to the next level. Now, he didn't specifically call it that, but there *is* a reason why Apple holds its Worldwide Developer Conference once a year; it's the same reason many other companies host annual gatherings and conferences. It's a whole lot easier to think in one year increments than it is to plot out a complete path towards a lifetime ambition.

From the Life Mission to the Vehicle to a series of Annual Missions, the Mission-Driven process progresses from your innermost passions to incremental real-world stages that bring your Life Mission to life in a substantial and concrete way. Simply put, it's "What" you need to do within your Vehicle to reach your goals.

This, then, is our version of the Golden Circle we discussed earlier:

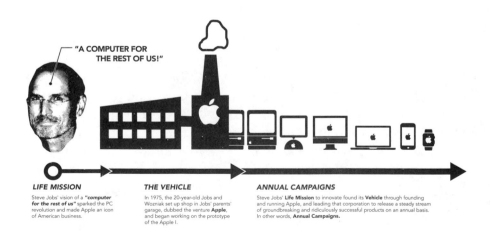

LIFE MISSION

Steve Jobs' vision of a *"computer for the rest of us"* sparked the PC revolution and made Apple an icon of American business.

THE VEHICLE

In 1975, the 20-year-old Jobs and Wozniak set up shop in Jobs' parents' garage, dubbed the venture **Apple**, and began working on the prototype of the Apple I.

ANNUAL CAMPAIGNS

Steve Jobs' **Life Mission** to innovate found its **Vehicle** through founding and running Apple, and leading that corporation to release a steady stream of groundbreaking and ridiculously successful products on an annual basis. In other words, **Annual Campaigns.**

As the graphic illustrates, the Life Mission starts deep within you, from vital aspects of your identity (your "Why"). The Vehicle then helps you connect your Life Mission to the outside world with through an infrastructure designed with that in mind (your "How"). Finally, your Annual Campaigns are engineered to move you closer and closer to your Life Mission through practical steps (your "What"). In this progression, you start from a place of pure ideals – and finally discover how you can put them to work in a less-than-ideal society.

In our forthcoming book on Mission-Driven companies, you'll discover an Action Process we've developed which is designed to help you work through these three stages yourself in order to transform your business into a Mission-Driven one. In that book, you'll also discover the incredible advantages being Mission-Driven bestows on your business or nonprofit organization. It's a lot of valuable information we don't have the space to include here (that's why we had to write a whole book!) – but trust us when we tell you that becoming Mission-Driven, when done properly, always helps you beat the curve!

About Nick

A 3-Time Emmy Award Winning Director, Producer and Filmmaker, Nick Nanton, Esq., is known as the Top Agent to Celebrity Experts® around the world for his role in developing and marketing business and professional experts, through personal branding, media, marketing and PR.

Nick serves as the CEO of The Dicks + Nanton Celebrity Branding Agency, an international branding and media agency with more than 2200 clients in 33 countries. Nick has produced large scale events and television shows with the likes of Steve Forbes, Brian Tracy, President George H.W. Bush, Jack Canfield Jack Canfield (Creator of the *Chicken Soup for the Soul* Series), Michael E. Gerber, Tom Hopkins and many more.

Nick is recognized as one of the top thought-leaders in the business world, speaking on major stages internationally and having co-authored 36 best-selling books, including *The Wall Street Journal* Best-Seller, *StorySelling™*.

Nick has been seen in *USA Today, The Wall Street Journal, Newsweek, BusinessWeek, Inc. Magazine, The New York Times, Entrepreneur® Magazine, Forbes,* FastCompany. com and has appeared on ABC, NBC, CBS, and FOX television affiliates around the country, as well as E!, CNN, FOX News, CNBC, MSNBC and hosts his own series on the Bio! channel, *Portraits of Success.*

Nick is a member of the Florida Bar, a voting member of The National Academy of Recording Arts & Sciences (Home to The GRAMMYs), a member of The National Academy of Television Arts & Sciences (Home to the EMMYs), The National Academy of Best-Selling Authors, and serves on the Innovation Board of the XPRIZE Foundation, a non-profit organization dedicated to bringing about "radical breakthroughs for the benefit of humanity" through incentivized competition, best known for it's Ansari XPRIZE which incentivized the first private space flight and was the catalyst for Richard Branson's Virgin Galactic. Nick spends his spare time serving as an Elder at Orangewood Church, working with Young Life, Downtown Credo Orlando, Entrepreneurs International and rooting for the Florida Gators with his wife Kristina and their three children, Brock, Bowen and Addison.

Learn more at: www.NickNanton.com and
www.CelebrityBrandingAgency.com

About JW

JW Dicks, Esq., is America's foremost authority on using personal branding for business development. He has created some of the most successful brand and marketing campaigns for business and professional clients to make them the credible celebrity experts in their field and build multi-million dollar businesses using their recognized status.

JW Dicks has started, bought, built, and sold a large number of businesses over his 39-year career and developed a loyal international following as a business attorney, author, speaker, consultant, and business experts' coach. He not only practices what he preaches by using his strategies to build his own businesses, he also applies those same concepts to help clients grow their business or professional practice the ways he does.

JW has been extensively quoted in such national media as *USA Today,* the *Wall Street Journal, Newsweek, Inc.*, Forbes.com, CNBC.com, and *Fortune Small Business.* His television appearances include ABC, NBC, CBS and FOX affiliate stations around the country. He is the resident branding expert for *Fast Company's* internationally syndicated blog and is the publisher of *Celebrity Expert Insider*, a monthly newsletter targeting business and brand building strategies.

JW has written over 22 books, including numerous best-sellers, and has been inducted into the National Academy of Best-Selling Authors. JW is married to Linda, his wife of 39 years, and they have two daughters, two granddaughters and two Yorkies. JW is a 6th generation Floridian and splits his time between his home in Orlando and beach house on the Florida west coast.

CHAPTER 3

THE MILLENNIALS GENERATION: HOW TO CAPTURE OUR ATTENTION AND BUSINESS

BY ALEX MORTON

Let's face it, the economy is down, the job market is terrible, student loan debt is the number one debt in America, all the baby boomers (a.k.a. our parents) are still working, and it's not 1960 anymore! The old way, the old system, the old ways of thinking and living life are simply out dated.

THE idea of going to school to get good grades, then taking out massive loans to go to college to get more good grades, then to graduate and get a job where someone tells you when to show up, when to go home, how much money you're allowed to make, and when you can pee / take your family on vacation. . . is literally insane. Oh, not to mention, you usually have to work 40 hours a week for 40 years of your life, only to then try and retire on 40% of your earned income. Sounds pretty foolish to me. And many of us Millennials aren't willing to take the status quo. Here's a question for you. When's the last time you went to a retirement party? Exactly, my point here people. It's time to wake up, get fired up, and take control of your life!

Now that that's out of my system I want to give you some background on this whole Young People Revolution phenomenon that has taken place in the world economy. It seems every company, every CEO and everyone with a brain is trying to tap into and ultimately dominate this segment of the market. Below I am going to tell you exactly why everyone is focusing on how to recruit millennials, attract millennials, and break into this marketplace. This year, 2015, the Millennial generation is projected to surpass the "biggest of all time" Baby Boomer generation as the largest living generation. Yep, you heard it here first, the Millennials are surpassing the baby boomers, baby! Us millennials are people aged 18-34. The Census Bureau projects that the Millennial population was 74.8 million in 2014. By 2015, Millennials will increase in size to 75.3 million and become the biggest group. Once one gets the attention and consumption from this market, one not only wins, but dominates. What we are talking about here is a big deal. The Millennials (YPR) are about to be the biggest living group of individuals. Pretty soon here, the Millennials are going to be running the entire world.

You may be asking yourself, "Why should I focus on young people? … Why should I go out there and try to attract young people into my business? … Why is this important, and how the heck can I even do this?" These are all valid and great questions. Again, I'm a young guy, excited about life, have earned a lot of money, and have traveled the world. I'm not writing this for an ego trip, I am writing this because I know I can help you tremendously. I am also aware that there are many "young people gurus" out there traveling around and speaking on these topics, yet they're 40 years old. That's like me trying to explain to you what it feels like to be on your death bed. I've never been on my death bed and don't intend to be on it any time soon. I built my organization from 0 - 15,000 people in all 50 states and 30+ countries and the majority of my group are young people. I know what I am talking about here and if you want to break into this segment of the marketplace, listen up, because I'm about to give you all my secrets.

Being one of the first people in a multi-billion dollar industry to crack this younger market wide open, there have definitely been some perks and also some punishments. Starting out, I was attending Arizona State University (81,000 students); yes, I said 81 freaking thousand, and I noticed how most of the students disliked being told what to do, when to do it, when to be in class, when homework and exams were due, all of that nonsense. I remember sitting in Hayden Library studying aka memorizing some random stuff about rain forest biomes thinking to myself, "How in God's green earth is this information ever going to help me make money, and this totally sucks how I am going to sit here for the next 8 hours in order to simply memorize facts, then vomit them all over the exam at 9 am, just so I can pass the course." You see, way before I got into my current company, I was hungry and looking for something to get excited about. Most of the time, walking on campus, it looks like a scene out of a zombie apocalypse movie or better yet, mindless robots stumbling all over the place. I know some of you are thinking I'm an ass, I hate school, I dislike college, and I have to admit you're completely wrong. I have a degree, my little sister has a degree, and I support school. I'm also not down on jobs I'm just up on opportunity. Re-focusing here, there are thousands of college campuses with hundreds of thousands of college kids roaming all over there. Again, most have no idea why they're there, most dislike class, and a lot of people are looking for an opportunity. It is literally the perfect storm of opportunity. If you are reading this and you're involved in business then in my personal humble opinion you should be focusing a lot of your time, energy, effort and money on capitalizing on this market. Back at ASU, I saw an enormous need to fill.

REMEMBER IN BUSINESS IT IS OUR GOAL TO SOLVE PROBLEMS AND FILL PEOPLES NEEDS.

When I saw the opportunity that allowed me to become a millionaire, eventually it hit me and it simply all made sense, and when things make sense, they make dollars, a lot of them! When I started my business back in 2011, I got very excited about what was possible. You see, I didn't need any guarantees, all I needed to know was that it was possible. It started with a small group in my dorm room and turned into a phenomenon. I now want to explain to you what I did, how I did it, and how you can 'blow it up' with your business. The YPR (millennials) are taking over the world, and if and when you penetrate this market, you can go from zero to hero in a hurry.

HOW TO GET THE MILLENNIALS INTO **YOUR BUSINESS**

We, the millennials are different types of people. We didn't really grow up playing tag or hide and seek. It was more like Nintendo 64 and Xbox. Point is, we are very different than the baby boomers and everyone else who came before us. We like things simple, hassle-free, easy, and efficient. We get bored easily, we all basically have ADD, and we want freedom. We want complete financial and time freedom. Again, I can't teach you chemistry, biology, or Japanese, but I can help you break into this marketplace. There are several things you must understand and master before you are going to successfully get 'us' to pay attention. Something to understand when approaching or talking to YPR's is that we would like you to be normal. We are young enough to remember how weird and creepy our 4th grade teacher was or our high school math substitute teacher. If you even remotely come close to resembling that, you're done before you even get started. Nobody likes being sold, especially us. If you come off crazy aggressive we immediately turn off. Instead of shoving your product or service down our throats and trying to "close the deal" its better to come off as a friend first, business associate second. Keyword here is "chill," this isn't the boiler room or Glengarry Glen ross. Relax and create conversation. We want you to ask us questions. We love talking about ourselves. Get to know us. I personally think that anytime you have a conversation with a YPR, your goal is to connect with them.

I think a good acronym for this is F.O.R.M = Family, Occupation, Recreation, and Motivation.

Once you get good at prospecting and connecting with YPR›s, within the first 5-10 minutes of conversation you should get 'them' talking about their family, what they do for work, what they do for fun, and what they are motivated by. When you talk to us you must genuinely get interested in knowing about us, not just faking it for a sale. When I speak all over the world I always talk about how everyone should always be asking great questions. In fact, I guarantee you are one question away from a major breakthrough in your business. Girls love to talk about themselves, guys love to talk about themselves, and Millennials really like to talk about themselves. So, you, being a professional business person, need to ask great questions to get us talking. If you can get a prospect talking enough about enough topics, you will find what I like to call the hot button.

Let's say you're an affiliate with a company that has an insanely healthy energy drink and you're getting compensated for the amount of sales volume that you and your team produce. Obviously, you want to prospect and eventually recruit people with big social networks, and those people are the millennials. You walk into a sushi bar or a Starbucks and you strike up a conversation with the waitress or barista. Your end goal as of now is to build the relationship, gather the contact information, and set up the next exposure. It is not to "slam-bam-thank you-mam" them into purchasing your healthy energy drinks and getting them excited about your business right off the bat.

We Millennials are visual people. If your end goal is to sell us anything, you should be utilizing tools. What I mean by tools for example is a great YouTube video, a vibrant brochure, and samples of your products! Later in my career, I didn't leave my condo without a cooler filled up with my company's products. Wherever I went, I sampled out the products. Every time I walked, and still to this day walk, into a gym to workout, I have my company's ready-to-drink protein shake, chilled, and ready to go. When I go out and have fun with friends, I always have some ice cold energy drinks in my pockets. Walking into a club or bar with bulging pockets may seem a little odd to some, but if doing that over and over again paid you $1,000,000, would you do it? Thought so. Also, if you're recruiting them into a company or organization, talk about the family atmosphere, high energy culture, and positive, motivated people they will get to surround themselves with. We "younger people" love being around high energy people and places.

One of the biggest reasons why our team grew quickly to 15,000 people was because everyone loved the 'campfire affect.' Our company's conventions, events, meetings were always focused on creating the greatest atmosphere possible. Also, something so small like a smile can cause such a big emotional shift in the other person. This one may sound quite funny to you, but you have no idea how many conversations and relationships I have created by simply smiling at people. Not too many people smile much anymore, so when you go out of your way to smile, people take notice!

Last, but certainly not least, you must be willing to do whatever it takes. If that means prospecting on a college campus for 4 hours in the hot sun or hanging out in a Starbucks for an entire day to meet new people, you must always encompass the attitude of doing whatever it takes. I can give you story after story over the years where I did a certain activity that I did not thoroughly enjoy day-in and day-out in order to grow my business. It's NOT going to be easy, nothing easy is ever worthwhile, but it will be WORTH it, I guarantee you that.

About Alex

Alex Morton was born October 21, 1989 in Houston, Texas. He is the only son of Marc and Sandi Morton. And he has one sister Maddie Morton who also works on his team, and has already hit a 6-figure income at the age of 21. He graduated from Bexley High School in Columbus, Ohio in 2008. He has a Bachelor of Science Degree in Communications from Arizona State University where he graduated in 2012. While Alex was a full-time student at ASU, he obtained an Arizona Real Estate License in 2009, and worked part-time selling and leasing condos.

Alex was introduced to Network Marketing (Vemma Nutrition) in 2011, and in March of 2014 at the age of 24, he became the youngest Royal Ambassador in his company›s(Vemma's) history, which is one of the top positions in their compensation plan. In March 2014, he hit the $1 million mark in career earnings, and has now earned over $2 million in career earnings by his 26th Birthday. He also helped develop 21 additional six-figure income earners on his team, which covered all of the USA, Canada, Mexico and 30 other countries around the world. He also assisted several hundred team members in qualifying for the 'company-paid-for' BMW's.

Career highlights: Alex was nominated for Distributor of the Year by the Academy of Multi Level Marketing Awards. Alex was featured in the book, *The Four Year Career.* Alex was also featured in an article in the Rolling Stone Magazine in 2014. He was also the youngest featured speaker in the history of Eric Worre's Go Pro Event in Las Vegas where he spoke to a live audience of 10,000 people plus a Live Stream around the World. Alex has spoken at Conventions around the world and has been interviewed in multiple podcasts including: addicted2success.com, Power Players with Grant Cardone, knowledgeformen.com. MLM nation.net, Awaken your Alpha on iTunes, among others.

You can follow Alex on:
Facebook- Alex Morton
Twitter-@AlexmortonYPR
Instagram-AlexMortonMindset, and
Periscope-@AlexmortonYPR.

You can also learn more about Alex at his website: www.AlexMortonMindset.com.

CHAPTER 4

UNLOCK YOUR POTENTIAL AND START A SUCCESS REVOLUTION

BY MARK T. ARSENAULT

Imagine you are in a place in your life where things feel hopeless, where past mistakes are thrown in your face daily, persistent reminders of your failure and obstacles to doing something positive with your life. Imagine facing people you dislike and distrust every day. There's no escaping them. Imagine sharing a home with them, with no locks on the doors or windows. How can you sleep knowing someone could literally stab you in the back or cut your throat while you sleep? Imagine facing constant pressure to break the rules, to harm someone else, or to abuse drugs. Imagine everyone you associate with feels hopeless, afraid and angry like you do. Any thoughts you express about making a change or being positive are quickly shot down and ridiculed. Imagine feeling like life holds nothing but more of the same, day after day, month after month, year after year. The drugs you have easy access to start looking like the only option to numb the pain and fear.

Many of us have had some of these feelings at one time or another. We all have our own prison. There are literal prisons, and there are others that we deal with. Perhaps you feel trapped in a bad relationship or stuck in a bad job (or a good job with bad management). If you feel a lack of freedom to do what you want to do and go where you want to go, you're living in a kind of prison.

There are a growing number of people who live the existence I described above every day in a very literal sense. They are the incarcerated; more than two million men and women incarcerated in United States Federal and State prisons, and County jails by the end of 2011 (source: U.S. Bureau of Justice Statistics) at a cost of nearly $300 billion a year.

From 2007 to 2012, I worked in a special assignment position in one of two large correctional facilities for a local law enforcement agency. I was assigned as the Intelligence Analyst in the jail's Investigative Services Unit (commonly referred to as "ISU" by the staff). While I was assigned to ISU, I had two life-changing experiences.

The first began in July, 2009, when I was diagnosed with colorectal cancer, which was linked to my use of tobacco products. That journey is detailed in my book, *Semicolon; Memoir of a Colon Cancer Survivor*. What's worth relating here is that for the year following my diagnosis, I was undergoing treatments, which included chemotherapy and radiation therapy, and two surgeries. To say the least I wasn't at my best. That journey through cancer put my mind in a very different place. It may well have contributed to how I came to my second experience: the creation of an in-custody gang diversion program.

While working in ISU, I was blessed to work with one officer in particular, Deputy Tammy Gillock. Together we had more than two decades of experience in dealing with gang members, both in cooperative and less-than-cooperative circumstances. We'd interviewed suspects and victims, received statements, confessions, and gathered untold amounts of intelligence, all with the focus of making our facility more secure and increasing the safety of the staff and the inmates. We were good at our job and to this day we have an excellent track record of establishing rapport with the inmates we interact with. Part of that came easier because of our understanding of what we called the "jail culture."

Tammy and I started identifying a growing number of inmates who showed signs of wanting to make different choices but not knowing how. We realized that we could use our investigative and interpersonal skills to reach people for change, to encourage them to choose a different path for themselves. To put it succinctly, we wanted to give hope, reduce recidivism and ultimately save lives.

We began working on an in-custody gang diversion program. We reviewed and hand-selected class materials, selected from an established evidence-based program, and we developed a curriculum. We added "free talk" time and a message of positivity to the program, what we termed "success strategies," as well as other non-traditional elements (such as opening each class with a music video and motivational video), that we felt would bolster the morale and thus, the participation, of the inmates in the program.

It took us a few months to put together, though it took nearly three years to get approval from the administration and some meager funding to get it started. Our program was added to the variety of classes offered through the reentry services program that resulted from recently-enacted prison realignment legislation. In July of 2012, our gang diversion program began and we co-facilitated our first class of 55 volunteer street gang members and associates.

I call them "volunteers" because every one of the participants voluntarily opted-in to the program, a program that had a zero tolerance for gang activity. You see, after each of our recruiting "presentations," which took about 10 to 15 minutes each, we had roughly two-thirds of the people we spoke to agree to at least try our program. That's nearly a 70 percent opt-in rate among gang members in custody, addressed in a group setting, to participate in an in-custody gang diversion program where they would not be allowed to "politic" or engage in gang activity. Many of our co-workers and supervisors at the jail were in utter disbelief at how many prisoners we spoke to were not only willing to try the program, but spoke up in front of other prisoners to do so. Now that's truly an example of 'beating the curve'!

At the classroom, the participants were greeted by me and my partner. We literally greeted each and every inmate as they came through the door, shook their hand, and thanked them for coming. We began reinforcing from the very first moment of class time that life was about choices. We reinforced that they made a choice to be there by welcoming them and thanking them. Some of them looked confused, while others smiled and soaked up the positive attention.

As they found their seats, we played a music video with the lyrics on the screen. We did this at the start of every class, and each song was specifically chosen for its positive message. After hearing the song and reading the lyrics, we would talk briefly about it and encourage the class to share what it meant to them.

After the song we usually shared a light-hearted, humorous video. It was solely intended to get people laughing and loosen up. Being in jail can be stressful. We wanted to do what we could to change the atmosphere, to allow them to "forget" the negative while they were in class.

The second video was motivational. We introduced the participants to a variety of speakers, from Eric "ET the Hip Hop Preacher" Thomas and world-renowned leadership expert, John C. Maxwell, to legendary speakers and authors like Brian Tracy, Tony Robbins, Og Mandino, Leo Buscaglia, and Jim Rohn. After the motivational video, we opened the class for discussion.

Following this opening session, which might last anywhere from 15 minutes to an hour, we got into the actual gang-intervention curriculum. This was, not surprisingly, the least popular portion of the class but they "endured it" because it was part of the program. And, frankly, they really enjoyed the rest of it.

It was amazing to observe how these men, many of them in and out of jail for all of their adult life, reacted to the information in these videos. We observed a noticeable shift in their behavior, how they thought and this was reflected in the choices they made on a daily basis.

For most of the participants, our program exposed them to many "firsts." Our class was the first time most of them were exposed to the concept of personal development. It was the first time most of them had even heard of the speakers. It was the first time most had been thanked by an officer (one man told me it was the first time an officer ever shook his hand). For most it was the first time they had "a good time" in jail. It was a change for everyone. It was a change in thinking, in expectations, and in attitudes.

By the end of the second session we asked them to come up with a class motto. They chose "Unlock your potential." It seemed appropriate on several levels, so it stuck. I'm fond of another saying, as well. "It's now o'clock," because there's no time like the present to start making positive change in your life.

Soon, they would enter the classroom, remain standing at their seats until everyone was inside when we would ask "What time is it?" In unison, all 55 inmates would shout "It's now o'clock!" Then we'd ask, "What's our motto?" They'd shout "Unlock your potential!" If we didn't feel their authenticity or sincerity we'd ask them again, and they would respond even louder. On several occasions the officers in the control room would ask us what we were doing that was causing the inmates to yell so loud. "Oh, you know," we'd say, "just doing our thing."

One of the memorable moments was about a month into the curriculum. Even after half a dozen class sessions, most of the participants still weren't opening up and actually talking much. To keep this in perspective, among inmates, talking about personal experiences in prison (or jail) with officers is considered "snitching" in jail culture. It isn't condoned by your fellow inmates. To reveal details about one's criminal life, about one's associates or one's gang to an officer is tantamount to becoming a target for beatings, or worse. But that was outside of this class. One of the rules of our program was that each participant agreed to leave "jail politics" outside the classroom. Until now, the "no talking" rule still held sway over the men in our class.

One afternoon, however, it all changed. I invited the class to share an experience they had related to the topic of discussion. Brad (not his real name), an inmate who'd been to prison and a leader in his gang, raised his hand.

"What have you got, Brad?" I said as I pointed to him. He went on to tell us about a situation he dealt with on the yard in prison. He related, with some detail, about the conflict he felt about a choice he had to make, and about the consequences of that choice. He also told us something that surprised me. He said (paraphrasing):

"I was all about my homies and the gang. But you know what? Every one of them is a dope fiend and they're going nowhere. It's all about doing dirt and coming back to jail or going to prison. And for what? So there can be more of us in there. I've got to do something different or I'm just going to die or, worse, rot in prison. Now, for the first time in my life I feel like I have a chance to take a breath and make up my own mind about what I want and what I'm going to do about it. So I just want to say thank you to you and Miss G."

Realizing we need to change is a start but making that public declaration, in the face of criticism from our peers, can be extremely difficult. When we do, however, it gives others around us the courage to do the same. Brad's courage to speak up and share his personal experience and honest feelings gave tacit permission to the rest of the class to speak openly and honestly. It was one of the turning points in our program.

The program continues to this day. As of this writing, the program has been running for more than three years. In that time there has only been one documented fight in the housing unit. Think about that. One fight in three years, in a jail housing unit occupied by rival gang members. Statistically it seems impossible but we made it possible by giving men hope, tools, and the permission to think differently and, thus, to change their lives.

Mohammed Ali said, "Impossible is just a big word thrown around by small men who find it easier to live in a world they've been given than to explore the power they have to change it."

We had an impact on all of them, however slight or great. What follows are some of the basic action steps we taught our classes. If they can help inmates, who came to us feeling helpless, oppressed and angry, make positive changes in their life, they can work for you in your life, too.

<u>Forgive yourself and let go of the past.</u> You have to have the courage to forgive yourself and give yourself permission to move forward in your life. Too many people get stuck in the past, clinging to mistakes that paralyze them into inaction. Your future really has nothing to do with your past, nor on someone else's opinion of your past. Your future is a choice. Your history doesn't equal your destiny. I would often tell my class, "What you did yesterday hasn't a damn thing to do with what you do tomorrow! It's about your choices starting today."

<u>Become an intentional student.</u> We all know that other people are having success in life. What makes them different from us? Knowledge and action. That's it. Personal development is key. The more we learn and the more we put that knowledge into action, the more successful we will become. My mentor once told me, "You should always be growing." We have to be intentional about learning. How did that person become wealthy? How did this person become happy? How can I achieve the

same thing that person did? It's not rocket science. If someone else has done it, you can find out how they did it and do it, too.

Choose the right kind of pain. Life will always bring us pain. It's human nature to try to avoid pain but here's a secret – you can't avoid pain. But you *can* choose what kind of pain you will endure. Jim Rohn said, "We must all suffer from one of two pains: the pain of discipline or the pain of regret. The difference is discipline weighs ounces while regret weighs tons." In the military we were told "Pay me now or pay me later." It's the same philosophy. You must be willing to sacrifice to grow. Sometimes the sacrifice is easy and sometimes it's difficult. My mentor, John Maxwell says, "You must give up to go up." Be willing to be uncomfortable, to sacrifice who and what you are for who and what you could become.

You can free yourself from your own negative circumstances. Your circumstances do not define you. Other people do not define you. *You* define you. You have the freedom to become what you were meant to be. Grab hold of the truth and begin a success revolution in your life.

It's now o'clock!

About Mark

Mark Arsenault is a John Maxwell Certified Coach, Trainer and Speaker. He is also the founder of Success Revolution, a company dedicated to bringing positive mindset and motivational training to individuals and organizations. He is also the founding Director of GAATES, Inc., a 501(c)(3) nonprofit dedicated to reducing recidivism and helping ex-offenders through personal development, career readiness, and success strategies.

Mark is a top selling and award-winning author and award-winning author of a number of books, including *Semicolon; Memoir of a Colon Cancer Survivor.* Mark has studied, researched, written and spoken for more than fifteen years in the fields of history, business, corrections and psychology.

He's been quoted in *SUCCESS Magazine, USA Today, The Wall Street Journal, The Washington Post* and *The New York Times.* He also appeared in a national commercial for the CDC *Tips from Former Smokers* campaign in 2015.

Prior to founding his company, Success Revolution, Mark had a successful career in law enforcement and corrections, where he co-created and co-facilitated a successful in-custody gang diversion and mindset program for state and county inmates. He has also run a successful publishing business and is a decorated U.S. Air Force veteran of Desert Shield and Desert Storm.

Mark is happily married and has two children. He is active in community and donated time as a volunteer speaker with several community programs as a way to "pay forward" what he's gained from his study of personal development.

To learn more about Mark's work, visit his web site: http://MarkTArsenault.com
You can follow him on Facebook: https://facebook.com/marktarsenaultcom
and on Twitter: @marktarsenault.

CHAPTER 5

THE GIFTS IN THE CHALLENGES: COMMITMENTS THAT LEAD TO A LEGACY

BY CAROL ROYSE

What happens when a single moment changes everything? I found out in 1985, because everything in my life changed in an instant—my 42-year-old husband passed away from a massive heart attack, abruptly leaving me as a single mother of two children, Tim who was 16 and Vikki who was 11. *It was hard to process and became worse when I learned that there was no life insurance to help sustain any kind of standard of living.* What I had in my checking account and a small savings account was it. **The rest was up to me!**

When I inventoried my skills I didn't get very far. I had plenty of experience volunteering, *but with skills that could earn an income I was starting at a deficit*. I had to learn how to support myself and my children...FAST. My first thought was to get a job as a clerk somewhere—a place where I might work my way up as I gained experience. A friend suggested something different. She felt that I had the drive and personality to become a Realtor. I'd never thought of working in real estate before, but took her insight to heart. Thirty days later, I was enrolled in real estate school.

I HAVE A LICENSE. NOW WHAT?

It took me forty-five days to get my real estate license. Now it was time to find a home for it. *Where to go was a huge decision.* There are many real estate offices of all sizes. *What was right for me?* After some research, I went with the top company in Phoenix. **Being associated with the best right from the beginning was logical**. There was just one problem— they preferred to hang the licenses of realtors with experience and a proven track record. I had neither. They didn't offer training, mentoring, or coaching, either. It was a major challenge, but I refused to let it defeat me. It was not the time to be timid.

I progressed from fear to motivation to observation very quickly— baptism by fire. Through some tenacity and expressed confidence in my potential to become an elite agent for the company, they allowed me to hang my license there, but due to my inexperience I had to start at a smaller office. That was okay! There I was, me and thirteen high performing males at this office, and they were skeptical of me because I was a woman with no experience.

What's the best way to alleviate skepticism? *Remove all doubt through hard work and determination.* That's what I began doing.

IT'S OUR ACTIONS THAT SHOULD DO THE TALKING.

One of my biggest fears about going to the office every day was that I wasn't doing enough, or the right things. I'd think, *please don't ask me to leave!* I knew I should be doing something productive, but what? Scouring the MLS and reading manuals was not going to give me opportunities. **Then I had an idea—I needed to observe the highly successful realtors and start copying what they were doing**. Why create something different if there's already a proven formula?

Watching these experienced professionals was enlightening. They'd send out a newsletter and then I'd copy it and send out my own. Of course, I had no money for mailing them so I'd "pound the pavement" to hand mine out. It took a lot of time, but I had time. When they'd run ads in the larger newspapers, I'd create ads in the inexpensive community newspapers. *Then I kept taking actions, repeating and moving forward, and I also waited...and waited.* I learned quickly and then my efforts began to show through with the sweet sound of my phone ringing. **Within ninety days I was getting calls from interested buyers and sellers**. I'd begun to become a master at copying and constantly testing the market.

WE GROW THROUGH GAINING EXPERIENCE AND DELIVERING RESULTS.

I'd already gotten further than many new agents, but it was time to go all out. I treated each day like it was "live or die" for my career. And within fourteen months, my efforts and results showed. I out-produced most of the agents in my office. *It felt incredible and I began accepting that I was absolutely meant for the career that I had chosen. I didn't need to re-evaluate, only look ahead.*

When I reflect back upon how all this transpired I still get excited. My vision didn't just involve surviving the day, despite it being a noteworthy goal at times; it also involved securing my future. I did it, too, becoming one of a handful of agents that could do the amount of business that I did—both in numbers of home sales and volume. Today, when people ask, "What did it take to get there, Carol?" I know the answer. It took:

- Commitment
- Dedication
- Coaching
- Vision to know where I wanted to go and how to get there
- A spirit of perseverance, regardless of what may be "lacking"

Today, I'm submersed into an entirely different culture than the one I walked into back in 1985. I have a team of sixteen people—five administrative and eleven listing/buyer agents. Each one of them is a reflection of our training and systems, which have resulted in a very high level of customer service standards. My team receives opportunities to grow based on what I have learned, and wish to teach. **I am now the Realtor with longevity, experience, and a keen sense of what it takes to be a successful business owner. I have a lot to offer**. Many of those realtors I emulated in the beginning couldn't do that. *That wasn't going to be my story*!

EMBRACING WHAT IT TAKES
TO BECOME A SUCCESS STORY.

Back before "coaching" was a buzz word, I found other ways to grow my real estate expertise. I did it through seminars, reading business books and seeking out high-producing Realtors who were willing to share their knowledge. I became an expert at:

- Understanding the business
- Promoting my business
- Creating meaningful client connections
- Assembling a great team

Despite these personal efforts that did pay off, it was not until 2007 when I joined the Craig Proctor Millionaire Training Systems, that this led to a fundamental transition in my approach to real estate—one that kept me focused on the future, not the past. **Real estate trends are volatile and can change—frequently**! John Maxwell stated, "Teamwork makes the dream work." We all achieve more through teamwork, and I am so proud of my team. Those two kids I was once worried about supporting—Tim Evans and Vikki Royse Middlebrook—are now my business partners, along with their spouses. I am their coach, as well as their leader, and we are a family business with a commitment to bringing the highest level of knowledge and performance to every buyer or seller we come in contact with.

Through my coaching and leadership, I have been able to design plans that helped us stay solvent and prosperous during times when other realtors— "successful realtors"—had to call it quits. For example:

- Through teamwork we all achieve more. Our team survived the brutal foreclosure downturn from 2005 to 2012. Business went from strong to struggling in six short months. **Without a different market aside from traditional sellers, we weren't going to make it**. I sought out big banks in hopes of securing REO accounts, offering them a well-trained real estate team with a proven system, not just a realtor. Working with big banks was not easy. There is a huge learning curve; however, this new distressed inventory saved our business. As a matter of fact, during the foreclosure debacle, I was able to pay off debt and build a reserve. It was not a good time for many, but it helped me to bring out my entrepreneurial traits and my team rose to the challenge.

- Blazing trails in the changing market. By early 2012, the Arizona market was coming out of the REO and foreclosure boom. Through many strategic moves **I guided our team back to a transition into the traditional market ahead of the curve and did so in a way in which we didn't lose any momentum**. Many of those who stayed completely vested in the foreclosure market were forced out of the business because they did not adjust, or make efforts to adjust in time. If I'd stayed in the moment, I would have missed the shift. I give a lot of credit to Gary Keller, founder of Keller Williams Realty International, as well as his bestselling book *Shift*, in which I was quoted about this topic.

Hard work and dedicated efforts are a major part of the battle when it comes to the real estate industry and being successful in it for the long term. It's tough work, which is why you see so much turn-over in the industry and a plethora of short-term realtors. *All that happens, often with many excuses, while my team and I continue to grow, increasing our market share.*

Working *on* business brings success much faster than working *in* business. I had to decide if I wanted to sell one home or thousands, and work to realize my goal. Through this, I transitioned from Realtor to business owner and CEO of my real estate business. My role became one of leadership, training, coaching, and holding individuals accountable to maintain the vision.

CREATING DISTINCTION

The rainmaker needs to constantly monitor and test their message to the market. You must be on the cutting-edge of technology and market trends. There is no room for complacency, and keeping your eyes on the road ahead is imperative. You cannot lose focus! Entrepreneurs know that you must change before the market changes or you'll constantly be playing catch-up, which will starve your profit, productivity, and growth.

Customer service is key to success. Everyone espouses customer service, but few go the distance. **Once you have a customer, do everything possible to keep that customer**. Few things are more costly than finding new customers. Successful ways we develop and keep customers—home sellers, homebuyers, and investors—are:

Strong data base referral marketing. **Relationships with current and past clients are everything**. We strive to give our customers a positive experience in their transaction, because we know they are a wonderful resource for us to capture new business. Maximizing this resource we already have is smart, and while it's not a new concept, it is one that is often attempted ineffectively.

Our team has a customer service representative. The job description is to keep our current buyers and sellers happy, almost like a concierge. **Our goal is to show and demonstrate our commitment to our home buyers and sellers through excellent communication and assistance**. Our customer service representative combined with our top of the line closing department makes for a complete and satisfying experience for our clients.

Customers and clients are the lifeblood of a business and prospecting for the kind of clients we want to work with is important. I am a marketer thinly disguised as a real estate agent! **I effectively utilize direct marketing to gain new clients and name recognition**. I don't assume that people know me. I also use many non-traditional consumer programs to attract and capture new clients and customers to our team, and I do it consistently, because that is what's necessary. The message has to constantly be tested so you know that you are offering what consumers want.

Through our coaching mentor Craig Proctor, I developed the Guaranteed Sale Program, which reverses the risk for the home seller. Exceeding the expectations of a new customer or client will move them to a "client-for-life" status. I always want to emphasize the WIFM (what's in it for me), for our clients.

Always seek out new venues to connect with new customers and clients. As CEO, it's my responsibility to increase our customer base. **I've done this by researching the demographics of my marketplace and finding a radio station whose audience matched that**. *Now, I do a radio show for an hour every week, speaking directly with the consumer about real estate, investing, mortgages, and through the use of "expert* *contributors" in related fields of financial planning, insurance, and tax planning.* I have a broad audience and it's allowed me to expand my team to the outer reaches of our county. It's made for a dramatic increase in my business and the bottom line.

My years in the marketplace have taught me that sellers want their home sold fast for top dollar and with the least amount of hassle to them. Buyers want to see homes that match their home-buying criteria and not to have their time wasted. This is what our team wants, too! I use a systematic approach to bring consumer programs that benefit our clients, as well as risk reversal. This sets us apart favorably.

What we create today should be inspired by what we wish to leave behind.

For me, my legacy is what I get so excited about when I think of all those years' worth of hard work. *I've sacrificed so much, but gained even more.* Words cannot express how exciting it is to see that through leadership and coaching, I have created something that I can hand over to my children—Tim and Vikki—to run with after I retire. I have faith in their abilities to carry on in this industry they've grown to love as much as I have. And as a mother, that feels amazing! All of this is happening because my actions match what I teach. That is the way a true leader operates.

Staying ahead and not playing catch-up are one of the messages I act upon for my team. These things are secondary to what we have to do every day for clients, and it isn't always easy. There are days when it might be easier to procrastinate, but I always remember: **it's these little things that set a person and their team apart**. The willingness to learn the business better than other Realtors, while still being passionate about it, is how we succeed. Through our teamwork, we have helped over 7,000 families find new homes and sell existing homes. We have seen children grow up, babies born and parents retire. It is a true blessing that cannot be counted in dollars.

Every day I am motivated by the knowledge that my legacy is built by what I do and not what I say. *It's more than having a place for others to hang their license.* My growth and success has been made even better by my loving husband of twenty years, Tom Oteri. Thank you!

About Carol

Inspired by the unexpected and drawn to results, Carol Royse is a top-producing Realtor at Keller Williams Realty who is widely known and acclaimed in the Greater Phoenix area. She is the CEO of The Carol Royse Team, bringing over 30 years' worth of experience with her, which always proves beneficial and revolutionary to the team's success. Carol works in an industry that has seen it all—the times where business "just happened," as well as the times where strategy and innovation were critical to "making it."

Back in 1985, Carol experienced the unexpected when her husband passed away unexpectedly of a massive heart attack, leaving her the sole provider for her family. Knowing that she had to do something—and quickly—she decided to pursue a real estate license, an action she credits a friend for. At that time, she entered into a market where the competition was intense and the best companies to hang your license at were only interested in those who'd already proven themselves. This was her first sales challenge and she excelled, growing her business by leaps and bounds. Today, Carol's team consists of 18 Realtors with sales totaling over $500 million. In addition, she's a sought out expert on real estate, and even hosts her own radio program – which airs weekly to a target market that is eager to tap into her abundance of knowledge about the market in her area.

Carol's team is also highly praised by both clients and herself. This was evidenced by exciting news for Carol recently. She was named as one of the *Top Ten Women in Business in Phoenix,* an exciting honor that acknowledges just how far she's come and the impact she has to those she connects with. And like all proud mothers, she's particularly fond of her partnership in real estate with her two children—the ones she used to worry about supporting—Tim Evans and Vikki Royse Middlebrook. Not only are they an intricate part of her team, but their spouses are too. It's a family business where everyone takes care of each other and together they all triumph.

Carol's expertise is also sought out by real estate professionals. She has co-authored the book *Death of the Traditional Agent and Rise of the Super Profitable Real Estate Team* with Craig Proctor and Todd Walters, and is a chapter contributor to the book *Beat the Curve* with Brian Tracy. While real estate sparks her greatest passions, Carol also enjoys time with her family, her team, and delights in opportunities to take the occasional trip to Hawaii. Boys & Girls Club is also a charity that is dear to her heart and which she supports wholeheartedly.

You can reach out to Carol Royse at: Carol@CarolRoyse.com

or call: 480-797-2724 to learn more about how Carol's visionary approach to real estate can benefit your life's goals.

CHAPTER 6

7+2 = HAPPINESS, LOVE, AND PEACE

BY DONALD PET, M.D., DIRECTOR, THE EDUCATIONAL COMMUNITY

In today's nuclear world where multiple tribes possess weapons with ultimate destructive power, we have created a race between nirvana and Armageddon. The answer to finding personal happiness is the same as the answer to the BIGGEST puzzle facing us today:

Why is it that we fill our world with fear, hate, scarcity, and war when we want (and need) happiness, unconditional love, abundance, and peace?

If you are concerned about the state of the world, popularizing the seven essential word-switches and the two still secret universal love-creation skills is the easiest, quickest, most effective solution to both problems. The 7+2 formula will popularize Einstein's solution to prevent human catastrophe and create sustainable world peace: "*We shall require a newer way of thinking*." (**ANWOT**)

Here are additional benefits. You will:

- Assume responsibility for your own happiness and love needs, so that you will welcome love from others rather than depending on it.

- Become your own lifelong friend and traveling companion 24/7.

- Own the most powerful anti-depressant.

- Free your energy from blaming to use your best to do your best.

- Become an: *each one, reach many* teacher of love-creation.
- Answer the universal questions: *Who am I?* and *What is my purpose?*

Here's the deal. Learn the seven critical word-switches that free the wish-granting genie within each of us, and the two powerful, secret happiness and love creation skills. When you experience the power of *a newer way of thinking* (ANWOT) you will want to pay the 7+2 formula forward to your loved ones and contacts ... as *your* gift!

You will become one of the one million love-creation teachers needed to create the domino effect that will circle the world. Together, we will make our world the safe, happy, sustainable home we all want.

What is a word-switch? Word-switches replace common problem-causing words and symbols that dominate our established tribal way of thinking. The seven word-switches turn on energy that has been shut down; redirect blaming energy to assume personal responsibility; stimulate puzzle-solving imagination using common sense instead of mindless obedience; redirect the focus of thinking to our similarities and shared benefits instead of our differences; call forth our highest intentions, *reciprocity* and *The Golden Rule*; and prevent the mindless unleashing of the innate *fight or flight, survival of the fittest* instinct.

Word-switch 1: Substitute *I can* for *I can't, Why bother, What's the use, To hell with it, F*** it*, and other "give up" words that shut down our energy factory.

Word-switch 2: Substitute *I allow* for *they (he, she, it, God) make me ...*

Word-switch 3: Substitute *I could* for *I should, have to, must.*

Word-switch 4: Substitute *both ... and* for *either/or,* a phrase that divides the world into two categories.

Word-switch 5: Substitute the universal puzzle-solving sentence: *What will make things better for me and you (us and them) for now and the future?* for the problem-causing sentence: *My way is the only right way.*

Word-switch 6: Substitute *energy* for *anger, fear*, and *anxiety.*

Word-switch 7: Substitute *urgent* for *emergency* and classify each issue as *high, medium*, or *low*.

These seven word-switches awaken us to the universal Truth of Reciprocity, which is commonly expressed as The Golden Rule. They inspire us to educate ourselves in the mental skills that transcend tribal love to create unconditional global love. Word-switches add our discoveries of conceptual moral-spiritual Truth to our growing knowledge of material-physical Truth. They elevate the intentions of our animal brain to the puzzle-solving portion of our human brain. Word-switches free the wish-granting genie within each of us to selectively upgrade dangerous thinking from instinct and tradition to create the wiser solutions required for today's issues.

Our animal brain functions like sorting machines that divide things into categories according to superficial characteristics: big from small, safe from dangerous, our tribe from their tribe. Our human brain creates symbols that allow us to imagine what is deep and wide; near and far; past, present and future. Imagination is our tool to add conceptual reality, viz. The Golden Rule, to our animal brain's excellence in managing physical reciprocity among organs. Imagination provides us a newer way of thinking (ANWOT) that emphasizes similarities above differences.

ANWOT reveals that the principal that elevates life to greater sophistication is reciprocity. When units cooperate, evolution progresses; extinction is the outcome when units take but give nothing to the system. Reciprocity is expressed through various iterations of The Golden Rule. A modern version is *"Love our self unconditionally with the abundance that overflows to enrich the world."*

Which brings us to the 2 in the 7+2 formula – the two secret universal love-creation skills:

1. Emotional self-endorsement

2. The Reasonable Best Measure of *Self*-worth

Love is the direction of energy for the benefit of someone (including our *self*) or something. Every life form contains an energy-producing factory. For us to survive and elevate ourselves to higher spiritual levels we must teach ourselves to add unconditional love to tribal love.

Until we learn to provide our own minimum daily requirement (**MDR**) of happiness and love, we remain addicted to forces beyond our control to sustain our well-being. The *self*-affirmation skills we require are discouraged by contemporary society. Let's make the secret love-creation skills common knowledge!

SECRET LOVE-CREATION SKILL #1: EMOTIONAL SELF-ENDORSEMENT

Few people know how to emotionally endorse themselves. Can you imagine being able to create good feelings with the same ease that you "naturally" feel angry, guilty, ashamed, or depressed? You can! ... if you learn how to endorse yourself emotionally and practice doing so. *Self-*endorsement is the secret of love-creation.

During our tender, malleable years, we lack the equipment to emotionally endorse ourselves. Survival requires "others" to provide the nurturance and love we need. Our educational system not only fails to routinely teach us to direct love energy to ourselves, it tells us we are self-centered, egotistical, and wrong to do so. Love and recognition from others are worth working for but when we take responsibility for our own emotional MDRs, love from others becomes a bonus rather than a necessity. When you're less needy, it is easier to be a lover than a love "junkie."

Good feelings stir us to continued action. Immediate emotional satisfaction sustains the work and practice required to attain the rewards of every important skill. It allows us to enjoy the work we do now in order to attain more satisfaction later.

Here's wonderful news. We are already well-practiced in emotionally directing love energy. We stomp our feet and yell with abandon at sports events, applaud and cheer a musical performance, know how to get that baby to smile and the dog to shake its behind and wag its tail. We even express our enthusiastic approval to food: "Wow!" to that chocolate ice cream sundae. The skill is there! We simply need to direct emotional endorsement to our *self*.

Take time each day to provide for both your physical and your emotional well-being. After you exercise, or while you're eating breakfast, take a few moments to consider your emotional MDRs. You can give yourself MDRs anytime and anyplace, but if you become accustomed to doing so at certain times, you will form the habit quickly. Make a short, positive statement to yourself: "Atta girl! / Atta boy!" Or use detailed imagery to create a self-endorsement fantasy.

Would you like to turbo-charge learning emotional *self*-endorsement skills? Apply *"secondary endorsement."* Secondary endorsement is endorsing yourself each time you engage in the very worthy act of emotionally endorsing yourself!

Like forging through a jungle, unless it's regularly maintained, the new path will soon be overgrown until not even a trace remains. Neglecting your emotional needs causes *self*-putdowns to re-appear and soon overpower the new habits. Secondary endorsement is the maintenance that keeps the path of self-endorsement clear.

Behavior that is rewarded is repeated! With practice, secondary endorsement will become automatic and effortless. Give yourself credit each time you endorse yourself. You will be pleasantly surprised to discover that secondary endorsement will rapidly build mental muscles that you will be proud to own.

"Hurrah! Congratulations to me for endorsing myself. That's worthy of a special bonus. I deserve to endorse myself for endorsing myself."

"Pull-ups," i.e., *self*-endorsements, serve you better than putdowns. When you endorse yourself for endorsing yourself, you pull yourself up and keep yourself up. As you recognize that you're endorsing yourself, enthusiastically call forth images such as blinking lights, musical accolades, and cheers as your signal to automatically trigger the secondary endorsement you deserve for endorsing yourself.

As you begin to feel consistently good about yourself, you'll notice that people will enjoy being with you and seek out your company more often. *And* you can add your new, upbeat attitude to your list of emotional MDRs.

Here is a special bonus. As you create the MDR of *loving-my-self* pullups, you will attain the highest expression of unconditional love: forgiveness. Forgiveness = for + giving. The hardest form of love is forgiving one who has done real or perceived harm to us. Remember the most powerful words ever spoken: "Forgive them; they know not what they do." Begin with *self*-forgiveness.

SECRET LOVE-CREATION SKILL #2:
THE "REASONABLE BEST (RB) TEST" OF SELF-WORTH

Most people evaluate their self-worth by the "outcome" of what they do. *The RB test* is an "input" measure. It emphasizes your efforts, not the results of your efforts.

This skill would be simple if we were not so strongly indoctrinated to not practice it. In any situation, simply recognize when you're doing your reasonable best and endorse yourself for doing so. You will create and maintain positive feelings about yourself no matter what you are trying to achieve. You can only control your input into a situation. The outcome is usually influenced by many factors that you can do little or nothing about, so it's unrealistic to expect that you can control it. Yet most people have been taught since childhood to regulate their feelings about themselves by focusing on the outcome.

Do you still depend on the outcome of your efforts as the primary measure of your *self*-worth? Consider these outcome measures that create an emotional response:

I'm OK if:
 He/she loves me
 I won
 My efforts worked out
 They accept me
 I got an "A"
 My salary is increased
 The audience applauds
 You understand
 They think I'm attractive
 I own a _____
 The kids do well
 I didn't make a mistake

You're utilizing healthy, realistic criteria to create positive feelings about yourself whenever you answer, "*Yes*," to the question, "*Am I doing my reasonable best?*" even if you don't attain the outcome you desire!

But isn't it natural to feel bad when things don't work out?

Of course! It's normal to experience hurt when things don't work out the way you would have liked, or when you've been treated unfairly. But applying *the RB test* balances your pain or disappointment. By creating a sustained level of positive feelings about your *self*, you can manage your discomfort while working to resolve it.

How do I know what my reasonable best is?

Your reasonable best is the best you can do in a situation considering your resources. Your intelligence is less than perfect. You have time restrictions and commitments to many obligations. If you're in doubt about what your reasonable best is, work with someone else to help set realistic goals.

Suppose I'm not doing my reasonable best? Don't I deserve to feel bad?

Certainly not! Improvement requires practice and patience; setbacks are to be expected along the way. Each time you recognize you aren't doing your reasonable best, you create an opportunity to improve until you reach the level of your reasonable best. Your appropriate response is to say:

> "I didn't do my reasonable best, but I'm recognizing the fact that I could be doing better. Only by recognizing an imperfection can I take the positive step of calling forth more effort and teaching my*self* to do better. I deserve to feel good for facing this shortcoming."

Most people beat on themselves when they discover they aren't the way they "should" be. Such "shoulding" on our *self* leads to avoiding facing faults. Becoming aware of shortcomings, imperfections, or mistakes *is* your reasonable best! *The RB test* prepares you to apply puzzle-solving and learn from your mistakes.

Putting our *self* down because we are less than perfect, less than we want to be, is a negative response that wastes our valuable energy without correcting the situation. The mistakes we make or our occasional poor judgment will probably lead to unpleasant consequences. Why pay twice by attacking our *self*-worth? Would you pay for your groceries and then get back in line to pay again?

Make *the RB test* a habit by asking frequently throughout the day, "Am I doing what I reasonably can?" If the answer is "yes," immediate, enthusiastic self-endorsement is in order. If the answer is "no," congratulate yourself for finding an opportunity to improve your efforts. Whether the answer is "yes" or "no," you will have created a win-win situation for growth and *self*-worth.

PUTTING IT TOGETHER

We are more than static human beings. We are dynamic humane becomings, a work-in-progress, on a mission to fill our world with happiness, unconditional global love, abundance, and peace. The root cause of war is the way we think. It can be stated in one sentence: *"My way is the only right way."* The cause of peace can be summarized in one word: *"Reciprocity,"* more familiarly stated as The Golden Rule.

ANWOT recognizes that we all come from a single source, our connection to one another, and the benefits of cooperation for mutual gain above confrontation to assert dominance. Our mission is gaining enough moral-spiritual wisdom to consistently direct our new godlike powers to constructive outcomes. Our survival and well-being requires us to combine our collective energy to elevate the way we think, feel, and act.

You are needed. Please join the EC to help start a movement to educate our population in ANWOT.

About Donald

Donald Pet, M.D., is director and founder of The Educational Community (EC), a privately funded nonprofit corporation whose mission is to popularize Einstein's solution to prevent human catastrophe and create sustainable peace. The EC offers the first and most comprehensive, scientifically-verified, self-taught curriculum that explains ANWOT. Our services are forever FREE to everyone, everywhere, every time.

Dr. Pet acknowledges the influence of Jerome Frank, M.D., Ph.D. (deceased), world authority on the causes of war and peace, his favorite mentor while training in psychiatry at Johns Hopkins and thereafter. "My passion is to inspire a movement that will allow my grandchildren and other loved ones to enjoy the opportunities I have experienced; surely I am not alone."

The EC web sites are forever FREE:
www.einsteinssolution.org: Two love-creation skills; a good introduction to ANWOT
www.lovingmenow.org: The skills to become a Love-creation teacher
www.anwot.org: A comprehensive curriculum to Einstein's solution = A Newer Way of Thinking.

CHAPTER 7

SIX STEPS FOR YOUNG ENTREPRENEURS TO BEAT THE CURVE

BY JEREMIAH RIVERS

The idea of starting your own business at the age of 23 can be quite scary and overwhelming. Despite my fear, that is exactly what I did. As most people, I started a business around what I knew and understood, countertop manufacturing. I previously worked for another countertop manufacturer for 7 years and thought: "I can do this." I had reached the highest management level at this company, reporting to the owner. Since I was only 23 and didn't want to spend the rest of my career at this level, I thought I would give this "business thing" a shot. I saved my money, paid off most of my debt and felt pretty good about my decision.

On December 15 2008, I officially incorporated River's Edge Countertops, Inc., right after the economic crash! I thought I was a hot shot at this point. My theory was I would work half as much and make just as much or more than I was making before. I hit the road and started selling countertops. At this point I was a one-man show and I thought I was living the dream. Then a problem hit. I had to produce what I sold so I was spending all of my time producing the work and no longer selling. Then the worst happened, I had no more work. I tried everything at this point just to make money for my family. I painted cabinets, incorporated new products and even sold candy for my grandfather-in-law's business.

After gaining no traction with all of this effort I recruited my friend, Heath Gray, to help me. I was aware of a product called recycled glass and talked to Heath about developing our own line of recycled glass and concrete countertops. He loved the idea and Heath went to work researching the products. He also found some other concrete products for overlaying existing countertops and floors. Because of this new information, I was excited again and we both hit the ground running. We spent about a year developing these products before we started producing it for the general public. We launched our products at the OKC home and garden show in 2010. It was a hit. We immediately had orders and people loved what we were doing.

Heath quit his job and started working with me full time in 2010. We were working countless hours and had orders coming in left and right. I hired a few more people and within a year, we moved into a new facility and got our first small business loan for $25,000 to buy some equipment. I really felt like things were going well until my wife pointed out to me that I was working more than I ever had before and was making half as much money. I took a step back and realized that she was right. At this time, I was doing my own selling, manufacturing, installation, bookkeeping, payroll, taxes and management – and I was not doing any of them very well.

In 2010, we posted a large loss in income and I was determined to do better the next year. In 2011, we picked up some big projects and our revenue was growing steadily. I hired a couple more people and we grew to a team of 6. I felt like things were really going well. We had several magazine articles done on the company and even one that was a national publication. Despite all of that excitement, at the end of 2011 we still lost money. I was tired, frustrated and I had to fire my best friend, Heath, due to the company not being able to support both of us financially.

At the beginning of 2012, I was beaten down and I wanted to give up. Then I met, Robert Garibay, who is now my business coach. I met Rob at a business-to-business networking event and we immediately hit it off. I expressed to Rob my frustrations and he said he could help me. I was broke at the time and could not afford to hire him so I decided to do a group-coaching class. During taking this class my eyes were opened to what a business really looked like. I realized I did not have a business

I had a job. That is when the real work kicked in.

In July of 2012, I decided I would sacrifice my pay and hire Rob as my business coach. Rob started coaching me one-on-one and I realized I needed to change some things. I developed a business plan to grow my company and bring affordable recycled glass countertops to the nation. I spent several months writing the plan and was ready to present it to some investors hoping to raise about $1,000,000. I presented my plan to several investors and after being told "no", or they wanted 51% of my business, I decided this was not the right path for me. Then I made the biggest and most difficult decision since I had started my business. I shut down that product line and transitioned into granite and engineered stone countertops.

In August of 2012, I officially started marketing granite and engineered stone countertops. I hated the idea of abandoning recycled glass countertops because I wanted to be different than everyone else and the market was flooded with companies that supplied granite and engineered stone. Additionally, I had a baby on the way, so I really needed to make money doing this or shut it down and go find a job. I didn't want to work for someone else, so I invested all of my effort into making this work. This was the hardest and best decision I could have made.

In the fall of 2012, we picked up our first builder for granite countertops. I still had about 5 employees and we were in the process of building a new building at the time. Rob was coaching me for free at this time since I could not afford to pay him and he really started to help me see what being a business owner was truly about. I started pulling myself out of doing the granite work and started looking at the big picture of where I wanted to take the company. This was when things really started getting exciting.

In the beginning of 2013, we completely shut down all products except granite and engineered stone countertops. Because of our focus, business was really starting to take off. By the end of 2013, we had grown to 20 employees and our revenue grew 380% in one year. I was able to hire my best friend, Heath Gray, and I now had the start of a thriving business. I was no longer doing manual work and I was now managing employees and focusing on business growth. Rob coaching me for free for almost one year was one of the best gifts I could have received from anyone. I was now able to pay him as he helped me focus on a big 2014.

In 2014, business continued to boom. We had just secured an $800,000 loan from our bank for us to purchase our first round of digital manufacturing equipment from Park Industries. By the end of 2014, we were the first fully digital stone manufacturing company in Central Oklahoma. This was a very important move for us, since we were having a major problem with keeping our labor force. Being located in Oklahoma, we have a lot of competition with oil companies for labor. Unfortunately, we cannot pay what oil companies pay so it was hard to keep good help. Fortunately, part of our team was very dedicated and hard working. We knew that for us to grow we needed to minimize our risk with labor and use machines. This allowed us to keep our A-Players and still expand the company at the same time.

In 2014 and early 2015, we received several prestigious awards. We received the Metro 50 award for being the fifth fastest growing company in Oklahoma in 2014, and in 2015, I was awarded the National Entrepreneur of the Year award by ActionCOACH in Las Vegas. We also just learned that we have qualified for the Inc. 5000 as the one of the fastest growing companies in the United States!

All of these awards are exciting, but it is not why I own a business. I own a business because of the impact I can have on my team and my community to give others the opportunity to provide for their families and work for a purpose. I could not have this impact if it were not for the six main things I have learned over the past few years.

SIX PRINCIPLES TO BEING A SUCCESSFUL YOUNG ENTREPRENEUR

#1. – Have a plan.

First and foremost; have a plan for the business and for yourself. I don't necessarily mean a business plan. This is helpful, but I mean a plan of what you want the company to look like in 1, 5, 10, 20, 50 years. Have realistic expectations of how many employees, the size of facility, how many locations, your revenue, and how you will market to get these numbers. The second part is to have a plan for personal growth. Your company will never grow bigger than you. If it does, then it will quickly implode. You have to be constantly learning about all aspects of business and grow yourself as a leader.

#2. – Set realistic expectations.

In todays society there is a real issue with the decline of young people starting businesses. This has a two-fold root cause. The first problem is that so many young people saw their parents suffer from the great recession and do not want to take the risk. The second problem is that you hear the media consistently talking about huge technology companies that grew from nothing to billionaires in a few years. I applaud those extremely rare entrepreneurs who were fortunate enough to do this. However, the truth is much closer to Steve Jobs' famous quote: "I'm always amazed at how overnight successes take a helluva long time!"

America still needs young people to pursue the American dream and own manufacturing, service, and other types of businesses. You might not end up a billionaire, but you can live a healthy lifestyle and have a huge impact on your employees by providing them with an opportunity to work for a small business that cares about them and their success.

#3. – Get a Coach!

I cannot stress the importance of this enough! This was the single most important thing I did. You do not always have to pay for it at first. You can find a family member that has a business or a person in your community. It just needs to be someone older than you that has the right experiences to help you see the big picture and help you grow your business. I do recommend hiring a professional coach when your company can afford it.

#4. – Hire people better than you.

This was the second best thing I have done outside of hiring a coach. The last thing you want is a bunch of "you clones" running around trying to lead your business. It may sound good at first, but I promise you, it will be a disaster. I focus on hiring people who are better than I am in the area of my company that they serve. This has helped me have the confidence I need to properly delegate to them so I can focus on big picture items.

#5. – Create Relationships.

One of the most powerful ways we have grown our business is by creating raving fans with our customers and suppliers. We have a supplier, Cosentino, who has become one of our biggest allies for growing our business. With their support and our relationship with their team, we now can offer new products at better pricing than we can from any other company. You also have to create strong and long-lasting relationships with your customers. The economy has changed and people can easily educate themselves. They don't want to be sold. They want to buy from someone they like and trust.

#6. – Set goals and accountabilities.

The last thing is to set goals and accountabilities for yourself and your team. There is nothing worse than having a bunch of A-players on your team and they have no idea if they are doing good or bad, since there is no accountability or goal set for them. Set daily, weekly, monthly, quarterly and yearly goals for yourself and your team.

SUMMARY NOTES

The most important things are to believe in yourself, surround yourself with people who are better than you, and be constantly learning and applying these things to your life. No matter if you own your own business or if you work for someone else, if you do these things you will be successful.

About Jeremiah

Jeremiah Rivers, CEO of River's Edge Countertops, is passionate about creating a one-of-a-kind experience for his customers. Jeremiah has over fifteen years of experience in the countertop industry. After many years of working in the countertop industry, Jeremiah incorporated River's Edge Countertops in 2008 as the first step in his journey toward creating this award-winning company.

Jeremiah is a powerful innovator in his industry and an entrepreneurial mentor. River's Edge is the most automated technologically advanced countertop manufacturer in Oklahoma by using fully digital CNC cutting and polishing machines. Constantly pushing River's Edge and himself to the next level, from our flagship product custom-made recycled glass countertops to becoming the first fully digital manufacturing countertop company in Oklahoma, Jeremiah is always looking for ways to improve quality and lower cost

Jeremiah's personal mission is to contribute to and impact the community and surrounding economy. He believes in the value of each one of River's Edge employees, continually offering education and training opportunities as well as emphasizing that all can be better and live better. Jeremiah Rivers believes in using his success as a business owner to transform lives and communities for the better.

Jeremiah has received many awards over the years, and most recently he was named North America Entrepreneur of the Year by ActionCOACH at the 2015 awards banquet in Las Vegas. In 2014 and 2015, River's Edge Countertops received the coveted Metro 50 award for being the fifth fastest-growing company in central Oklahoma. Also in 2015, his company made the Inc. 5000 list as the 517th fastest-growing company and the 18th fastest-growing construction company in the United States.

Considered a pioneer in his industry, he is often asked to speak and teach at various granite and stone events throughout the country. He recently had an article written about him in *Stone World* Magazine.

Jeremiah has a beautiful family – wife, Tiffany and son, Eli. He loves his business ventures and enjoys spending time working on his business. Jeremiah also loves to travel, cookout with family and friends, golf, and spend time with his family.

If you would like to learn more about Jeremiah's story or River's Edge Countertops, please visit:http://www.riversedgecountertops.com/
https://www.linkedin.com/pub/jeremiah-rivers/28/931/495

CHAPTER 8

THE WORD ACCORDING TO LUKE

BY LANCE LUKE

Aloha!

When I was growing up in Hawaii, my Christian Chinese Hawaiian family practiced certain values of honor, reputation, respect for others, sincerity and loyalty. There is a Hawaiian word Alaka'i – which means to be humble and to lead with good example. Others will follow your lead when you have gained their trust and respect.

During my college days, I once asked a wise man a very important question. "What is the secret to making money?" The wise man said to me "Help people first and the money will come" That wise man was my father, Sam Luke who, by the way, continues to be my trusted advisor to this day.

I always had a passion for fixing stuff. I still do today except in the field of construction management as a construction engineer and inspector. Managing a construction project from start to finish is a heavy responsibility.

Qualities of a construction manager should include the following:

1. Acting as the advocate for the Owner.
2. Remaining objective.
3. Striving for a project being on time and on budget.

4. Ensuring the plans and specifications are being followed.

5. Being a team player.

Responsibilities of a construction manager should include the following:

1. Finding out the needs of the Owner.

2. Finding out the needs of the building.

3. Working with the architect and engineer.

4. Finding and working with the general contractor and sub-contractors.

5. Approving and monitoring the construction schedule.

6. Helping with permits and inspections.

7. Negotiating the construction contracts.

8. Reviewing change order requests.

9. Approving payments to the contractors.

10. Completing punch list inspections and following up on warranty documents.

The Board of Directors of a Condominium or Community Association has a fiduciary responsibility to maintain the property in a good state of repair and protect all owners from financial hardship. To this extent, what do you do when your Condominium or Homeowner's Association property is in need of repairs or replacement of a major common area component? Projects such as roofing, siding, concrete spalling repair, plumbing, HVAC, asphalt paving and even exterior painting require proper planning to ensure a successful outcome.

For a major project, many Associations go through a three-bid process. The Board reviews the bids and will typically award a contract based on the overall cost, quality of materials, availability to start, contractor's reputation, or simply the lowest bidder. By following this process, there is a higher risk that the project may not be successfully completed. How many times have you heard people say they thought there was a warranty – only later to find out that the manufacturer would not honor it because the installation was not completed in accordance with the manufacturer's guidelines.

Here are some other reasons a construction project may go wrong:

1. Contractor not licensed, bonded and insured.
2. Contractor not specialty licensed for the specific trade work completed.
3. Lack of appropriate bidding and/or contract documents.
4. Inability of contractor to meet the construction schedule.
5. Contractor lacks experience and/or the technical expertise required.
6. Contractor not following plans and specifications.
7. Unexpected cost-overruns and numerous change orders.
8. Contractor, sub-contractor, or material supplier files a lien on the property.
9. No building permit.
10. Building code violations.
11. Lack of or no communication with owners.
12. Board or Owner expectations differ from the agreed upon scope of work.

When considering a major project, the construction manager should be the first person hired. With a Construction Management Agreement, the construction manager is retained directly by the Association; therefore, is not affected by conflict of interest. The construction manager coordinates permitting, design, and construction issues, and interfaces, on behalf of the Board, directly with the architect, engineer, contractor, and other construction industry professionals involved in the project.

Construction managers can provide you with sound guidance and assistance through all phases of the construction process. They can also provide assistance with development of cost of construction estimates; control the scope of work; obtain and negotiate bids; consider optimum use of funds throughout the project; schedule and coordinate work; offer assistance in avoiding delays, changes, disputes, and cost-overruns; communicate directly with Board and Management Company; and documents compliance with the project specifications through progress and final inspections.

A good construction manager will strive to deliver the best possible project on time, within budget, per plans and specifications and with the least amount of disruption and inconvenience to the Association and to individual homeowners. All construction projects have challenges, but by hiring a professional construction manager, you will have a representative who will bring control to the process and minimize the numerous risks.

A good construction manager will save the cost for his services by making the design and building repair and renovation process more efficient.

A good construction manager will save the cost or fee for services by his effectiveness through the construction process. If nothing else, he can save you big headaches and hassles on your project.

Hiring a Construction Manager does not cost, it pays!

"If it ain't broke, don't fix it" was the old axiom that is obsolete when it comes to maintaining Community Association property. The problems will not get better if nothing is done. It's as simple as that. Be smart and seek professional advice. There is major significance in using outside expertise and subject matter experts.

If your association needs legal advice, you consult an attorney. Likewise, if your association needs a tax advisor, you consult your CPA. So, it makes common sense that if your Association needs construction advice, you hire a Construction Manager. Specifically refusing to seek outside advice when no board member is an expert on the topic at hand, could be construed as failing to act in the Association's best interest.

Some board members are reluctant to hire outside professionals or to pay for any service they think they can do themselves or don't need. That is a fallacy that could prove very very costly.

A Professional Construction Manager helps level the playing field. Construction managers keep the Contractor honest, and assure that someone is on your side. Consider the construction manager as the "eyes and ears" of the Owner.

In Hawaii, the word Aloha means hello and goodbye.

Remember, if life throws you a curve, **Beat The Curve.**

And that's the word according to Luke.

Aloha!

About Lance

Lance Luke has been in the construction industry for over 35 years. He is a former general contractor and worked as a construction and project manager for real estate development companies. Currently he owns an independent construction management company. He has experience in design, home inspections, construction inspections, construction management, reserve studies and real estate development. His specialty is in inspection and construction management for condo association buildings and commercial properties. Recent types of projects worked on include concrete spalling repair, painting, roofing, waterproofing, asphalt resurfacing, plumbing re-piping, electrical retrofit and structural wood repair. He provides construction oversight and progress inspections for residential and commercial projects.

Mr. Luke holds a Bachelors of Science degree in Civil Engineering, and Masters and Doctorate degrees in Building and Construction Management. He has held the following designations for many years:

CCI - Certified Construction Inspector

CCPM - Certified Construction Project Manager

CCC - Certified Construction Consultant

CHI - Certified Home Inspector

Lance Luke serves as an expert witness on construction and real estate litigation cases. He is an Advisory Board Member for the State of Hawaii Regulated Industries Complaints Office, as an expert consultant. His expertise is helping to resolve complaints filed with the Contractors' License Board.

He has written numerous articles on construction and inspection, which are published in both local and national print media. He conducts up to six presentations a year to the construction, real estate and property management industry including educational seminars.

Mr. Luke is a qualified insurance inspector for Research Specialist Inc., and an approved HUD inspector for Interstate Professional Group Inc. He is also listed as one of America's Premier Experts and Marquis Who's Who in America 70th Anniversary Edition.

Lance Luke is a former member of the Structural Engineers Association of Hawaii and the American Bar Association and served on the Real Property/Probate Law Division and the Forum for the Construction Industry. He is or was a former member of the following Professional Associations:

- Construction Management Association of America (CMAA)
- The Construction Specifications Institute (CSI)
- Hawaii Building Association (HBA)
- International Code Council (ICC)
- International Concrete Repair Institute (ICRI)
- National Institute of Building Sciences (NIBS)
- Roofing Consultant's Institute (RCI)
- Structural Engineers Association of Hawaii (SEAH)

You can contact Lance at:
LanceLuke@HawaiiBuildingExpert.com
www.hawaiibuildingexpert.com
(808) 422-2132

CHAPTER 9

MAKING THE CASE: PRINCIPLES THAT EVERY POWER LAWYER SHOULD LIVE BY

BY MELISSA SOSA, ESQ.

MY MISSION STATEMENT

My name is Melissa Sosa. I am the **wife** to the best husband in the entire world, a **mother** of three children whom I dearly love, and I am a **legal advocate** who serves as a voice for those who cannot speak for themselves. My calling is a noble one, and my purpose, like that of John Adams, is to provide for my clients the hope of equal justice.

MY BACKGROUND

I grew up in paradise—Key West, Florida. Key West is a small island city located at the southernmost point in the United States, only 90 miles from Cuba. I hail from a long line of 'Conchs' whose genealogy (on my mother's side) traces back to the Bahamas where my 'Loyalist' kinfolk fled during the American Revolution. Conversely, my father's genealogy traces back, in distant party, to Abigail Adams, the mother of John Quincy Adams II who was our nation's sixth President. Life in Key West was idyllic to say the least. Quick trips to the beach (whether before, during or after school) was not an unheard of treat for my friends and me in high school. In fact, although I realize it would probably lead to his arrest and my suspension in today's world, my choir teacher used to let us leave school to go buy Cuban bread and 'café con leche' as long as we brought him back some too. Life was in some ways utopic. The atmosphere was laid back and sunny. Anything was possible. If you weren't sure of that, you only needed to ask the fire-breather who performed nightly during sunset at the now famous Mallory Square. This was the backdrop of my life and the foundation for my idealistic understanding of the world.

I was six years old when Sandra Day O'Connor became the first female to serve as a United States Supreme Court Justice. When I was in about the fourth grade, I remember wanting to dress like her for a school Halloween event. I never imagined that my classmates would not know who she was. In the end, I attended the parade as a fictional character and can remember feeling particularly frustrated that no one else my age seemed to know or care who Sandra Day O'Connor was. She was NOT just some old lady!

By the way, do you know which two founding fathers died on the exact same day? If not, don't worry – I am about to tell you. John Adams and Thomas Jefferson, the bitterest of rivals who grew to become the best of friends despite their very different views, both died on July 4, 1826, fifty years to the date of signing the Declaration of Independence. How is that for coincidence?

My parents are part of the baby-boom generation. They grew up in the sixties, in the era of John Kennedy's "New Frontier". My father's family was poor and my mother's family was among the working class. My parents achieved the quintessential 'American Dream' and, through hard work and determination, raised my siblings and me in such a way that changed my destiny. From my father, I learned the principles of hard work and honesty. From my mother, I learned the principles of self-determination and what it means to be 'tough as nails.' My life would not be what it is today without their presence and influence.

MY PASSION

History and Law have always been my great passion. Consider if you will the following quote from the Declaration of Independence: "We hold these Truths to be self-evident, that all Men are created equal, that they are endowed by their Creator with certain unalienable Rights, that among these are Life, Liberty and the Pursuit of Happiness." Did you consider the words or just read them? If it was the latter, try again – ponder the words. What does it mean to 'hold certain Truths to be self-evident'? If these self-evident truths are 'unalienable' then how have we landed where we are today?

The four words above the US Supreme court building read *Equal Justice Under Law* but if I know anything now, it is that *Justice* is neither blind nor equal. It takes a skilled litigator to even out that playing field, and passing the bar exam will not be sufficient.

In 2002, I entered the legal world as a bright-eyed, noble-minded, young woman who had eagerly traded in the laid-back, island-style life of her youth for the big bad world of **Practicing Law**. That's right, I became a lawyer . . . who had to work with other lawyers. It is hard to describe what the 'real-world' of lawyering did to my idealistic view of the world, especially the practice of law.

To describe the experience with imagery, try to imagine the following scenario:

A beautiful yellow balloon, floating gracefully up and away with its shimmering string glistening in the sun, reaching farther into the expansive blue sky towards clouds yet untouched. Prior to its earthly departure, however, a few nasty bull ants attached themselves to the balloon's shimmering string and began traveling up towards its helium-filled enclosure. Now, we all know that in order for this balloon to maintain its shape, momentum and altitude, its structure would have to remain intact. Not surprisingly though, with their dagger-like legs, those nasty bull ants began creating tiny little holes in the balloon's exterior resulting in helium leaks and eventually leading to a steady decrease in altitude until it finally fell back down to earth, laying limp and shriveled, a fractional reflection of its former perky, optimistic self.

After a few years of practicing law in the real world, I felt just like that little yellow balloon – limp and shriveled and a fractional reflection of my optimistic self. I understood why most people hate lawyers. After all, I hated most of them and I *was* a lawyer! I found most of the attorneys I came in contact with to be untrustworthy, conniving, manipulative and arrogant. I asked myself over and over again why I had become a lawyer, as if searching for a justification for my career choice. I continued to hold on to the idealistic views of my youth and the belief I had as a child that the practice of law was a noble calling, but those ideals and beliefs seemed to be battered on a daily basis by the real world actions of these so called 'officers' of the court.

MY TRANSFORMATION

It is said that behind every successful man is a strong woman. The reverse is true for me. I happen to be married to the best man I know, and it is he who helped revive the optimism of my youth so that I could once again make my way to the clouds. Hubby challenged me to stop whining about what I didn't like and figure out how to do things my own way. After all, that is one of the blessings afforded to those who live in this great country that I love so much – freedom to innovate. With that, I decided to open Sosa Law Office, P.A. and do it MY way.

With no salary and a HUGE law school loan to pay off, I had to figure out how to make a living selling my services in a market that was already oversaturated with lawyers on every corner (not to mention the market crash in 2008 which, to my knowledge, was the worst since the great depression), and a general distrust on the part of the public towards members of the Bar in general. Thus, I began to develop for myself principles that I encourage every young lawyer that I mentor to use in her or his career.

Every power lawyer must have a story, and so must every case! As of July 1, 2015, there were 83,799 attorneys in Florida who are both *eligible* to practice and remain in good standing with the Florida Bar.[1] How are you, the attorney who is starting her practice now or who is trying to reinvent himself in a new and ever-changing economy, going to set yourself apart from the other 83,798 attorneys such that your clients not only seek you out specifically, but they refer everyone they know, like and trust to you as well?

Just as my life's mission is clear, so must my firm's mission be. The same principle is true for each and every client that I, or you, agree to represent. Is their story one that you can tell? If so, tell it well. If not, walk away. Following the principles that I have developed over the

---

1. https://www.floridabar.org/tfb/flabarwe.nsf/f6301f4d554d40a385256a4f006e6566/47fc0a8f415a11d285 256b2f006ccb83?OpenDocument

years will help you lay the foundation for a law practice more successful than you can wish for. These principles are not simply overnight actions, but they are consistent and thoughtful steps to be taken daily, pondered periodically, modified, and lived until they become part of you. Practice these principles, in life as well as business, and there will be no one who can stop you!

P – PROCESS

O – OWNERSHIP

W – WEALTH MANAGEMENT

E – EXCELLENCE

R – RESPONSIBILITY

Regrettably, there is not enough room in this single chapter to review each of these very important principles. Notwithstanding, I simply cannot close out this chapter and fail to address PASSION. While not a foundational principle, passion is a characteristic that is quite essential for any attorney who intends on representing clients in a court of law. It happens to be a huge motivation for me, and I find that if an attorney lacks this one characteristic, he or she will make a **very poor trial lawyer**.

Passion is defined as an *intense, driving, or overmastering feeling or conviction.*[2] We associate the word passion with many other things as well, including intimacy, religion, conflict, etc. However, passion as used in this chapter refers to one's ability to argue a point with sincere and dignified conviction. I posed the question earlier about whether your client's story was a story you could tell well. Many attorneys are tempted to accept a case simply because the person seeking assistance is ready, willing and able to pay, or perhaps because the attorney is simply in need of additional income. DON'T DO IT! If you manage your life and practice well, you won't feel the need to accept whatever case walks through the door, and you will develop a clientele that will return to you over and over again in the future. That kind of business will yield a return on investment greater than any marketing piece, even the largest, most expensive billboard you could ever possibly purchase.

The one thing that I find holds most litigators back from expressing passion in their arguments is fear. Fear of what the other attorney will

2. http://www.merriam-webster.com/dictionary/passion

think, fear of what the judge may think, etc. Honestly, I have found that there is nothing easier about my job than to wipe the floor of a courtroom with a 'litigator' who is afraid. Like a shark to blood, a skilled litigator can sense fear in an opponent and will surly strike at any and every opportunity. Don't think for one second that having passion means that you are never scared. You can be as scared as you want. Let the fear propel you—convert it into conviction as you present your case.

The best antidote for fear is practice . . . so practice up.

I'll see you in court!

About Melissa

Melissa Sosa, Esq. is the President and CEO of Sosa Law Office, P.A. With a passion for history and the founding of The United States of America, Melissa naturally gravitated to the practice of law as a vocation. Melissa began practicing law in 2002, and decided to do it "HER WAY" in 2005.

Melissa's Mission Statement sets forth that she is a wife to the best husband in the entire world, a mother of three children whom she dearly loves, and a legal advocate who serves as a voice for those who cannot speak for themselves. Melissa believes that her calling as an attorney is a noble one, and her purpose, like that of John Adams, is to provide for her clients the hope of equal justice.

Melissa is a graduate of Florida State University and Stetson University College of Law. Melissa has been recognized by The American Academy of Trial Attorneys as a *2015 Premier 100 Trial Attorney* and in 2014, Melissa was recognized as a *Top 40 Under 40* by The National Trial Lawyers. Melissa has advocated cases that were reported in *The Pasco Tribune, The Tampa Tribune*, and the Center for Responsible Lending.

You can reach Melissa at:
Melissa@SosaLawOffice.com
www.SosaLawOffice.com
www.MelissaSosa.com

CHAPTER 10

SUPERSIZE YOUR SOCIAL SECURITY

BY LEASHA WEST,
MSFS, CHFC®, CASL®, NSSA®, CLTC

One of the most important financial decisions for a retiree is when to begin taking Social Security. Most retirees are not aware of the 8000+ unique Social Security claiming strategies that exist and are not informed of their options. Those who are aware consult with a certified National Social Security Advisor® (NSSA®) and are handsomely rewarded with additional retirement income over their lifetime.

Early vs. Later Factors to consider:

- Ability or desire to continue working
- Cost of waiting (breakeven point)
- Affect on future Widow Benefits
- Personal finances (BIGGEST factor)
- Current and anticipated health
- Life expectancy
- Coordination of spousal benefits

The majority of retirees treat Social Security like a "land grab" and take it as soon as they are eligible at age 62; however, failure to collaborate with a certified NSSA®, assess their situation and "run the numbers" can result in a serious loss of monthly and lifetime income.

One of the biggest concerns people have is that the Social Security system will be insolvent…. "Is Social Security really going to be there for me?" People are afraid if they don't take their Social Security income when they turn 62, that it may not be available later on. As a result of this fear, 80% of retirees file before their Full Retirement Age (FRA - see chart) and unknowingly lower their percentage of benefits for themselves and their spouses – permanently!

Full Retirement Age (FRA)	
NOTE: If you qualify for benefits as a survivor (Widower) your full retirement age may be different	
Birth Year	FRA
1937 or earlier	65
1938	65 and 2 months
1939	65 and 4 months
1940	65 and 6 month
1941	65 and 8 months
1942	65 and 10 months
1943-1954	66
1955	66 and 2 months
1956	66 and 4 months
1957	66 and 6 month
1958	66 and 8 months
1959	66 and 10 months
1960 and later	67
If you were born on Jan 1 of any year you should refer to the previous year. If you were born on 1st of the month, your benefit (and FRA) is figured by the previous month.	

Most baby boomers (born between the years 1946-1964) have not saved an adequate amount of money towards retirement. Although many have done a good job in saving, the biggest portion of their retirement savings is held in employer-sponsored plans such as 401(k)s, IRA's, etc. To make matters worse, taxes will have to be paid on the funds distributed from these accounts. What many don't realize is that the tax they will owe is not just on the amount that was distributed from their IRAs (which the government counts as taxable income) but also up to 85% of their Social Security benefits which are taxed as a consequence of the IRA withdrawals! This results in double taxation as taxes were already deducted from the Social Security tax on your earned wages and then taxed again on your income.

Nearly all Social Security claimants think their Social Security income is, or will be, tax-free. Discovering the facts of taxation on Social Security

Provisional income =

Your adjusted gross income + Any tax-exempt income (including interest form municipal bonds – often a core component of retirement portfolios) + 50% Social Security income for the year

is quite the shock to say the least. As explained in the aforementioned paragraph, up to 85% of Social Security income may be taxable due to what is known as provisional income or combined income.

Provisional income is comprised of your adjusted gross income plus any tax-exempt interest, plus 50% of your Social Security benefits.

Several sources of income can trigger the provisional income taxation thresholds (see chart) as well as impact the taxation of your Social Security check. These income sources include, but are not limited to:

- Distributions from 401k or IRA account(s)
- Wages, pension income
- CD, money market, savings interest
- Dividends from stocks, bonds, mutual funds

Filing Status	Provisional	Income Levels
Single Taxpayer	$25,000 - $34,000	Over $34,000
Married Filing Jointly	$32,000 - $44,000	Over $34,000
S.S. Ben. Subject to Tax	50%	85%

As you can see, it's critical to work with your NSSA® early on, in order to map out a distribution strategy of your existing resources, while being mindful of minimizing taxation on your Social Security check. When and how Social Security is taken directly impacts the longevity of retirement assets and your income stream. Planning ahead cannot be emphasized enough!

In order to 'Beat the Curve', there are multiple strategies to SUPERSIZE your Social Security income. Let's explore a few:

COORDINATION OF SPOUSAL BENEFITS

- You must be at least age 62

- Exception: you can be any age if caring for the worker's minor child (under 16) or disabled adult child subject to the Annual Earnings Test

- Your spouse must be receiving Social Security retirement, disability benefits, or if at Full Retirement Age: file & suspend

- Duration of current marriage = 12 months or more; Duration of former marriage = 10 years

- You can receive a maximum of 50% of your spouse or ex's benefit at Full Retirement Age

- You'll receive the higher calculated benefit amount, based on your own or your spouse's work record

Understand two things:

1. The longer you wait to collect, the more you will receive every month in the long term.

2. Your spouse (current or ex) can collect 50% based on your work record without taking their own benefit.

Most people think when they retire, they'll be collecting Social Security benefits based solely on their own work history. However, "spousal benefits" are available which allow you to collect a monthly check up to 50% of whatever your spouse (current or ex) is collecting.

So here's how it works…

- First, one member of the couple (let's say the wife) files for benefits as soon as she is eligible. Right now, that's age 62.

- Simultaneously, the husband files for spousal benefits at 50% of hers. The husband does NOT file for his own benefits at this time; instead, he waits until age 70. By doing so, he delays filing for his own benefits. The longer he waits to file, the more his benefits will be worth.

- Once the husband's benefits are maximized, he files for his own benefits. The wife is then able to "step up" her benefits to the higher payout. (She can collect her benefits plus file for the spousal benefits… up to the total amount that her husband collects.)

- This strategy also locks in a higher Widow's Benefit for the surviving spouse (presumably the wife). The Widow's Benefit is 100% at the time of death; so whatever the deceased spouse was collecting or eligible to collect, that amount is now what the surviving spouse will receive.

A few more guidelines:

- Preferably, the higher-wage earner should collect spousal benefits when eligible and delay their own benefits to maximize the payout.

- If you are not eligible for a spousal benefit when you file for retirement benefits, you can take a spousal benefit when you become entitled or delay until Full Retirement Age.

- Both spouses must have an earnings history.

- You cannot collect both the spousal benefit and your own benefit at the same time.

- Both spouses cannot collect spousal benefits from each other simultaneously (not applicable to ex-spouses).

Recap: The basic strategy is the one spouse files and the other receives their spousal benefit; a few years later, the other spouse files for their benefit and the other one receives their spousal benefit.

NOTE: Every situation is different, consult a National Social Security Advisor® to determine the best strategy for your circumstance.

Coordinating spousal benefits can raise your Social Security up to 30%!

DELAYED RETIREMENT CREDITS

This strategy allows people to predictably plan the timing of collecting their Social Security benefits in order to maximize their Delayed Retirement Credits (DRC).

After reaching Full Retirement Age, for each year you postpone claiming your Social Security, your income is increased by 8% every year until you reach age 70. This is a permanent increase of 32%.

When you file at age 62, you're electing 75% of your Full Retirement Age benefits. By postponing until age 70, you receive 100% of your Full Retirement benefit plus capture all the Delayed Retirement Credits totaling 32%.

Example of Monthly Benefits
Consequences of when you file

Age 62:	$750
Age 66 FRA	$1000
Age 70 FRA + DRC	$1320

Postpone and prosper!

If you were born after 1960, there will be 30% reduction in benefits if taken at age 62

Another factor to consider in SUPERSIZING your Social Security is the ability or willingness to continue working. Why is this important? Check it out - your monthly Social Security payment is calculated using the highest 35-years of earnings (not necessarily the last 35 consecutive years). The calculation includes an inflation factor for every year up to age 60. What this means is that your wages in the year you turn age 60 are no longer calculated with the inflation factor applied; instead, Social Security uses your actual wages from that year forward. So for every year that you continue working past age 60, these sacred peak earning years replace earlier years of lower wages - which translates into an overall higher average of your 35-year calculation! Armed with a higher 35-year average from your work record, coupled with a 32% increase from acquiring your Delayed Retirement Credits can 'Beat the Curve' in retirement and substantially boost your Social Security payout.

Understandably, not everyone can wait to take their benefits and SUPERSIZE their Social Security income. For some, claiming early is an absolute necessity and they need the immediate income. For others, they simply don't understand the financial ramifications they are imposing on themselves. It's not uncommon for folks to later learn that they could have greatly increased their lifetime income by making an informed decision. The fallout of improper planning not only consists of lost income but also stiff tax consequences which could have been minimized or eliminated.

Working with an NSSA® will help you decide the best course of action.

START STOP START OR SUSPEND AND RESTART OR VOLUNTARY SUSPENSION

The Social Security provision of *Suspend and Restart*, also referred to as *Start Stop Start* or *Voluntary Social Security Suspension*, allows many early claimants to earn their Delayed Retirement Credits despite filing prior to their Full Retirement Age. This rarely-exercised technique helps individuals and couples recover additional lifetime income.

The strategy goes like this:

- Upon reaching Full Retirement Age, you can file for a *Voluntary Suspension* of benefits, and temporarily suspend receiving your monthly Social Security income.

- During this suspension, you will be accumulating your Delayed Retirement Credits of 8% per year.

- If you are married, you can potentially receive your spousal benefits during this time.

- At age 70, you will file to restart your Social Security income and receive the new payment amount with a 32% pay raise!

- The new hike in pay will supplement the lifetime income and enhance the Widows Benefit.

The *Voluntary Suspension* provision allows you to SUPERSIZE your monthly Social Security income check; the new, elevated monthly payment is nearly the same amount as you would have received had you waited to Full Retirement Age to claim.

WORK ONLY WITH A NATIONAL
SOCIAL SECURITY ADVISOR®

The vast majority of brokers, financial advisors and /or planners, investment representatives and insurance agents are NOT educated, experienced or certified in the area of Social Security. Their work revolves around investment management (stock market), selling securities, annuities, mutual funds, etc. Accountants and tax professionals are focused on their chosen field of practice which involves tax preparation, auditing, and bookkeeping.

None of these professionals are trained or qualified to advise on any aspect of Social Security claiming strategies or income planning for retirees.

> Be very cautious of financial professionals hosting local Social Security Seminars or Workshops; this is the latest craze for annuity hunters.
>
> To locate an NSSA® in your area visit:
> www.nationalsocialsecurityassociation.com

Be cautious of financial professionals and/or planners who host Social Security seminars or workshops; this is the latest craze for annuity hunters. Let me explain: Social Security is a white-hot topic and the quickest way to get a retiree's attention. Therefore, financial professionals and insurance agents who are under tremendous amounts of pressure to make sales quotas are jumping on the Social Security education bandwagon in order to draw a crowd to their seminar. The idea behind the Social Security seminar is to introduce the retiree to the individual and their firm and present a generic, canned Social Security presentation – in return, a fancy Social Security report is generated for the retiree to take to their local Social Security office. With that being said, the UNQUALIFIED professional conducting the seminar does not answer live questions about Social Security or provide adequate consultation beyond the seminar. However, they will contact you to follow up and discuss moving your investments to that firm.

These Social Security Seminars are dangerous and irresponsible. As of this writing, there is no legislation to regulate the advisement of Social Security. I anticipate forthcoming legislation in the future as mistakes and complaints mount up. I'll say it again for good measure...

Work ONLY WITH a Certified National Social Security Advisor®

www.nationalsocialsecurityassociation.com

A WORD ON LOCAL SOCIAL SECURITY OFFICES

Local Social Security administration personnel help the public with filing and servicing routine claims, case management and processing information requests. They are not going to review the cost of living, build out a lifetime income plan or help SUPERSIZE your Social Security benefit. Essentially, they are "order-takers", NOT money-makers or wealth-protectors. The Social Security staff is typically not allowed to tailor customized claiming strategies or to offer Social Security recommendations for single, widowed, divorced or married couples. Thus, scheduling an appointment with the Social Security office and presenting them with a fancy report is futile. Thankfully, the area of Social Security planning is quickly emerging in the specialized field of retirement planning and working with an NSSA® can allow you to take control of your retirement income, make informed decisions and 'Beat the Curve'.

About Leasha

Leasha West, known as America's Retirement Authority, is a highly decorated Marine Corps veteran and respected community leader. With the explosive success of her firm West Financial Group, Inc., she is now recognized as one of the nation's leading experts in retirement planning.

As an award-winning and multiple best-selling author, Leasha was selected as one of America's PremierExperts® and is frequently quoted in the *Wall Street Journal, USA Today, New York Times,* and *Inc. Magazine,* as well as featured in several publications and news outlets commenting on retirement issues. She has shared the stage at distinguished conferences across the country with legends of business, Hollywood, politics and sports – such as Steve Wozniak, co-founder of Apple, Eric Trump, NFL Hall of Famer and 3-time Super Bowl Champion Michael Irvin, Fashion Mogul Donna Karan, Oprah's life partner Stedman Graham, Supermodel turned Supermogul Kathy Ireland, George Ross of the Donald Trump Organization and Celebrity Apprentice, NY Times #1 Best-Selling Author Dr. John Gray, the lingerie tycoon of Europe Michelle Mone, Arnold Schwarzenegger and the World's #1 Wealth Coach, JT Foxx.

Leasha's combined knowledge and celebrity status has solidified her as a retirement planning guru, as she is frequently called on by local and national media for her ability to communicate, teach and transfer her innovative and rarefied financial skills.

Leasha's leadership skills have made her a powerful force in her community; she serves on the Boards of Directors for numerous non-profit and for-profit organizations. As a result of Leasha's outstanding volunteerism, she was awarded the President's Volunteer Service Award by President Barack Obama.

In addition to her community involvement, she is a multi-year member of the Million Dollar Round Table, was named to the Circle of Excellence by the Women in Insurance and Financial Services (WIFS), is a member of the National Ethics Association and was chosen as one of North America's Elite Women in Insurance by Insurance Business America Magazine.

Educationally, Leasha holds a Masters Degree in Financial Services and the prestigious designations of Chartered Financial Consultant®, Certified Long Term Care, National Social Security Advisor® and Chartered Advisor for Senior Living®. She is the official spokeswoman for The American College.

Leasha has intensity, contagious enthusiasm and amazing passion for helping baby boomers, seniors, and retirees preserve and protect their portfolios, maximize their Social Security income, make sense of Medicare, generate income through solid cashflow and use growth to offset inflation.

Through Leasha's strategies and inspiration, retirees are likely to avoid probate court and protect their assets, investments and savings from losses due to volatile markets, needless taxation or an extended illness. She has personally helped thousands of clients retire in the comfort of their homes rather than being cared for in a nursing home.

If you are retired or retiring soon, and would like to learn more about securing your retirement in any economy, visit Leasha's websites to read articles, watch videos and receive free special reports:
www.westfinancialgroup.com or
www.americasretirementauthority.com

You can connect with Leasha at:
leasha@westfinancialgroup.com
www.twitter.com/LeashaWest
www.facebook.com/LeashaWest
https://www.linkedin.com/in/leashawest
https://plus.google.com/+LeashaWest

CHAPTER 11

HEALTHY *FROM THE INSIDE OUT*: INFUSING EASTERN PRACTICES IN A MODERN WORLD

BY LUCIA AU

I spent much of my childhood in Hong Kong, not as part of a wealthy family, but thankfully as part of a wise family. Like all families from the region, there was never a time when the realization of who had money to who didn't was made clearer than if there was a health concern—whether a minor ailment or something more significant. If you had money, you paid for the medical help you needed based on those Western medicine practices. And if you didn't…well, you relied on something a bit more traditional—those Eastern holistic practices that had been handed down for many generations and were there to help us manage conditions the best we could. *This was something that my mother understood—always—and for this, I've never been so thankful.* She inspired me long before she realized she did.

For those who are not familiar with the differences between Western and Eastern medicine, let me explain. When you are at an appointment with a holistic doctor (based in Eastern wisdom), **the appointment is**

about more than just your noted symptoms. Attention is also paid to the larger picture, including:

- Your eyes
- Pulse
- Tongue
- Complexion and its color
- Diet
- And . . . your specific concern(s)

Based on the conversation, the holistic doctor will then recommend specific herbs for you and write them down for you to hand to a herbalist to get filled. But you are not done.

With the herbs that you need in hand, you'll go home and make what it is they recommended for you. *Then something truly amazing happens*: *Slowly and usually surely, from the inside out, you begin to feel better*. It's quite common to experience relief within 24 hours! How does this work? It's really quite simple. If you have a minor ailment, **adjustments to a diet plan can help you realign the balance of your body**, working to create "ying/yang."

Today, I am in my mid 60s and I live a disease-free life, which makes me an exception. However, I know this does not have to be the case. I also realize that what I have access to is a gift that is meant to be shared with others. *Helping just one person realize what it truly feels like to feel great from the inside out is inspirational and my calling*. Today, I call on all of you who strive for balance in some way to begin experiencing what I'm sharing with you.

GOWNS AND THE GIFT OF BETTER HEALTH

It's a blessing that my life stage is disease free, because I have a great mother that knew how to nourish me since the day I was born.

~ Lucia Au

Since I was eight, I felt like I was born to be a wedding gown designer. I loved it and I could sketch creations for hours upon hours, drawing the attention and admiration of adults and teachers. They told me to consider it, and I did, and I loved it! Although this is not where I have ended up, I do see a tie between my personality, the way I've used my gifts, and what I offer people as a Certified Health Coach.

I have always had these amazing opportunities to connect with people for the important events in their lives—their memories in the making— and play a part in that. It's a truly incredible, rewarding experience. Here I am, involved in people's lives, learning their personalities and likes so I can make this beautiful creation for them. However, in reality, what's more beautiful than "us" as a creation. I feel this part of me comes alive when I help connect people with that perfect dress, **yet there's this other part of me that is highly influenced by my mother and my health** that is thinking, *Lucia, there's something bigger meant for you.*

Here's a riddle for you: What does a Custom Gown Designer and a Certified Health Coach have in common? The answer is that we both know how to tap into what is necessary to make a person feel healthy, whole, and beautiful *from the inside out.* Gowns are gorgeous, but we are drawn to the smile on the face that relays what a woman is feeling inside from wearing it, not to mention the look of their partner when they see them in it. *When it comes to health, there is also an inner radiance that can easily be detected when someone is truly healthy internally.* It naturally shines outward. And this is my passion and why I view what I do as something more than "holistic." I am very much focused on "wholistic," which has led to inspiration and success for one person at a time.

FIVE CHINESE SUPERFOODS

Through watching my mother prepare countless herbal
dishes and tonics to keep my family healthy, I have learned how
to be the one who doesn't accept disease as a part of aging.
I do my best to defy it, and help others do the same.

~ Lucia Au

Superfoods are so called because they are considered very rich in nutrients, antioxidants, polyphenols, vitamins, and minerals. These are natural ingredients that our bodies crave, helping us to operate better internally so we have the energy, joy, and health that we all want in our lives. *I have yet to meet a person who does not want to be as healthy as they can be.* Many times, they just don't know how to go about achieving that goal, thinking that it is too difficult or they are too stuck in their ways. I have exciting news: **it is not impossible and it may be easier than what you think**! You do not need to diet to give your body what it needs; you can incorporate five Chinese Superfoods into your diet so your body and organs starts to get what it craves to be at its best. Of course, *making wise food choices is always helpful, but it is not everything*. The five foods listed out can be found at local health stores, as well as from reputable online resources if you live in a smaller community where you don't have easy access to them.

1. **Astragalus**: This is a herbal root that comes in long slices and has been used in Chinese medicine for centuries as a restorative tonic. It's sweet and has warming effects on your organs that help you with aging, improved energy, and stimulation of your immune system. It's also used as an adaptogen, which helps to increase your general resistance to stress and disease.

   Recent research has also suggested that astragalus can slow down the aging process by "turning on" an enzyme called telomerase (hTERT), which is linked to expanding the lifespan of your DNA. These types of benefits add up!

2. **Ginseng**: The three varieties of ginseng are: *Korean*, which has hot healing properties; *Chinese*, which has mild heating properties; and *American*, which has cool heating properties. Their names stem from the countries in which they are grown. Regardless of the variety of ginseng that you may choose to use, all of them offer healing properties for the following conditions:

   - Malnutrition
   - Chronic fatigue or general weakness
   - Heart
   - Stomach
   - Liver malfunction
   - Menopause

3. **Medicinal mushrooms**: Mushrooms that promote better health contain lentinan, which is a polysaccharide that bolsters the immune system and has been noted to have anti-tumor effects. The mushrooms that fall into this category can easily be incorporated into food for a

tasty boost, and include:

- Reishi (red)
- Cordyceps
- Maitake
- Shiitake

4. **Goji berries**: This is the superfood that most people have heard of, as you can get it in juices, teas, wines, supplements, and various other forms. Plus, they can be eaten raw, cooked, or dried. In Asia, goji berries have been eaten for centuries to promote longevity, but they are also known to help manage diseases such as diabetes, high blood pressure, fever, and even age-related eye problems.

5. **Dang yui (Angelica)**: This root is for women with menopausal and menstruation disorders, but it is also good for men, too, because it enhances the blood, alleviates pain, helps the bowels, and can decrease swelling.

These five superfoods are simple to incorporate into the diet for your entire family, giving everyone their best "wholistic" advantage. I wanted to share a recipe with you that incorporates all five of these superfoods into one recipe! I do appreciate the struggles that people can have to make better choices at times, but love guiding those who wish to learn how to make it easier to become that healthier person you envision becoming.

Longevity Herbal Chicken Soup
(4 servings)

This has been a favorite of mine for a long time! It's good for the immune system and excellent for strengthening energy (qi), particularly during cold and flu season. The broth is "double boil," where the soup is steamed inside a container so that the broth is very clear and intense. Doing this is important, as it is the most effective way to extract the pure essence of the herbs into the soup. Plus, this is very easy to make!

Ingredients:

1 whole chicken (3 to 3-1/2 pounds)

4 cups boiling water

1 cup rice wine, preferably Shaoxing wine

5 slices of Astragalus

3 slices of Dang Qui (Angelica)

10 dime size slices Chinese Ginseng

10 pieces Cordyceps

1 tbsp. of Goji Berries

Salt

Instructions:

Rinse and soak the herbs in boiling water for 20 minutes.

Rinse the chicken with cold water, and remove any visible fat from the cavity.

Place the whole chicken in a heat-proof pot with lid.

Stuff half the herbs in the chicken and place the rest around the chicken.

Pour the boiling water and the rice wine over the chicken and the herbs.

Cover with aluminum foil and lid.

Fill steamer with water up to the base of the rack.

Place cover pot onto the rack inside the steamer.

Cover and steam on high heat for 2 hours.

Season to preferred taste with salt and serve.

Enjoy…

THE FIVE PILLARS OF GOOD HEALTH

"Balance is the key to our food and our health."

In Chinese medicine, the number "5" is very significant because the number implies balance. Balance is necessary in all that we do in life, and particularly important in how we treat our bodies on a daily basis. After all, our wonderful and diverse bodies are the vessels that will take us on the greatest journeys in life and help us achieve all the things we set out to do.

Things come at us from all directions in the world we live in, and if we do not remain strong, they can negatively impact us. Think of the body as the center of your universe and all those outside forces as gravitational pull. Don't you want to remain strong and poised? *The Five Pillars of Good Health can help you do that so you remain focused and grounded—in other words, balanced.*

1. Use moderation when you consume food; avoiding excesses of spicy, sour, fried, or sweet foods. Don't overindulge in beverages in place of solid food.

2. Enjoy small portions of a wide variety of foods.

3. Cut your food into smaller pieces to ensure uniformity in cooking, as well as making it easier to share with others. This is a wonderful way not to overeat.

4. Eat fresh food as much as possible over anything processed—there are great ways to make fresh meals just as quickly as "convenient" meals.

5. Eat according to the climate and season. You do this by knowing your *ying* and *yang* foods.

THE YING AND YANG FACTORS

We have many things we can do to help ensure that our bodies are balanced and able to respond to any changes that come our way.

~ Lucia Au

Whenever our bodies have imbalance, they will naturally try to compensate and correct on their own. This may work for a bit of time, but without adjustments, the body will have a tougher time of it as life goes on. We have the ability to help our bodies by ensuring that transitions are less taxing. These changes are based primarily on:

- **<u>Our body types</u>**:
  - *Ying body types* are known for being: listless or lacking energy; thin and pale-faced; vulnerable to infectious diseases; relaxed, easy going, and quiet; and, sensitive to cold.
  - *Yang body types* are known for being: hyper and energetic; heavy set; flushed complexion; restless or impatient; and, not sensitive to cold.

- ## **The seasons (five, in total)**:
    - *Spring* – which is associated with sour (wood) and has the liver and gallbladder for corresponding organs.
    - *Summer* – which is associated with bitter (fire) and has the heart and small intestine for corresponding organs.
    - *Late summer* – which is associated with sweet (earth) and has the spleen and stomach for corresponding organs.
    - *Autumn* – which is associated with pungent (metal) and has the lungs and large intestine for corresponding organs.
    - *Winter* – which is associated with salty (water) and has the kidney and bladder for corresponding organs.

Taking into account the seasons and our body types, we are able to bring variety into our diets throughout the year while also addressing the proper types of food to maintain better internal health. These wonderful ways to improve our chances of having a more physically, therefore emotionally, prosperous life are the "wholistic" approach that I teach my clients. *I show them what the best seasonal foods are, guide them in lifestyle adjustments, and watch exciting results happen.* It's as beautiful to see as it is to be a part of.

GIVE 100% TO YOUR LIFE

When I can help even one person find a way to give 100% to their life, I feel success and experience joy for their results.

~ Lucia Au

From a little girl on, I have always liked to give 100% to everything that I tried. I always knew that in order to do that, I had to make sure I had the energy and balance to succeed. This is not a desire that's exclusive to me, either. **And this is why I am so passionate and purposeful in my every action, so I can show others what 100% does feel like. It's amazing**!

Do you like the thought of having better health without the need for medicine to make it happen? Is the idea of having a full, productive day doing what you love or being around those you cherish inspiring? If you see the excitement in living life in a grander way, I am so excited about the potential I can help you bring out, making it so you are healthy *from the inside out* as you give 100% with less effort than you may have ever thought possible.

Today is your day!

About Lucia

On a life's journey that started in Hong Kong and then took her to Canada, and eventually the United States, Lucia Au has met amazing people and been witness to many incredible things in her life. With her career as a design teacher, and wedding dress and evening gown designer, she has always brought out the inner beauty of women through fashion, because she understands what it is that makes a person positively radiant from the inside out. This love, combined with a great awareness of how Chinese medicine is beneficial to the body, turned into a merger of Lucia's soul and purpose. She found that through being a Certified Health Coach, she could help every person who longed for it, to receive a higher quality life.

Upon moving to the United States in 2007, Lucia noticed that so many people's health needs were not being met by the Western medicine practices of the culture. It was a profound experience that brought her back to her roots, as well as the way she lived her life, and she knew that helping people to live vibrant, balanced lives was something that she must do. After all, why help people create happy moments through design if they couldn't reflect on those events later in life.

Lucia graduated from the lucrative Professional Training and Certification Program from The Institute for Integrative Nutrition in New York City in 2013, and also holds a degree in Human Ecology from University of Manitoba in Manitoba, Canada. Further degrees include a Grading and Sorting of Rough Diamonds Diploma from the American Institute of Diamond Cutting, and a Fashion Design Diploma from the Fashion Institute of Hong Kong. Lucia has also been the recipient of several awards based on her design experience and has made appearances on numerous Canadian television shows such as CTV and CKND, while also being a contributor to *Canadian Living* Magazine and *Style Manitoba* Magazine. Now, she can also add author to her list of accomplishments as she shares the excitement of when Chinese medicine meets Western lifestyles.

Surrounding herself with her passions, Lucia is also an avid cook and well known by her neighbors, friends, and peers as an excellent French pastry chef. Those same people often refer to her as "Super Mom," due to how she pursues everything she has with gusto. Her pride and joy are her four daughters, all who are successful in their chosen endeavors and have also given Lucia a name that she truly cherishes—that of Grandmother. With each day bringing the promise of adventure and a personal guarantee to give it her best, Lucia continues to blaze trails and help people connect to the type of health that will allow them to go the distance in whatever it is they love to do.

You can contact Lucia Au at: luciaau9750@comcast.net
Or call her at: (708) 800-8249.

CHAPTER 12

THE NEXT BEST PLACE TO INVEST

BY PAUL LEE

How do you determine the next best place to invest?

In 2005, I was heavily invested in San Diego. The real estate market had been fantastic for several years and a variety of indicators were signaling that we were near or at the top of the market and it was time to exercise my exit strategy. Knowing now what was about to happen with the mortgage meltdown, I'm very glad I had an investment plan, was paying attention to the market indicators, and that I followed my plan. *Lesson 1. Have an investment plan. Notice if it's working. Adjust your plan if it's not.*

I hadn't decided where or how to invest next, so with an open mind I began searching for types of investments that were new for me. I decided to join a friend for a four-day seminar about constructing highway billboards and leasing the advertising space. It was an excellent seminar, with plenty of great ideas. Although it seemed like a good business model, it just didn't feel like the right business for me. So, I kept looking. When I was planning this trip to Dallas, I decided, after the seminar, to visit another friend in Austin. I flew to Dallas, did the seminar, rented a car and drove three hours South to visit my friend.

I had heard, from several sources, Austin was a great little city. I only had one day in Austin to visit my friend and see what was so great about Austin. During my one day, I could see Austin was indeed a special place. After a little research it seemed undervalued and just the place to begin a new investment plan. In 2005 a nice neighborhood a few miles north of downtown Austin named Crestview had cute, little, old houses for about $100,000.00.

While values had gone absolutely through the roof in San Diego, Phoenix, Las Vegas, and many parts of Florida, values in Austin remained relatively low. Longtime residents didn't consider Crestview to be cheap, but it was considering the neighborhoods charm and proximity to downtown Austin. At that time, and still today, I consider downtown to be Austin's "beach front". As nice as the lakes are, for most people, including myself, downtown is the main attraction. Today, a teardown in Crestview would be over $300,000. Of course, not every neighborhood has seen that level of appreciation, but the areas closest to downtown have seen the largest rise in value. Some neighborhoods have seen even greater appreciation. Homes in the South Congress neighborhood of Travis Heights have seen values appreciate from the formerly highest prices of just under $700,000 into the millions now.

People want what they want, and will pay a premium to get it. For many home buyers, the purchase of a new home is an emotional decision. Areas that are the most affordable and close to the "beach front" are likely to appreciate because demand is highest and these areas are what the largest number of buyers can afford. Investors shouldn't let emotion guide their decision making. They should however, be aware that many home buyers will be emotionally driven in their choice of a home. A high value that seems crazy to some investors, may be a price an emotionally-involved buyer is willing to pay.

One thing I love about investing in real estate is that shifts in the market happen relatively slowly. It's not like the stock market where you can lose everything literally overnight. Noticeable changes in the real estate market usually happen over months. If you're working with a real estate professional that is an expert in an area you're watching, your agent will notice when things are changing and will know a great opportunity when it hits the market. Every investment plan should include an exit strategy with plan B and plan C contingencies. If you're paying attention to the signs of a changing market, you can see opportunity developing and you can see warning signs of a cooling market. So, what indicates a market that is likely to produce opportunity?

Here are a few things to consider:

1. Desirability: If for you, a place has that certain something, a quality you can feel, chances are others will love it too. The question is, when will the word get out, and when will a tipping point of popularity happen for the area? For years now Austin has been on many "Best of" and "Top Ten" lists. This popularity has dramatically increased in recent years. Twenty years ago, the people of Texas knew about Austin's great music scene, the beautiful Hill Country, and of course the University of Texas. Texans knew Austin was a special place, but it wasn't nearly as well appreciated outside Texas. Roughly ten years ago, events like ACL, SXSW and UT beating USC in the Rose Bowl, began to bring increasing attention to Austin nationwide. Lately, with a new F1 race track, a growing foodie scene, and a thriving, diverse economy, Austin is becoming an international destination. This brings us to the next indicator of a real estate market with great potential.

2. Economically: Expected future growth can be foreseen in the form of low unemployment rates, low vacancy rates, major employers moving headquarters to an area or expanding operations. A strong presence of companies in a growing industry and a wide variety of industries are great indicators. These days technology companies are thriving and Austin has become a second silicon valley of sorts. The film, gaming and music industries in Austin are also booming. Fortunately, there is so much more to Austin's economy. Austin is the capital of Texas and as such, has a large government employment presence. The University of Texas, with over 50,000 students is a huge contributor to Austin's economy. These areas of the local economy won't change with a slowing national economy, so there is some stability. Tourism has always been strong in Austin, but this is the case now more than ever.

Which areas of our economy will be the driving forces in the near future? A few possibilities are, alternative energy, healthcare for the aging baby boomer generation, nanotechnology, biotech, environmental technologies or even the space economy. These industries tend to develop in clusters. Perhaps these communities will see dramatic growth soon. The good news for real estate investors is you don't need to know well in advance. If you know the signs to look for, and you're paying attention, you can buy at the beginning of a growth pattern and make a bundle. If the number of people moving to an area is increasing, and unemployment is low or dropping, these are obviously good signs.

Will the availability of water be so relevant in the future, that cities like Portland and Seattle could draw people and businesses? Notice trends in population growth. Are people moving to the country or are urban areas growing taller to accommodate increasing demand? I believe urban growth and increased density will continue to be the trend. However, big profits can also be made by identifying small towns with special qualities before the the word gets out and they become increasingly popular.

Now that you've identified a city or region and have narrowed down the specific neighborhood to watch for a good investment opportunity, develop your plan of action and be prepared to act quickly, because you're not the only one looking for a great deal.

As part of your plan, as I said before, have a plan B, in case your original plan isn't working the way you'd hoped. For example, if you bought a property in 2006, using money that was borrowed from the equity of another property and you were rehabbing the property using lines of credit, you were about to have a real problem and you weren't alone. This very scenario happened to thousands of highly-leveraged investors. If you had another resource, like actual money in the bank, rather than a line of credit, at least you could finish the project. Then you'd have the problem of trying to sell when few people could qualify for a home loan. If leasing this property could bring in enough money to cover the expenses while you wait for the market to change, you'll be ok. Would the property be a good short term vacation rental? You could try finding a buyer willing to pay a premium for a seller financing situation. The point is to be prepared for surprises. If possible don't put yourself in a position where you have to sell or you have to refinance.

Self-evaluation is also very important. Is this working? Is my plan realistic? Create templates and systems to be consistent and efficient. Having a great team in place is also important. Share your plans with an excellent lender, Realtor, CPA, attorney and have a list of contractors you're confident will do good work in a timely fashion. What does it take to be successful? The truth is that it depends. People have different strengths. Find your strength and use it. Don't let non-experts in a field tell you it can't be done. Find people who are excellent at their job, make your goals clear to them and trust them to do great work for you.

When I was in college, I had a landlord who at first meeting didn't impress me much and certainly didn't appear at all successful. He drove an old truck that appeared ready to break down at any moment, and he certainly didn't dress to impress, looking less like a serious businessman, and more like he just woke up in an alley. After getting to know him over time, I learned a few things about the man. In many ways he was an average man, but as it turned out, he was a man with a plan. This man had figured out his strengths. He had his system for success. He knew what to do, and he took action according to his plan.

After several months I learned this average Joe owned, in addition to the near beachfront fourplex I lived in, many other rental properties in desirable areas all over North San Diego County. At one point, I had reason to come to his house and was amazed. He had a huge, beautiful home, overlooking the polo fields in Del Mar, and his wife had the biggest diamond I'd ever seen. This regular guy had figured out how to identify the right areas for investment, found great deals, developed a system to manage his properties and created fantastic wealth for his family. My point is, if he can do it, so can you.

Many people live their entire lives never figuring out how to utilize the talents and strengths they possess. As Dr. Wayne Dyer said, "Don't die with your music still inside you." Find your strength and develop your systems. Then apply them in a way that will help you achieve your goals.

I wish you the best of luck with your future investments. While you're hoping for luck, also make a great plan.

About Paul

Paul Lee is a Top Producer Realtor and was rated in the 2014 *Texas Monthly* as a Five Star Professional.

In Paul's words: "My client's success is my priority. I do everything I can to negotiate the best possible deal, protect their rights, and keep them well informed about the process and the specifics of the transaction in real time. Buying and selling property doesn't need to be stressful. When you're well informed and prepared for the process, it can be an exciting and fun experience. I will keep you informed and prepared for the likely events before they unfold. If you're an investor or simply looking to find a quality home in a great neighborhood for your family, I'd love to work with you and help you achieve your goals."

Paul has a BA in Economics from SDSU. He has been a Member, since 2006, of the Austin Board of Realtors®, the National Association of Realtors® and the Texas Association of Realtors®.

CHAPTER 13

OUR BODY'S TRANSITION FROM YOUNG TO OLD — HOW GENETICS LEADS TO UNDERSTANDING

BY DR. ALEX GOLD, MD, FAAFP

Before we know it, time has passed by and our youth has turned into age, but without the wisdom of why.

~ Dr. Alex Gold

Being young evokes positive qualities in us, such as vibrancy, energy, and this feeling of invincibility. Really, it's hard to accept that anything will ever change. Then it does, leaving us wondering how the thirty-something version of us managed to leave the building without us fully realizing it. Have you ever asked why? *Why does aging have to be so shocking to us*? How could some people live to be 125 while others lives end so much sooner? The main reasons this happens are:

- Lifestyle choices
- Compromised cells
- Genetics

It's in genetics that my passions lie. In fact, my love of my field of geriatric medicine was a great catalyst for me to get me thinking about how I could help people increase their chances of reaching a fulfilling life that may be blessed with longevity. I'm not talking supplements, herbs, and other commonly-used techniques to help in this process. I am talking about genetics! *Through genetics, our body offers us an abundance of information about us—specifically. We are not reproductions, as much as we are customized blueprints based off of genetics.* Tapping into this potential wealth of knowledge is not only logical, but a way to emphasize prevention of certain diseases over just management of them. This is exciting!

THE CURRENT TRENDS

It's time to divert attention and resources to disease prevention, instead of management.

~ Dr. Alex Gold

Most of us are quite passionate about causes, especially those that support eradicating some type of disease or another. After all, most of us have been impacted by a disease in some way, whether we have contracted it or we've seen how someone we care about suffers from it—possibly even passes away from it. It all seems so senseless, doesn't it? This research is valuable and necessary, and I'd never say nor think otherwise. This is what else I believe in as adamantly—**a logical extension of this research targeted toward treating diseases that currently exist in a body would be to evaluate exactly how they began**. This driving force is what is guiding me away from solely focusing on treating only what exists. *I'm called to use my love of science and my many years of experience to learn more about how it all begins.* The answers to this are inside of us!

No one just gets fatally sick overnight of a disease. Things such as high blood pressure, high cholesterol, and cancer build up over time, gaining in strength as we move on in years. Stopping it or hindering it is best served before it begins, right? It's logical, but this type of logic is impeded by some factors that are pretty tough to control, especially insurance. *Most health insurance is focused around diagnosis and management of a disease that's manipulated our body.* **This is not the way it has to be**.

The thoughts of our potential to use genetics to help adjust the course of aging and how we manage it is exhilarating to me, as well as my own questions and curiosities about how I can contribute to solving this big mystery! I spend my days at my practice, Gold Vitality Center, and my nights and weekends doing research. I strive to find new ways to use what I've learned from my patients to help me learn more about the science of genetics. This immersion is what will drive the science, and ultimately, will drive the results.

BRIDGING THE GAP

The merger of research and patient care is long overdue.

~ Dr. Alex Gold

There are certain things that we understand when it comes to money and where we choose to divert it for research. *It is easy to grasp why we want to invest multiple billions of dollars into curing cancer, because anyone who learns they have it, hopes to become a survivor.* Some may say that survivors are fortunate because of what they've learned about the value of their lives. And of course, they are! But… **If a survivor could make a choice to have avoided their disease over living through it, they'd likely choose to avoid it**!

Physicians rely on scientists and scientists rely on physicians. This is easy to accept; however, did you know that physicians and scientists barely ever interact or cross paths? It is true. Unless you are someone like me, a rather unique combination of physician and scientist, you never have a chance to make the connection. Most people like to see the same doctor and when it's time to see a specialist for a condition, they seldom change once they've established the connection. This tells me one significant detail: *physicians are a wealth of information about how people change and digress in their lives*. This is useful—essential, really! Why wouldn't a scientist or researcher that is truly set on a cure want to have access to real people's real information and progress?

I've practiced medicine in both Dallas and LA, my current location. When I was in Dallas I recognized that I had a much older client base, which forced me to specialize in geriatrics, because I wanted to fully understand aging and all that came along with it. Always passionate about learning and curious about solving, I absorbed so much information and that was fantastic. Then I moved to LA, and the culture was a bit different. My average patient was quite a bit younger. I thought, *it's fascinating how the body changes as it ages, but why does it?* And that became my spark idea. I wanted to take all this knowledge I had about the aging body and my interest for science and research and create a union of sorts, where both sides of the medical spectrum could feed off of each other. It didn't seem that anyone else was doing it, so I decided to begin bridging the gap.

Bridging the gap is something else that is logical in theory, but there are challenges to it, ones which I am willing to take head-on, because this is that important! The journey has begun and it will continue on to:

- **Raise awareness for the prevention cause—the cause fully committed to giving every person the opportunity to understand their genetics a bit better**. Just because a certain disease—such as heart disease or certain types of cancer—have been passed down from generation to generation, doesn't mean that anyone has to accept that fate or possibility without question. Through a partnership with their physician that leads to a stronger understanding of their specific genetics, they can be proactive and reach a greater potential in their lives—both in quality of it and longevity.

- **Show people an exciting new path about how their humane financial contributions can positively impact lives before disease has its chance.** Of course, there are never 100% guarantees in anything, but when it comes to offering people opportunities to avoid what they previously thought was "inevitable," things get quite exciting. Hindsight is 20/20, and who wouldn't have chosen to donate to prevention before they lost someone they cared about or found out that they were in an epic battle for their own lives?

The energy about this is intense and it's catching fire. I've spent countless hours starting to create the connections—a think tank, if you will, between scientist and doctor—to start the ingenuity rolling. Honestly, I cannot think of any better gift to give my patients and every person in this world.

WHAT TOMORROW HOLDS

As everything changes and evolves, so can our quality of life through gaining a better understanding of genetics.

~ Dr. Alex Gold

All the advances we have had in medicine and understanding the human body better all started with a vision. *Along with that vision came the acceptance of, no matter how much we think we know, we still have a lot to learn.* There is such great tenacity in the human spirit, though, and we really do crave to "know it all." That drives us and motivates us.

My research and my efforts are still in their infancy stage, but I wanted to share with you three exciting things that I believe can happen—and not only for future generations, but for our generation, too.

1. **We will find a mechanism to extend our life spans**.
   This mechanism involves research and understanding of all humans, as individuals. There are certain genetic tendencies and traits that we can grow this research from to gain that understanding, but it will take time and funds. And like all complex things, it will involve many questions, trials, answers, and retrials—then repeat. This mechanism may be something as simple as a custom supplement that works to keep our genetics stronger and less vulnerable to compromise. It's the next step and a sound one, health-wise. It moves us beyond simple awareness and adjustments to lifestyle, although those are wonderful contributors to longevity.

2. **Society will demand that the same scientific attention be paid to researching prevention as it is to disease management**.
   I know my passions and vision drive me, but I don't see any way that another person couldn't be excited about finding ways to access what our bodies have in store for us. Genetics allows us to do that, and through that, we can look at our children, parents, spouse, and even ourselves in the mirror and think, "There's a great chance for a disease- free life." Wow!

3. **Physicians' roles in helping their patients will shift to sharing the good news about prevention, compared to the tough news about how they will help you "manage" whatever disease you may have**.
   People get into medicine as a profession because they have this burning desire to help others in some meaningful way. They may choose general practice or a specialty, but they understand that they can use their intelligence and all those years of very hard work to make a positive difference. With the merger of genetics research and a physician's wisdom, this desire to make a difference will surge to a higher level—one that borders on utopia.

A tomorrow that has those three things listed out is an exciting one for me to participate in. It inspires me to work harder when I'm tired and it encourages me to continue pursuing this idea.

TAKING MY VISION VIRAL

Suddenly fighting against the "inevitable" has become considerably more exciting.

~ Dr. Alex Gold

Through using the highly finessed and comprehensive world of pharmaceutical development and adding a new twist to it—alternative medicine—we can target problems that we are genetically predisposed to, and alter their destiny. *The time to sit back and wait, maybe even pray and hope that we don't find ourselves sick, is over*! With motivation, money, and mastery we can give everyone the opportunity to extend the time of their human experience in this world—the next year will come and tomorrow will provide an opportunity. But today, that's when this must begin.

With one chapter it's hard to share a world of change, which is why I invite more conversation from those who want to have it. *Everyone has the ability to participate in the prevention of diseases and realize that genetics don't have to be as scary as we may think they are.* **They are exciting, especially when they can answer so many of the questions that linger in many of our minds**. The "what-ifs" of genetics can be tapped into and answered.

About Dr. Alex

Alex Gold was born and raised in Kiev Ukraine to a Jewish family. His immediate family survived through the thicket of World War II by living in Siberia until the war was over. But with that trauma in mind and anti-semitism still an influence on the job, his family were Jewish in the home, and hid under a Ukrainian last name in public. At the ripe young age of 25, Alex worked his way through medical school and became a practicing Urologist. Just at the time when he had a taste of affluence in medicine the USSR began to crumble. With a bad economy and poverty on the rise, so was anti-semitism.

Alex knew it was time to move on and took a one-time-shot at an opportunity to come to America. His parents and brother were soon to follow. Once he arrived, he had complete culture shock. Everything was new – from nationalities he never met before to electric doors at the airport. It would prove to be challenging however, especially not knowing the English language.

Alex picked up odd jobs in a Tarzana California hospital cleaning utensils. That's when he made the decision that he would practice medicine again. Alex studied seven years for the medical boards, looking up each word and translating it from English to Russian – so he could memorize the English term. Alex finally passed the test, but that was just the beginning of his hurdles to achieve his dream of practicing medicine again. The fierce competition from American-educated doctors and other foreign doctors for spots in a residency program was daunting. After applying to so many residency programs the denial letters piled up leaving Alex in a near state of depression. He could barely get out of bed when he received a call for an interview to a well-established residency program at the University of Texas - South Western. He packed his clothes and drove to the Lone Star State with a moments notice.

With a background as a surgeon, they saw his knowledge as superior for their highly-esteemed family practice residency. While in residency he would be reborn again! He was still Jewish, but now he was American. He was so proud to gain his American Citizenship, and up to this day he will joke that he was born in Texas. As much fun as he had in Texas, Alex never let his goals fall short. He knew he would make it back to Los Angeles and work on his dream of developing a regenerative medicine center. His moto was always move where you want to live and then open your own business.

Now Dr. Gold is a practicing physician with a thriving medical practice in the heart of Santa Monica where he resides with his lovely wife and two young sons.

CHAPTER 14

PURSUING FINANCIAL CONFIDENCE

BY STEVEN F. ST. PIERRE, CPA, CFP®, MSA

We all look forward to the "golden years." Although our vision of this ultimate period of our lives may be different, the concept is the same: to be able to have enough financially to do what we want without having to work anymore. Our parents used to work their entire lives for a company and on their last day, they got a gold watch and a pension for life. They added their social security benefits and accumulated 'nest egg' to this and learned to live within their means. For us, successfully reaching this point in our lives takes a plan.

My father worked for the Boston & Maine Railroad starting when he was 18 and ending when he retired at age 62. He collected his gold watch and his pension while being able to spend more time doing what he enjoyed. I was one of seven kids, having two older brothers, two older sisters and one of each that were younger. My mother had a full-time job managing this brood, as most did in those days. Raising seven children on a brakeman's meager salary was challenging, but they did a good job. We might not have had everything we wanted, but we had everything we needed. That included a good education beginning with 12 years of Catholic schools and concluding with college, graduate school and even a doctorate degree.

At an early age, I learned that if you wanted something, you had to work for it. For me it began with a local paper route and working my way up the employment food chain. This instilled a good work ethic along with a desire to better myself and my circumstances. I chose a career in accounting following in the footsteps of my older brother. After a few years of practicing with a local CPA firm, I attempted to pass the CPA exam, but failed. I continued to pursue this lofty goal, meeting with the same negative results on the second and third tries. I'm not sure if it was the Irish heritage that I inherited from my mother which made me so stubborn, but I continued on my path unabated and the fourth time was the charm. I still remember the words of encouragement from my brother each time I received the negative results. He said "they don't ask you how many times you took it; they just ask if you passed."

My brother and I eventually created our own CPA firm. For the first few months we practiced out of his garage in which we had a daycare center for our toddlers in one stall and our desks in the other. We eventually sent the kids off to school and rented some office space. After practicing together for 10 years, I came to a horrible conclusion: I hated accounting because it dealt with history, but loved planning because it dealt with the future! This created somewhat of a mid-life crisis for me even though I was only 38 years old. I thought long and hard about what I wanted to do when I finally grew up.

Around this time I had been referring my accounting clients to other professionals for things like investing, insurance and estate planning. As I began to sit through these meetings and experience what these professionals did, I concluded that the industry was built around products and not process. In those days, if you needed to invest money, you went to see a stockbroker. If you needed to buy insurance, you called an insurance agent. Or, if you needed to put your estate in order, you made an appointment with an attorney. What became apparent to me was that regardless of what the problem was, their products quickly became the solution. It resembled someone trying to fit a square peg into a round hole.

I also observed that these various professionals worked in separate silos and very seldom, if ever, interacted with each other. This left the client feeling that they had covered all their bases, but I found that there were side effects and interactions in these processes that created gaps in the coverage. For example, I had one client tell me that he had done his estate planning with a well-known and respected law firm and he was all set. I asked him to allow me to review his documents to double check for him. I was surprised when he handed me a sealed envelope from the law firm. This envelope contained his planning documents along with a letter from the attorney instructing the client to look over the documents and to call to set up another appointment to come in and sign them in front of a notary. Obviously he didn't know this because he never opened the envelope and no one bothered to follow up with him! I was seeing this problem arise in other clients' financial lives as well, and it frustrated me.

At the same time, my personal life was getting more complicated, having had three children of my own who would someday need educating and elderly parents that would need long-term care. In addition, my wife and I would like to one day enjoy those "golden years" we had heard so much about. It was these factors which compelled me to enter the field of financial planning and wealth management. I spent the next year getting licensed for securities, advisory services and insurance. And if that was not enough, I studied to take the CERTIFIED FINANCIAL PLANNER™ exam. I took it, and passed on the first try!

I then began to develop my *Financial Confidence Process*, the goal of which was to create a comprehensive planning process that would help people address their financial concerns in a holistic manner. The concept and design was simple enough that anyone could understand it and it started with a vision meeting. At this meeting, we determine not only *what* the client wants to have and do in their life, but more importantly, *why*. We determine their vision, which determines what their goals and priorities are. This helps us design a plan that will provide them with a road map from their present position to where they ultimately want to be. It also provides us with a measuring stick and guide to monitor their progress.

I believe that to solve any problem you need to commit three (3) things:

- Time
- Money
- Mindset

Out of the three, which do you think is most valuable? Some believe it is money, but that's not really true. Our most valuable resource is time, since we all have a limited supply. That is also illustrated when we talk about the value that time can bring to us when it is on our side.

The flipside is that it can also hurt us if we wait too long before taking appropriate action. Knowledge in and of itself is useless unless used to create change. So once you decide to commit, you need to take action!

In addition to committing time, money and mindset you will need to determine four (4) things to create positive change:

1. First you need to <u>determine what you want</u> for an outcome. This is where the vision meeting comes in. Through this process, we become crystal clear about what we want to accomplish and why. The why is extremely important – it is what motivates us and is usually something we want to avoid (pain) or something we want to move towards (pleasure).

2. The second step in the process is to <u>determine what you have</u> currently in the area you want to change. This process will quantify your present net worth, cash flow and related resources – in other words, what you own, what you owe, how much you make and how much you spend and save. It is also used to review what things you may have already done in this planning area and how successful they have been. This step is like going to a new doctor who will document your medical history, review your current medications, take different measurements and perform tests to assess your current state of overall health.

3. The third step in the process is to <u>determine what you should do</u> to make improvements in the various planning areas. This is the part of the process where the strategies come in, but instead of trying to pound the square peg in the round hole, we will seek strategies that are a custom fit. The strategies should provide you with increased progress towards your objectives. At this point, you'll want to be aware of any conflicts of interest that may exist in the implementation of these strategies. In the best of situations, your objectives and your advisor's objectives will complement each other. This step is like going to a doctor who gets paid a bonus for keeping you healthy instead of one who gets paid a stipend for recommending a drug. He chooses what is best for you and gets rewarded for it.

4. The final step in the process is to <u>monitor the results</u>. Like all processes, the *Financial Confidence Process* is built on the concept of continuous improvement. To get from where you are

today to where you want to be tomorrow takes a plan. Like a road map from a starting point to a final destination, there is a constant monitoring of progress. It is through this monitoring process, and the continued tweaking of the plan, that you can work towards your financial goals. It only makes sense!

Well now you know it will take three (3) commitments and four (4) steps to improve your financial confidence. We can now talk about the four (4) areas of your financial life that need to be consistently monitored and improved to guide you towards the "golden years." They include (1) investment management, (2) income tax planning, (3) risk analysis and (4) estate planning. These will comprise the four areas that you should monitor along with net worth and cash flow.

Unlike our parents, who received a pension when they retired, we must provide for ourselves. This means that every one of us should consider learning about investment management and decide whether we should attempt a do-it-yourself approach or find someone we trust enough to put our financial life in their hands. Long story short, the DIY investor is like the person who represents themselves in court: they have a fool for a client! If you were about to have brain surgery, would you be searching YouTube for a video on it hoping to save money? Of course not; you will work hard to find the best surgeon out there. You will ask family, friends and associates for referrals and you will meet with the doctors personally before making your choice. This area deserves no less importance – *it is your lifeline!*

If you thought making money was hard, you should try keeping more of it. A smart man once said that the only things in life that are certain are death and taxes. Once again, this is an area that can have a dramatic effect on your wealth. Take it from a guy who has been a tax preparer for over thirty years. The good news is that you are responsible as an individual taxpayer to calculate what you owe. A little tax planning before executing taxable transactions can have a dramatic effect upon your ultimate tax bill. Once again, you will have to determine if you are going to try it on your own or find a guy . . . you already know my thoughts on this.

Now we come to the part of our program where we talk about risk analysis. Simply put, if you are putting in all this hard work trying to turn dreams into reality, you'll want to consider what things may knock you off track. If you can anticipate these things, you can try to protect against them. What am I talking about, you ask? Why insurance, of course! It is one of those necessary evils that should not be ignored. What type of insurance, you ask? Many types may be necessary at some point in time, but not all are necessary all of the time as this depends on your individual situation. They include health, dental, homeowner's, auto, umbrella, life, disability and long-term care to name a few. There are too many to review in depth, but needless to say, many may be necessary, and for this you should consider finding a guy (or a gal) to help you out.

Finally we get to talk about everybody's favorite subject...death! What is it about traditional estate planning that causes us to cringe? Could it be that we are mostly talking about the end of our time on earth? Yup! Instead of this approach, I try to get people to focus on life, living and legacy. Estate planning documents can help protect the people you care most about should something happen to you. You can also determine how you will be remembered by planning on who will receive benefit from your assets. I'll give you a clue...there are only three candidates, two of whom you like and the third, not so much. Your wealth can be used to benefit your loved ones and charities if you plan properly. If it were up to me, I would disinherit the IRS/Federal Government, but that's just me!

So to summarize, we need to commit three (3) things – money, time and mindset – to help work towards solving a variety of problems. Once we have committed, we need to determine four (4) more things – what we want, what we have, what we should do, as well as how we are going to monitor the process – in order to focus on the outcome we seek. The only way we will know if we are getting the results we seek is to monitor and tweak our process. We will need to repeat this process for the four (4) financial areas in our lives:

- Investment Management
- Income Tax Planning
- Risk Analysis
- Estate Planning

If you follow this comprehensive 3-4-4 approach, it can help guide you towards better financial health and you can begin focusing on enjoying life in your "Golden Years."

[The opinions voiced in this material are for general information only and are not intended to provide specific advice or recommendations for any individual. This information is not intended to be a substitute for specific individualized tax or legal advice. We suggest that you discuss your specific situation with a qualified tax or legal advisor. Securities offered through LPL Financial, Member FINRA/SIPC. Steven St. Pierre is not affiliated with the authors of other chapters in this book.]

About Steven

Steven F. St. Pierre, CPA, CFP®, MSA is a widely recognized Financial Educator, Author, Speaker, Accountant and Financial Planner. You may have seen or heard Steve as a guest on various TV or radio programs discussing a variety of financial, business and tax-related issues – including WMUR TV9, WZID and WMUR in Manchester, NH; WSMN in Nashua, NH, and WZLX in Boston, MA.

Steve is a dynamic speaker and he loves to share his knowledge and experience with the community as well as with other professionals, like the NH Society of CPAs, through his Financial and Tax Education Briefings. In addition, he regularly authors articles for the *NH Business Review*. Steve also shares his expertise by giving testimony before the state's legislature on various proposed bills.

As the creator of the *Financial Confidence Process*, Steve and his team guide their clients through the maze of choices they need to make in the areas of education, retirement, investments, insurance, income and estate tax planning. This holistic, integrated approach provides Steve's clients with the confidence they seek to fully enjoy their life, business and retirement.

Steve earned his Bachelor's Degree in Accounting from Plymouth State College, and a Master's Degree in Accounting and a Graduate Certificate in Taxation from New Hampshire College.

He is a Certified Public Accountant, as well as a CERTIFIED FINANCIAL PLANNER™. Steve is a Financial Advisor with, and offers securities through LPL Financial, Member FINRA/SIPC. He is a member of the American Institute of Certified Public Accountants, New Hampshire Society of Certified Public Accountants, New Hampshire Estate Planning Council, and Financial Planning Association.

Contact information:
To find out more about Steven and his Financial Confidence Process, visit:
www.FinancialAdvisorNH.com.

CHAPTER 15

CZ THE DAY! - SIMPLE C SUCCESS SYSTEM©

BY SUSAN F. MOODY

There is only one success – to be able to live
your life in your own way.

~ C. Morley

Imagine if you will that you are Dorothy in the Wizard of Oz. You wake up one day and realize you are not in Kansas anymore, that this is not the life you imagined you would be living and now it is your time to finally make your way back home. This home is that place in your heart that will make you happy; whether that is to change your career, start your own business, find the love of your life, or generally to live a more enriched, joyful life.

When you opened that door into the Land of Oz, you meet Glinda the Good Witch and she helps you clarify what it is you truly want, then guides you towards the path of the yellow brick road. While traveling down that road, you soon learn you have to be courageous as you run into your share of thrown apples and flying monkeys along the way. But, undaunted, you continue to do what it takes to talk to the Wizard, to find out how to get "home."

In your mind, you can clearly see your family and friends wondering where you are and when you will be getting back. So even though you are fearful of what you may need to do, you take a deep breath and dress for success in preparation for your return home. You thought you were ready, after all you made in to see the Wizard, but you find that just by asking to get home doesn't necessarily get you there. You have to prove yourself worthy of your request.

You have to go and get the witch's broom, or take some business classes at the community college, or update your resume in the format of the day, or post a photo along with your profile on that online dating site. There always seems to be "something" that sets you back along your path to success. But, just like Dorothy, you have to remind yourself of what you truly want, then recommit to the plan and do whatever it takes.

Now you are finally on your way, you make it into that hot air balloon and are taking off – and one more challenge happens. You watch the balloon sail off without you; . . . or your business loan falls through; . . . or the job with the interview you thought you nailed goes to someone else; . . . or you find out the person you are dating is not really who you thought they were.

Crying in frustration, thinking all is lost, Glinda reappears and reminds you that you already have everything you need within you to get back home. You must truly believe in the power of your dream; your definition of success and your reason for wanting whatever it is you want in the first place and that there really is no place like home. . . Or that your idea can be a successful business. . . Or that you deserve a better paying job. . . Or that you will meet the love of your life – whatever it is you truly want.

You see, I believe we all have much more potential than we realize. I also believe that we all deserve to live a life we love living. I have found that just like Dorothy's story in the Wizard of Oz, there are six essential elements for achieving the success we all desire:

- Clarity
- Confidence
- Course
- Courage
- Commitment
- Coach

I call this my Simple C Success System©.

1. The first 'C' is <u>CLARITY</u>:
   You need to clear all the clutter in your mind to see the true picture of what you really want. You and I are both familiar with the conventional symbols of success (nice house, luxury car, expensive toys, etc.), but if that is not how <u>you</u> personally define success, you will find yourself still disappointed with life once you have obtained these material possessions. Take some time and really think about what it is that you want in life as it relates to your health, wealth, career and relationships.

2. The second 'C' is <u>CONFIDENCE</u>:
   To feel confident in who you are and what you want, you will need to further explore each of your goals that make up your definition of success. Why is each one important to you? What are your core values? How will it make you feel when you achieve your goal? If you are not significantly attached to your objective, it is harder to stay motivated to do the work necessary to achieve the goal. So, what is the *real* driver behind what it is you truly want in your life?

3. The third 'C' is a <u>COURSE</u>:
   What are the steps you need to take to get you from where you are today to where you want to be? Personally, I start with just making a long "To-Do" list of everything in my head (no matter how overwhelming it may seem at the time) and simply put those ideas down onto paper. Then I start to organize them by recognizable themes – like money, research, support, education. This allows me to sort my list into smaller, more manageable steps under each of these categories. Then, this is the key; I place a due date by each step.

4. The fourth 'C' is <u>COURAGE</u>:
   Even when you have figured out what you want and why you want it; even when you have developed your action plan, taking the necessary steps to move you forward takes courage. An inner strength and resolve to move towards the life you desire to live. To work on moving forward courageously, again I encourage you to write down your fears. I found that when I list my fears on paper, I can address them more logically and even surprisingly, cross a few off the list. The rest? Well, when my desire outweighs my reluctance, I do the things I need to do anyway!!

5. The fifth 'C' is <u>COMMITMENT</u>:

If you are not totally committed to achieving your definition of success, then it will be easy to walk away or make excuses when the path chosen and course outlined does not go 100% according to plan. The one guarantee? Things will not go 100% according to plan. I find it very helpful to elicit support from an accountability partner. Someone who will regularly check in with me to be sure I am staying on track. The main attributes of an accountability partner include: respect, open-mindedness, confidentiality, and compassionate honesty. Think about your circle of influence and determine if you already know someone who could fill that role for you.

6. The sixth 'C' is a <u>COACH</u>:

While you are following your path to success, it is tremendously helpful to have a strong support system in place. In my experience, friends and family are not always the best choice when following your heart. They sometimes don't understand what you are trying to accomplish or maybe even why you want to change your perfect (in their eyes) life. That is why I recommend a coach and mentor so that you will have your own personal, experienced lifeline supporting you all the way through the process – someone who believes in you sometimes more than you believe in yourself. And also, someone to cheer and celebrate your successes along the way.

Long ago I decided that I wanted to live life on my own terms, which basically meant to do what I want to do when I want to do it, making enough money to be able to live my chosen lifestyle. Making the transition to creating this life for me did not come without some stumbling blocks and lesson-learning failures, now considered "feedback."

Back in 1992 when I realized I was a smart woman who had made some stupid choices, I knew I needed to make some changes in my life. I was very clear on what I didn't want, but not too sure of what I did want. Once I took some time to figure out the "what" and the why, I needed to come up with an action plan. Those first three C's came pretty easily to me. The tough part was actually making the necessary changes and being committed enough to my goals to make them happen. Fortunately for me, my drive to succeed overshadowed my doubts. In my book, *Cz the Day!* I go into greater detail of my history and how I learned the steps necessary for me to succeed and create the Simple C Success System©.

The key for me was tapping into my own inner wisdom to trust myself enough to do what was best for me. I don't know if it is the same for everyone but, for women in particular, we seem to struggle with self-worth. We tend to place more value on others than we do on ourselves. I got so caught up in what others thought I should be doing that I had lost sight of what was important to me.

Once I made the leap to accepting that "Destiny is made by choice and not chance," I vowed that moving forward I would make the best choices for me; that I wanted to be able to live my life for me and no longer give others the power to make my choices. Needless to say, that was a big 'Ah-ha' moment for me – and one that changed my life forever.

It is actually quite interesting to me that I seem to give the impression that my successes have come easily or that opportunities have just been handed to me. In actuality, I have trained my mind to be ready when an opportunity presents itself. And how am I able to recognize these opportunities? Because I am very clear on what I want in my life and my reason why. I like to say I work "backwards" – meaning I start with the end in mind.

That is why Clarity and Confidence are the first 'C's in the Simple C Success System© I focus on what I want to have, not what I don't have, and why I want to have it. Plus, I admit that I like the challenge of figuring out how to get whatever it is I want, especially when others tell me it is impossible!!

I have also been described as fearless; which as I have already disclosed, I am not. I am an analytical by nature and can research things to death. I prefer to take calculated risks and always try to have a backup plan in place. The one definitive is that I am always committed to my goals. Once my mind is made up, it is tough for me to give up or change direction. That is why it is important to have someone like a coach or mentor in your corner keeping your best interest in mind. I sometimes do need a "reality" check!

Bottom line, the Simple C Success System© outlined here is what I have used repeatedly to create and bring into my life the success I have achieved to date. It has helped me to start multiple businesses, purchase several investment properties, take numerous cruise vacations and generally enjoy my happy, healthy life. I truly believe this system will work for you as well, the operative word being "work." I would just like to point out that while I said the system is simple, I didn't say it is easy.

The one thing I do know for sure, however, is that whether you are trying to realize your dream, achieve your goals or reach your highest potential to live a happier, more fulfilled life, there will never be a better time than right now to start. *If you are truly ready to achieve your personal definition of success, then take action now!* The sooner you start, the sooner you will be living the life you would really love to be living!!

CZ THE DAY! ~ SUSAN

Simple C Success System©

Clarify: Know how you define success and what goals are important to you.

Confidence: Identify who you are, your core values, and be sure your goals are in alignment.

Course: Develop an action plan with the steps and deadlines needed to accomplish your goals.

Courage: Be able to ask for the help you need or do what scares you anyway.

Commitment: Come up with solutions to situations as they arise. Figure out a way to make it happen.

Coach: Have someone who believes in you, inspires you, empowers you and mentors you to success!

About Susan

Susan F. Moody is a Certified Business, Success and Life Coach who, for over 20 years, has been working with clients of all ages, helping them define their goals, build their dreams, accelerate their results and create richer, more fulfilling lives.

Susan graduated from Mount St. Mary's College in Los Angeles with a degree in Education. Throughout the years, she has held many titles both personally and professionally having worked in small companies and large corporations. She is also a self-proclaimed serial entrepreneur having owned and operated over ten businesses.

Susan has been a sole proprietor, a franchise owner, a business partner, CEO of an LLC and President of an S Corp. Through these companies, she has sold products and services generating multi-millions in sales dollars. She has served on the board for the Small Business Administration's (SBA) Women's Roundtable, been mentioned in Entrepreneur's *Small Business Magazine* and featured on KFNX Talk Radio as well as NBC, ABC, CBS and Fox affiliate television stations speaking on creating a business that makes a difference and makes money.

Susan became a Certified Coach through Coach Training Alliance in 2003 and received a second certification through Life Mastery Institute in 2013. She became a Coach to facilitate and nurture others on their personal path to success. Susan provides coaching, mentoring, workshops and retreats for individuals and groups ready to embrace change.

She is the creator of the Yes! U Can Success Coaching Program and the Simple C Success System, writer of *Ask the Wise Woman* advice column, and author of the *4BNU Tween Mentoring Program* and *Cz the Day!* Susan is also a featured coach in Dawn Billing's book *Coaching for Results* and a co-author in Brian Tracy's book,, *Beat the Curve.*

Susan currently resides with her husband in the Phoenix area and is a member of America's Premier Experts, the Southwest Valley Chamber of Commerce, Networking Phoenix, The Conscious Community, Gals Prepared to Succeed and the Phoenix Chapter of NAWBO.

For enjoyment, Susan spends time by Oak Creek in Sedona, reading, writing, wine tasting and cruising around the world with her family and close friends.

For more information on working with Susan or to discuss speaking opportunities:
Susan F. Moody - Founder and Director - U-SUCCEED Coaching Programs

email: susan@u-succeed.com
direct: 623.734.7377
toll free: 855-U-SUCCEED
website: www.U-SUCCEED.com

CHAPTER 16

LIVE YOUR LIFE'S PURPOSE AND UNLEASH YOUR JOY!

BY PATRICE TANAKA

The two most important days in your life are
the day you are born and the day you find out why.

~ Mark Twain

I can pinpoint the exact moment when my life really began. It was upon sharing my life's purpose with an executive coach I had sought out five months after 9/11 when I was depressed and in a malaise I couldn't shake. I was not alone among New Yorkers who lived through that terrible day. What haunted me most was the idea that nearly 3,000 people went to work that morning in the Twin Towers and didn't return home that evening. I wondered what they were thinking in their final moments. If it were me, I thought I'd be trying to convince myself that I'd done everything I most wanted to do in life and that, perhaps, I was *"good to go."* But, I knew that many of the people who died that day were young, in their 20's and 30's, and probably not thinking of their mortality and probably not *"good to go."* Like most of us, they lived as if they'd have a future long enough to do everything that was most important to them. Sadly, they did not.

Suzanne Levy, my executive coach, had insisted at our first session that I re-think my purpose in life as a starting point for our work together. I was annoyed at her request because I was depressed and had little energy to envision a grand purpose for the rest of my life. But, Suzanne insisted that she couldn't help me until I could identify and articulate my life's purpose. Two weeks later at our next coaching session, I told Suzanne that my purpose in life was simply, "To choose joy in my life every day, to be mindful of that joy, and to share that joy with others." I told Suzanne that if I could live my life this way every single day that I think I could be *"good to go"* no matter how much or little time I had left.

"SO WHAT BRINGS YOU JOY?"

When Suzanne asked me the natural follow-up question – *"So what brings you joy?"* – I was stunned because I had spent so much time rethinking a life's purpose that would allow me to be *"good to go"* whenever it was my time, that I hadn't thought about the answer to that question. Suzanne prodded me until I finally blurted out: *"Dancing."* My response surprised me and only after some discussion with Suzanne did I remember my long-forgotten childhood dream of "dancing like Ginger Rogers." It's the reason I moved from Hawaii, where I was born and raised, to New York City where it seemed that Ginger and Fred, elegantly clad in flowing evening gown and tuxedo, were always dancing to a big band at some swank Manhattan supper club in their Hollywood films.

That longing to dance like Ginger Rogers brought me to the Big Apple, however, once I arrived I became laser-focused on my career and fulfilling an endless number of professional and personal obligations, including caring for a sick husband with a terminal brain tumor, and building a business with 12 colleagues after leading them in a management buyback from the hot, creative advertising agency, Chiat/Day, to start an independent, employee-owned PR firm. We were very successful and only eight years later PT&Co. was named the *"#1 Most Creative PR Agency in America."* I was, however, totally stressed and burnt out from fulfilling commitments to everyone else but me. My childhood dream of dancing like Ginger Rogers had been long forgotten until that coaching session with Suzanne.

When Suzanne learned that I couldn't even remember the last time I went dancing, she gave me homework: book yourself a dance lesson. So, at age 50, I took my first-ever dance lesson at the Pierre Dulaine Dance Studio and quickly fell madly, passionately in love with ballroom dance. Soon, my dance lesson became the highlight of my week. I was laughing and having fun again. I was living my life's purpose and *"choosing joy"* and joy came flooding back into my life.

This total "transformation" in both my personal and professional life was so profound that I felt compelled to write a book entitled, *Becoming Ginger Rogers...How Ballroom Dancing Made Me a Happier Woman, Better Partner and Smarter CEO*. I wrote *Becoming Ginger Rogers* to share how discovering and living your life's purpose can totally transform your life and take you places you never imagined nor dreamt possible. And, I don't use the word *"transform"* lightly. I am happier now than I've ever been in my life, I lost 25 pounds and my business is eight times bigger than it was BEFORE I took up ballroom dancing.

FINDING YOUR LIFE'S PURPOSE

When you know your life's purpose, it is energizing! You can more quickly identify and choose those "actions" that support your purpose and bypass those that do not.

And, when you are living your purpose, you are at your most "confident" and "powerful." Exhibiting "leadership" comes naturally and easily because you know what you want, you know what you're willing to fight for, and when you fight for something you know what you stand for, and so do others. And, in the process, you define who you are.

It's a sad truth that most of us can more easily cite our organization's business "purpose" than we can articulate our own individual life's purpose. Many of us have read the growing body of research that "purpose-driven" vs. solely "profit-driven" companies outperform the S&P 500 significantly – 1681 percent growth over a 15-year period vs.118 percent for all S&P 500 companies.[1] Being a purpose-driven organization, it seems, is definitely the way to *beat the curve.*

Extending the idea of being "purpose-driven" to individuals, especially leaders of organizations, it seems, would result in even more successful professional and personal lives. Yet fewer than 20 percent of leaders can distill their own individual life purpose into a concrete statement, according to the authors of *From Purpose to Impact* in the May 2014 issue of the Harvard Business Review. The authors go on to say that "the process of articulating your purpose and finding the courage to

1. *Firms of Endearment: How World-Class Companies Profit from Passion and Purpose, Feb.2014,* Rajendra S. Sisodia David B. Wolfe & Jagdish N. Sheth

live it—what we call purpose to impact—is the single most important developmental task you can undertake as a leader." Being a purpose-driven leader is the way that we, as leaders, can *beat the curve*. I know this to be true from first-hand experience.

WHAT I LEARNED FROM LIVING MY LIFE'S PURPOSE

By living my life's purpose and pursuing my joy, I learned some invaluable lessons that made me happier than I'd ever been. It transformed me from "Ayatollah Tanaka," what one colleague once dubbed me, to "SambaGrl," who is a much nicer person and a better colleague and business partner. Pursuing my joy of ballroom dancing taught me so many business and life lessons, including the importance of "close partnering," which helped me in co-founding two other PR agencies, CRT/tanaka (2005) and PadillaCRT (2013), the largest, employee-owned PR agency in America, where I am "close partnering" with 200 other amazing employee-owners.

Other valuable lessons I learned from pursuing my joy of ballroom dancing, which have helped me to succeed on and off the dance floor, include:

- **The importance of being fully present in life.** Dancing well requires that you execute your "present step" full-out and fearlessly, because this is what "produces" your next step or your "future." Moreover, beating yourself up over some misstep you just made is like being stuck in the past, which has the domino effect of messing up your present step and your future step. So, the only safe place to be when ballroom dancing is fully present, dancing full-out and fearlessly. I've found this to be a great metaphor for business and life.

- **Perfectionism is overrated and inhibiting to growth, the willingness to take risks and innovation.** Great dancing is not about executing each step perfectly so much as it's about dancing full-out and fearlessly. Because of ballroom dancing, I try to focus on doing a task full-out and fearlessly rather than sapping my energy worrying about doing it perfectly and making myself and everyone I work with afraid to make a mistake.

- **Practice failing to succeed more quickly.** Learn what you can from each failure and apply it going forward to help you succeed. Professional dancers don't view themselves as ever "failing." For them, it's all about continual improvement. Our Dyson vacuum client always said he learned to succeed from producing 5,127 "failed" prototypes until he finally invented the DC01 vacuum, the world's first bag-less vacuum, employing "cyclonic" technology.

- **Close partnering is key to success on and off the dance floor.** Being a strong and active follower – as women are in ballroom dancing – is as important a role as being the leader. Both are critical to the success of any team endeavor on or off the dance floor. My former partner, Frank de Falco, the one who dubbed me Ayatollah Tanaka, once said had it not been for ballroom dancing, I could never have sold my agency and let someone else take the lead. He astutely observed that because of ballroom dancing, I truly understood and appreciated the important role of follower. This is what enabled me to sell my first agency, PT&Co., to Carter Ryley Thomas and form a larger, mid-size, national agency, CRT/tanaka, and, more recently, to sell CRT/tanaka to create PadillaCRT, the largest, employee-owned PR firm in the U.S. My current agency is much bigger and more successful than my previous agencies because the "missteps" I made in my previous businesses helped me to better succeed today.

- **Visualizing your dreams is the first step in manifesting them.** Many professional dancers actually visualize themselves performing before they even step onto the ballroom floor. They see themselves executing every step, every figure, full out and fearlessly. They feel the excitement of the audience and hear the roar of the crowd. Now, I, too, visualize and set an intention for every outcome I want to achieve, beginning with a "subway meditation" on my commute to work to setting an intention for every meeting that I'm in and every initiative I undertake.

And finally,

- **Pursue your joy with a sense of urgency** because when it's our time, we want to be *"good to go,"* having done everything we most wanted to do and knowing that we lived and loved full-out and fearlessly.

AMAZING THINGS HAPPEN WHEN YOU LIVE YOUR LIFE'S PURPOSE

All of the amazing things that have happened to me since I began "pursuing my joy" would not have happened had I not first identified my "purpose in life." Everything flowed from discovering my life's purpose: "To choose joy in my life every day, to be mindful of that joy, and to share that joy with others."

Finding your purpose in life makes clear what's most important to you. And, when you "take action" you begin to attract what you want in your life, including things you hadn't even imagined or thought possible.

Taking action to live my life's purpose has resulted in:

- Writing a book on the lessons I've learned from ballroom dancing.

- Being invited to serve on the board of a wonderful, global non-profit organization, Dancing Classrooms, which brings ballroom dance into public elementary schools. This non-profit is the "perfect marriage" of my passion for ballroom dancing and my personal mission of helping children become strong, confident, productive members of society.

- Creating Joyful Planet, a Business & Life Strategy Consultancy, to help people identify and live their life's purpose and, in doing so, unleash all the success, fulfillment and joy available to them. I am doing what I love and what I do best, leveraging my creative problem-solving abilities to help individuals and organizations move forward more successfully and joyfully in business and life.

FINDING YOUR LIFE'S PURPOSE

If you have not yet discovered your life's purpose, here's a brief instrument I developed to help you get started. It involves a series of questions. Don't overthink when responding, just jot down the first things that come to mind.

1. What did your eight-year old self most love to do? What did you dream of becoming when you grew up?

2. What are you most passionate about? What makes your heart sing and soar?

3. What are your talents and special gifts? What do you love doing or feel supremely qualified to teach others?

4. What are your most heart-felt core values?

5. What is the one word/theme/character trait that captures who you are, your personal ethos and what is most important to you?

6. What is your biggest dream in life?

7. What is the unique way that you want to contribute to the world? And, what do you want your legacy to be?

After studying your responses to these questions, write in 5 to 20 words (or thereabouts) how you would leverage your greatest passion and talent to make a difference in the world. The most powerful life purpose statements are expressed in a way that is energizing, distinctive and memorable. Your purpose should not simply be a string of words (because they're not as galvanizing as a declarative statement) and it should contain words and ideas that delight, energize and excite you.

My life's purpose, as I mentioned earlier, is: *"To choose joy in my life every day, to be mindful of that joy, and to share that joy with others."* If I were to distill this down even further I would say: *"Bring joy to the world!"* My life's purpose is easy to remember and delights and excites me every time I recite it to myself and others. And, yes, I strongly recommend that you take every opportunity to state your life's purpose aloud and to share it with others, especially people who support you and want the best for you. Reciting your life's purpose is very affirming and can quickly communicate, even to perfect strangers, who you are, what's most important to you and what you are focused on achieving in life. It attracts those you want in your life and, conversely, helps filter out those you don't want to attract. It also helps people understand how they might most effectively engage with you.

Being able to identify and articulate your purpose is like having your own personal North Star, helping you navigate through life. Moreover, it's the ultimate calling card to introduce you in a way that is specific to you and deeply profound, memorable and succinct, which is essential in a time of sharply-decreasing attention spans.

To *beat the curve*, discover and live your life's purpose is the single most efficient thing you can do to unleash the joy of a more rewarding and fulfilling professional and personal life.

About Patrice

Patrice Tanaka - *Chief Joy Officer, Joyful Planet LLC*

Patrice Tanaka is a serial entrepreneur, having co-founded three award-winning, PR and Marketing firms and, most recently, Joyful Planet, a Business and Life Strategy Consultancy to help people discover and live their life's purpose and, in so doing, unleash all the joy available to them. "Through Joyful Planet, I am doing what I love and what I do best, leveraging my creative problem-solving talent to help individuals and organizations move forward more successfully and joyfully in business and life," says Patrice.

Joyful Planet is the culmination of Patrice's experience and award-winning track record in creative problem solving for some of the most successful global brands. The only reason I started my first PR agency, PT&Co., was to avoid firing four talented colleagues when we lost our biggest account, explains Patrice. The best solution I could come up with was to lead my colleagues in a management buyback from advertising agency, Chiat/Day, to co-found an employee-owned PR agency in 1990. Within eight years, PT&Co. was recognized as the *"#1 Most Creative"* and the *"#2 Best Work Environment"* among all PR agencies in the U.S.

Prior to starting Joyful Planet, Patrice was Co-Founder, Chief Counselor and Creative Strategist for PadillaCRT, the largest employee-owned PR agency, and the 15th largest independent PR agency in America. "I am proud to have been part of co-founding a purpose-driven agency committed to helping clients achieve their business purpose," Patrice says. Previously, she was Co-Chair, Chief Creative Officer and *whatcanbe* Ambassador for CRT/tanaka, an entity she helped co-found in September 2005 with Richmond, Va.-based Carter Ryley Thomas.

Patrice has been honored by many PR, marketing, business and civic organizations, including the Public Relations Society of America ("Paul M. Lund Award for Public Service"), The Holmes Group ("Creativity All-Star" Award), New York Women in Communications ("Matrix" Award), Association for Women in Communications ("Headliner" Award), Girl Scouts of Greater New York ("Woman of Distinction" Award), *Working Mother Magazine* ("Mothering That Works" Award), Asian Women in Business ("Entrepreneurial Leadership Award"), University of Hawaii ("Distinguished Alumni" Award), among others.

Born and raised in Hawaii, Patrice graduated from the University of Hawaii in 1974, became an editor at Hawaii Press Newspapers and, following that, PR Director of the Hotel Inter-Continental Maui in Wailea. In 1979, she fulfilled a life-long dream of moving to New York City. Patrice joined Jessica Dee Communications, a PR agency she helped to build, which was acquired by Chiat/Day Advertising in 1987.

A widow since 2003, Patrice lives in Manhattan. She devotes much of her free time to serving on the boards of non-profit organizations dedicated to helping women and children, including the Girl Scouts of Greater New York, Dancing Classrooms, and the American Friends of Phelophepa (the South African health care train). Patrice is also a ballroom dancer and author of *Becoming Ginger Rogers…How Ballroom Dancing Made Me a Happier Woman, a Better Partner and a Smarter CEO* (2011).

CHAPTER 17

THE FIVE PILLARS FOR AN UNSTOPPABLE COMPETITIVE ADVANTAGE

BY MELISSA D. WHITAKER

God steps into the suffering with us, and He takes it on himself, and He walks through it with us, and He uses it to create something in you that is unstoppable.

~ Kirk Cameron

It was 10:29 pm and I was sitting at our island in the kitchen doing the bills. Suddenly my husband came into the room looking very nervous and shaken up. What came next, I was not expecting. He told me that he needed $5000 from our personal finances and he needed it within two days. I became nervous and angry, and asked him what was going on. He began to explain that his motorcycle repair business was financially struggling and that he was too embarrassed and ashamed to tell me earlier. He thought he could turn it around and not have to bother me with it. However, even though he was very busy during the six months of warmer weather here in Chicago, paying for the commercial space and overhead during the winter months was killing the business. If we lived in a warmer climate year round, the business would have thrived.

Unfortunately, at this time, in January of 2012 our marriage was already hanging by a thread. So when this news came, many emotions came rushing in: feelings of anger, resentment, fear and betrayal. I was furious that he didn't speak to me earlier so we could have come up with a plan. Instead I felt pinned into a corner and had two days to figure things out.

You see this came at a very bad time for us. We just had our second baby in the year 2010, and I started my sales training and consulting business when she was only three months old. We also had a two-year-old toddler at the time and life was pretty crazy and stressful. Starting my business back then was a huge risk. I was the majority bread winner of the family and needed to make sure I was bringing home a large amount of money on a consistent basis to cover our bills and the life we have. I left an executive corporate job before my second daughter was born and had to make the decision if I was going to go back to working twelve to sixteen-hour days at another corporate job after maternity leave or start my own business. I desperately wanted to be a more present mom and wife, and definitely wanted more time with my children. However, I also knew that as a family we needed me to continue making the six figure income that I had been bringing home. So through a lot of prayer and talks with my husband back in 2010, we decided that it was time for me to start my own business. That way, even though I would still need to work a lot, I could have more flexible hours and work from home when I wasn't at a client location.

So for the first year-and-a-half of my business I made sure that I was in front of billable clients every day I could, all day long. For those of you who are in a service business like training and consulting, you know that you typically have to be in front of clients to be able to bill and make money (*or so I thought*). So that meant that I had to do all the administrative work at night. When you start your own business you wear all the hats: prospecting, appointments, proposals, closing deals, writing and teaching curriculum, invoicing, collecting, bookkeeping, etc. So my schedule looked something like this: work all day with clients, come home and make dinner for the family, give baths to our girls, spend a little time with them and then put them to bed. Then I would work from 12:00 midnight until 3:30 am pretty much every night. I would sleep for two hours and then start the next day over. How I kept up that kind of schedule for over a year is only by the grace of God. But I was determined to build my business quickly and profitably to take care of my family. My prayer when I started my business, and still is today, *"God, I will do everything you have given me the abilities to do,*

I just ask that you continually open doors and contracts so that I can provide for my family. If you keep opening doors, I will know that you are honoring this business so that I can honor my family by financially taking care of them and still having the flexibility to be more available and present. However, if the doors close, then I will go back and get a corporate job and do whatever it takes to provide for my family." God is good, and he has given me the strength and opportunity to have a thriving business.

So let's fast forward now to the night in the kitchen with my husband in 2012. Everyone who is married knows that marriage is tough enough, but when you throw financial challenges into the mix, it can get even tougher. As I mentioned before, my husband and I were already hanging by a thread. So this news felt like the straw that broke the camel's back. I felt angry that I had been working so hard around the clock to provide for us, and then to find out that the shop my husband was running had racked up a tremendous amount of debt that now we also had to recoup from. Then a couple of days later, I received a call from a friend who was worried about my husband and us as a couple. He informed me that my husband was struggling mentally and emotionally more than I knew. That threw me into a darker place.

As all of this was going on, I still needed to show up for my clients every day like nothing was happening. I needed to put my happy face on, be positive, ready to give and inspire my clients. It was a very tough time.

My husband and I were already in marriage counseling, but now we really had to fight for our marriage. We didn't like each other during this time, but we never stopped loving each other *(if that makes any sense).* We fought hard for each other for a long two-and-a-half-year process and it wasn't easy or fun. My husband and I prayed that God would help both of us work through the resentment we had for each other. During that entire time, I prayed that God would give me the strength, courage and the energy I needed to be fully present for my kids and my clients. I wanted to serve them in every way that they deserved. So, by the grace of God, my business thrived and grew every year.

Through this process with my husband, we both went through our own personal transformations. We had to take personal responsibility in what we each brought into our marriage and why it had reached the place that it did. I personally learned how important it is to be self-aware of how not only I am wired, but also how others are wired. And why that is so important not only in marriages, but also in business and everyday relationships around us. I learned that everyone wants to be seen, heard, understood and appreciated. I also had a lot of work to do when it came to vulnerability. You see, in business we are all taught to be strong, never show emotions, definitely never cry, and that showing vulnerability is weak. However, I have found that being human, being authentically real and therefore being vulnerable, is a **competitive advantage in business and in life.**

So as I started applying all of these lessons in my business, my business really took off. When people ask me how I built a thriving business in such a short time, I tell them that the following Five (5) Pillars are vital to anyone's success in business and in life:

PILLAR #1: HAVE FAITH

Through life, faith is what has elevated me to each new level, and has also kept me going during tough times. We don't make things happen on our own. Many people around us pray for us throughout our lives. We need to look to God, a higher power for guidance, direction and strength. Lean on God. Just remember that sometimes we go through tough situations so that we can learn a lesson and grow as an individual. God is more worried about our character than our comfort. We also go through hard lessons in life so that we can be used as a blessing to others along our path who may be struggling with the same thing. Just know that we each have a purpose and are here for a reason.

PILLAR #2: ANCHOR YOUR MINDSET

Every day in business, in sales, and in life we get to choose how we are going to show up. We are surrounded by negativity everywhere, so it is up to us to set the tone. We have to mentally and emotionally decide to make each day count. To make each day great! When we give off positive energy, we will attract positive results.

PILLAR #3: BE AUTHENTIC

Understand how you are wired and recognize how others are wired. Understand your strengths and challenges. Seek to understand others strengths, challenges and points of view. Show your human side. People in business and in person will appreciate that and trust will be built faster. Everyone is broken in some way. By sharing our hard lessons in life, instead of always acting like everything is perfect, we open the door for others to share and also be real. This is where real growth and healing occurs to allow for real connections. Your *competitive advantage* is caring about other people and being real *(vulnerable)*. If someone doesn't appreciate that, then don't align with them as a friend, a business partner, a spouse or a client.

PILLAR #4: BE DETERMINED

Whatever you want in life, be determined to get it. In business and in life you have to ask yourself, "How bad do you want it, what price will you pay to get it?" I definitely paid a price to fight for my marriage and to fight for my business. It took sacrifice, a lot of hours, and limited sleep. However, the outcome *(the prize)* was worth it. How determined are you to achieve the results you want in business, in a marriage or relationship, and ultimately in your life? My husband and I both share our story so that others will have hope and know that there can be beauty through the pain. We also want you to know that people and things in life that are important to you are worth fighting for.

PILLAR #5: TAKE A RISK ON YOURSELF

You are worth it! Whether you are contemplating starting a business, fighting for your authentic you, or fighting for a marriage; know that you are worth it. It may be risky, and you are not guaranteed the outcome you desire. However, you don't want to look back in your life and wonder what could have happened if you just tried. How would your life be different if you just took the risk to be uncomfortable? Believe in yourself. The magic happens outside of your comfort zone!

So through this entire journey, you may be wondering how my kids and husband are doing? They are happy, thriving, and doing magnificent. My marriage with my husband is abundant and we take steps each and every day to have an unshakeable love. He is my hero and my knight in shining armor. As for me and my business? We are UNSTOPPABLE! Are you going to choose to be UNSTOPPABLE?

About Melissa

Melissa D. Whitaker is passionate about helping people in life and in business. She takes a holistic approach to helping her clients achieve success from within. Her motto is *"Whatever you can conceive and believe, you can achieve."* Family is extremely important to Melissa, and is her ultimate driver in life. She especially wants her daughters to know that they can achieve anything they put their mind to.

Melissa is a Sales and Management Expert, Business Consultant, National Speaker and Coach. She is the co-author of the best-selling book *Pushing to the Front* with legendary Brian Tracy, and the Founder/President of Melissa Whitaker International where she helps executives and their teams achieve alignment and drive profitable sales.

Through her proprietary program called *MWI Total Sales Transformation System™* Melissa has helped thousands of sales reps and hundreds of companies achieve double digit percentage increases in their business within the first year of working with her and her team. The transformation process creates long term sustainable growth through creating clarity, finding ideal clients, increasing sales, accountability, mindset and faith. Melissa is passionate about making sure people feel seen, heard and understood in her programs and in the corporate world.

Her high-performance, customized training consultations and proven selling systems help you drive performance, generate new prospects, improve negotiation skills and ultimately win more sales.

Prior to founding Melissa Whitaker International (MWI), Melissa was the Director of Professional Development & Managed Print Services for a $40-million-dollar technology company and a Global Relationship Manager / Business Analyst for a $54.3-billion-dollar international organization. She has over 18 years of experience and success in sales, sales management, leadership, and professional development.

Melissa loves to travel, enjoys all outdoor activities and is very active in her church. She is happily married to her husband of ten years, has two amazing young daughters, and a very lovable 110 lb. Rottweiler. Melissa is also active in her community, and sponsors Compassion International and Foundation For His Ministry.

You can connect with Melissa at:
info@melissawhitakerintl.com
www.melissawhitakerintl.com
www.linkedin.com/in/melissawhitaker

CHAPTER 18

THE POWER OF LISTENING: A JOURNEY TO EXCELLENCE TO BEAT THE CURVE

BY ISMAEL CALA

I was born thanks to failed suicide attempts! My father gave me the gift of life because God would not let him take his own. He lost his left arm in an accident when he was 8. I never understood why until recently listening with all my senses to the story of my life narrated through the few pictures my mom was able to get taken in Cuba during my childhood.

While I was still developing emotionally, it was too much to understand losing my grandfather and then my aunt, and to have a father who had tried to hang himself several times. Something was not right, and I knew it. Our family had problems, but I still couldn't understand why we seemed to have a dark curse in our DNA and were under this spell's power for several generations.

With such a fragile mental health family history, I became a gladiator of the mind. My main purpose in life has been to become the master of my own voice, my body, and my mind, under the guidance and blessing of God, the universe, the light, and the higher power. My calling: to become a master listener to create a successful self in spirit, mind and body.

The relationship you have with the mind and spirit is sacred, and the secret of staying balanced lies in knowing how to listen to your inner being. As I grew more focused on discovering my own voice, one day I started to distance myself from those other voices I had given so much importance inside my head. I didn't know it then, but I was relying on the third ear, the sense of emotional detachment and skepticism. I began to question my own voices, and understand that they were not my real "I"; they were my fears speaking to me. The voice of fear silenced someone like my father who did have a very strong voice of his own, but didn't yet know how to tune in to it, or what to do with the other obstructive voices kidnapping his mind.

LISTENING TO YOUR OWN VOICE

Beyond race, religion, culture, and language, there are two kinds of people in the world: people who question, and people who think they have all the answers. Those who follow a path of spiritual enlightenment, in search of truth, learn to listen. And the others, who believe they own all the truths, never stop talking. Some people go through life asking questions, trying to find the answers, while others from a young age believe they already know everything including a false misconception of the meaning of life.

No matter what business or professional path or industry you are in, communication skills will help you beat the curve. Those are no longer soft skills but really solid ones that with creativity and innovation will avoid your work being replaced, displaced, dismissed, outsourced or automated by a robot.

Everyone should discover the fine art of conversation. I must admit that when I was younger, I felt the need to control everything, even conversations. But eventually I realized that the art of conversation could only happen when you are ready to approach it without any prejudgments. Generally, we would rather have a dialogue than passively listen to a sermon. The great philosophers have shared their passion for discovering the truth with more questions than answers. That's how electricity, the telephone, and the automobile came about, and that's how human evolution and technology have continued to develop even today.

Society has conditioned us to demand total instant gratification, which is more important than anything else. We don't have patience anymore. "Today" means "now." We ask for it, we demand it, we want it. That is why today people don't connect face to face, we try to communicate through virtual tools and social media, but our focus is always on us speaking and the secret weapon to engage is listening.

Of all the senses, hearing is my favorite. The ability to hear correctly, truly listening, is grand. One of the magical contrasts of human reality is the line between sound and silence. "You cannot teach a man anything, you can only help him find it within himself." This quote by the Italian astronomer Galileo Galilei is a guiding principle for success. Finding the answers is an act of self-enlightenment. The mystery of listening manifests itself in this way: when we understand with clarity, we carry the message and wisdom within ourselves.

OPEN YOUR MIND

Effective communication is open and receptive, and is determined by a desire to listen to the other person's point of view, not just to explain or (worse yet) impose our own. If we try to have a conversation based solely on our own agenda, we will surely not be capable of hearing our conversation partner's message. Obviously, each person has his or her own goals and interests in the conversation, especially if the interaction will result in an action or decision to be made. It's not about waiting for a result—or about letting go of our own point of view—it's about temporarily setting aside our own goals and ideals, while the other person explains theirs, to listen to them with the attention that they deserve. It's basically about being receptive, just as we hope others will be receptive to us. Actually, it is about focusing on the other's interests and not only on your own.

You have to enter into the conversation without any preconceived notions; the worst thing you can do is just follow some set-in-stone script. You have your own information and ideas, but you keep an open mind, to see what the other person is going to say.

A good conversation, or a good interview, is like a scale: on one side are your expectations for an exchange of ideas; on the other, the possibility of maintaining a harmonious relationship. Nothing positive can come from the head-on collision of two closed-off points-of-view, where neither is willing to listen to the other. Not a good conversation, or a good interview.

If we let our egos dictate how we act, we will never learn how to listen. We will only feed our own personal glory, and be incapable of sustaining healthy relationships with others, or with our selves. The ego annihilates the self. True empathy—putting yourself in another's place—cannot happen if the ego is the main star in our life's movie.

When we negotiate or have a dialogue, we are programmed to try and get things to come out to our advantage. Before we even start the conversation, we think to ourselves, "If I compromise, if I give in, I won't get ahead." But many opportunities are lost because of this narrow view.

NEVER STOP DREAMING

You should adopt good listening as a key to tolerance and personal growth. Just as I have tried to do in my career and life, I want you to move away from a rigid outlook, typical of people who don't listen. There is nothing worse than pretending to show respect with the sole purpose of manipulating, when there is no real interest in listening, connecting, and learning. Synergy comes about through a mystery we can all unlock: the mystery of listening.

But, in the quest to find your true inner voice, one of the greatest battles is going up against the ego.

I have been involved in plenty of complicated situations. That's why I understand the ego upsets, blocks and negates, when one gets out of "the zone". Like the Hindu proverb says, "Each person is a house with four rooms: the physical, the mental, the emotional and the spiritual."

Still, the ego is an engine able to move mountains if it is used in a healthy, positive way, like a megaphone to amplify our abilities and channel them as part of our personal growth process. For many people, living in poverty inhibits growth. Others try to escape it, understanding that the worst kind of poverty is mental, since it is harder to overcome. We are creative beings, of light and progress. That is the concept we must cultivate in our children and future generations.

The greatest inventions were born of brilliant dreams, pursued with determination and faith. And from the acceptance of failure, which is really just the chance to better shape a dream. Who could have imagined fifteen years ago that technology would turn our mobile phones into little computers? Whenever someone asks me if I am happy with all I have achieved, I always say, "There's still more left to do. I'm doing the best I can in the time I have, but I'm always looking ahead, dreaming and enjoying the present." Each person's story is unique according to the power of his or her dreams. The ability to dream defines the character of our existence in this world. Many people believe in luck, others don't. I am a tireless dream hunter, and believe in them because I now enjoy the results of so many years of faith and dreams come true. This is a world for dreamers. The extreme pragmatists have another mission: to execute the visions of those who dream. You either live your own dream, or someone else's. I discovered this a while ago. So, listening to your inner voice, you will be a more intuitive person and we know that in life there are calculated risks to take with just pieces of partial information. Those risk takers are people who listen to their intuition. Listening goes from the external conversation to the most intimate code of self-communication. That's the way you speak to yourself.

Sometimes we imagine expanding our horizons, but if we don't put a plan in motion like a military operation, nothing will ever happen. I don't just mean creating wealth, but the necessity of building new friendships and alliances. We get used to living with just enough, when we could be living with abundance. Surviving is stressful for almost everyone. I don't just mean in a material sense, with the consumerist obsession that keeps us perpetually unsatisfied. Enjoying the extraordinary means living fully, using our potential and surpassing the law of least effort.

LIVE ABUNDANTLY

If you really want to attract what you want, live abundantly; aspire to have more than you need. You will become a kind of talisman. Make your very essence an irresistible force of attraction to success. Think about how a bee heads straight for the honeycomb, and cannot resist pollen. In that way people, supporters and resources will come into your life. It's not about a negative ambition. Listen to your dreams and create a massive plan to get close to the dreams manifestation and let it go.

Following your dreams is a way of saying "yes" to the present while looking to the future. The past doesn't exist, it's history. I am not my mistakes, but I can learn from them. Now I am all dreams. They are the door to freedom from mundane limitations in a world dominated by the ego. Dreams founded on love and gratitude offered to others reveals the God that we all carry inside.

The power of listening to beat the curve starts with the power of smiling. A smile is the most powerful weapon in your arsenal for making a good first impression. Listen! Our eyes speak volumes while we listen. Good eye contact is very important, so the people we talk to feel valued and heard. After spending five years doing interviews every day for the international CNN en español network, I can assure you that the most important part of any human exchange is listening. That is what determines the quality, enjoyment, and emotional commitment of the conversation's participants. A conversation is not about how much you say, or how you talk. If that were the case, nothing memorable would transpire, because then people would be too preoccupied with the next question. A conversation is not a duel either, where each person is waiting for an opportunity to strike.

In conversation, the ideal is to function as a bridge of ideas more than an orator. To earn the title of good conversationalist, you must listen more than anything, and once in a while throw out an idea or thought to further develop the dialogue with the other person. This approach lets your conversation partners fully express themselves. In the end, they will feel satisfied because they were heard, and you will get credit for being a good listener, a rare thing in our world full of tweets and video chats, where real interpersonal communication has grown scarce.

If you're talking to someone, there must be a reason why. Find out what interests them, what motivates them, what makes them laugh or suffer. We can learn something from each and every person, because the experience of living is unique. Every personal story is worth hearing, and they can all teach a lesson. Beating the curve nowadays means being human, empathetic, warm, compassionate, efficient, caring, engaged, responsible. All of the above will be achieved if you decide to become a master listener to excel in business, negotiations and your life. Society tells you to stand up and speak out. My deepest strategic advice is to shut up more often and listen with generosity. That will be powerfully transforming and enlightening.

About Ismael

Ismael Cala is the Founder and Chief Creative Officer of Cala Enterprises, a multimedia content Production Company based in Miami. Cala's mission is to create multimedia and multiplatform strategic and inspirational content to better and empower people to live their full potential. Cala Enterprises produces training materials on leadership, sales, productivity and personal growth. It also creates motivational events that range from conferences and workshops to weekend retreats. Cala Enterprises has created successful business partnerships like the one established with the Chopra Center for online meditation experiences for the worldwide Hispanic market. Cala Enterprises also owns *CALA 3.0* – a digital magazine on Success, Leadership, Entrepreneurship and Wellbeing.

Ismael is a top Spanish radio and TV personality, best selling author, leadership and human development award-winning speaker and a syndicated columnist in over 23 countries. He has more than thirty years of media experience in Cuba, Canada, the United States and México. He anchors the primetime interview show Cala on CNN en Español, where he has interviewed numerous Heads of State, thought leaders, authors, business people and celebrities. Cala reaches – through CNN en Español – more than 41 million households in the Americas. Among his guests are the likes of Carolina Herrera, Larry King, Deepak Chopra, Gloria and Emilio Estefan, Jada Pinkett Smith, Elizabeth Banks, President Michelle Bachelet, Don Miguel Ruiz, Senator Marco Rubio, and Time's *One of the 100 Most Influential People 2015*, Jorge Ramos.

His books *El Poder de Escuchar, Un Buen Hijo de P...* and *El Secreto del Bambú* have become international bestsellers in the U.S. and Latin America. He is a social media influencer gathering more than five million followers on his Twitter, Facebook and Instagram accounts.

Ismael has shared the stage on major speaking events with Deepak Chopra, John C. Maxwell and Chris Gardner among others. Cala is also a sought after leadership and communication expert for corporations and the general public at large.

Born in Santiago de Cuba, he graduated with honors at York University (Toronto), attained a TV Production Diploma from Seneca College and has an Art History B.A. from Universidad de Oriente. He has studied along with world experts like Tony Robbins, John Maxwell and Deepak Chopra.

In 2013, he was named Iberoamerican Personality by the Iberoamerican Journalists Organization (Organización de Periodistas Iberoamericanos). In 2014 he received the

John Maxwell Leadership Award in the Media category, and also the *Palma de Oro*, from the National Mexicans Journalists Association of Mexico.

To learn more or to get in touch with Ismael, please visit: www.ismaelcala.com or email: Ismael@calapresenta.com. For bookings and speaking engagements, please email: manager@calapresenta.com.

You can also follow him on social media!
Twitter: @cala @calabienestar
Facebook: Facebook.com/IsmaelCala
Instagram: @ismaelcala
Periscope: @cala

CHAPTER 19

AESTHETICS OF THE HEART

DR. GERALDINE JAIN

Air guns—all the men in my family, young and old, they loved them. They were the toys my great grandfather, grandfather and then father loved the most. Apart from the air guns there were more serious firearms and rifles that were stored with great care. Vacations were meant for picking up the gun, calibre according to age, gathering all the boys and heading out to hunt as a pack. Pigeons were practice targets and then came the rabbits, wild boars and several small animals.

Everybody had guns at home till the Government of India prohibited personal possession of arms without a license. Persons possessing arms had to surrender them. But not before a fair number of animals had died standing up, healthy and happy, till the hunting bullet laid them down and made them trophies. I was surrounded by every manner of stuffed animal and photos of proud hunters with their kill. They were the men in my family. Heads of deer, antlers, mother and cub tigers stared down at us. Carpets, wall hangings or sofa covers would be the skin of some animal.

"Daddy, why are you killing all these animals?" I would ask when I was a little girl.

"God has made everything for man….and He made man to sing His glory," he replied.

173

I could never figure this out. Nor could I figure out how we could kill the hens that we nurtured as the sweetest little chicks, all with names that we had given them. When I saw Chiku or Lalli in a dish, I wept silently in the core of my being. I grieved day and night for those animal heads on the walls and the skins on which we sat. One day, unable to bear it any more, I gathered up all the skins and gave them away to anyone who would have them. My family was outraged and I never heard the last of it for many years to come.

No one realized that right from the darkness of the hunter's den, an animal activist was born and that birth would see me in future years as a fierce fighter for animal rights. While the men played with their toys of violence, I played with 'doctor sets.' With a fake stethoscope around my neck, I bullied my sister and her friends (with incentives like chocolates) to be my patients. Diseases were invented and injections with mock syringes were given freely. My playroom became my clinic.

I grew up in Bangalore, South India, like any other normal girl, till my face exploded in a minefield of acne. Acne became my very own personal nightmare. Angry red pus-filled papules erupted and grew, happy with all the popping and puncturing that I did in front of the unforgiving mirror. I had no one to guide me (oh, it's only an aspect of growing up!) and no one to tell me what to do. So I slathered calamine and mixed it with sulphur and ended up with burns. I covered my face with home remedies like turmeric and cow's milk cream and popped tetracycline capsules that were expensive then. I tried every lay technique. Acne devastated me, making me lose my self-confidence and sense of pride in my own identity.

So traumatised was I by acne, that I decided that skin was what I would work with. I would become a Dermatologist. My acne had decided my future. So I went to medical college and did a post-graduation in Dermatology. By now I was married, soon had kids, and settled in Jaipur, Rajasthan, in North West India. Now, armed with a degree, I needed a practice. Where, how? My two kids clamoured for my attention all the time. With some difficulty, I managed to find a slot for a dermatologist at Meera Hospital. Day after day, I sat idle in the polyclinic, very often with my little daughter, without any patients, twiddling my thumbs.

And then Priya came along one day. She was the daughter of a neighbour of one of the nursing staff. Twenty-two-year-old Priya walked in shyly with her face covered, head down, silent. I could see that she was in deep emotional pain. Slowly, I pulled up her face chin up. I saw that she had an uneven skin tone with blotched pigmentation. So, this was it.

"Doctor," she finally found her voice, "my parents are finding it difficult to find a match for me. My friends avoid me and I'm not invited to parties. I would rather die than live like this! I want to be fair!"

"Why on earth would she want to be fair?" I thought to myself. "Yes, she has an uneven skin tone, but why *fair*? She has such sharp features and is actually beautiful." India's obsession with fair skin is legendary. It is in our very DNA. Markets scream fairness creams from the rooftops. I have yet to understand why a country of beautifully brown people worships fairness like we do. I didn't know if I could make Priya fair, but I could try and make her happy.

I had only heard of the new kids on the block—chemical peels of Glycolic acid. I got the chemist to prepare a certain concentration for me. I started work on her, not only medically, but also constantly praising her sharp features, her lovely smile and her kind nature. Slowly I realised that along with the Glycolic peels, I was also peeling away her inhibitions and complexes while adding volumes to her self-esteem and confidence. Priya was soon a bride-to-be, confident and smart. Her friends began to come to me for treatment.

Thus, Aesthetic Dermatology had found me. I travelled all over the world picking up skills in the subject. Thanks to Priya, I stumbled into my niche, gaining steady popularity as a 'marriage' and 'beauty' dermatologist. I was the one to beautify young girls and boys perched on the threshold of their marriages wanting to look their best on their most important day!

Let's take Nivedita's case. She was called for an interview at a five-star hotel for a post at the front desk. She passed the interview with flying colours but was told to lose weight and get her acne cleared. A friend of hers sent her to me. She had done the rounds of several doctors and seemed pretty hopeless as she sat in front of me, crestfallen. She said she hardly ate, but her weight didn't decrease. She had coarse hair on her chin. I scheduled a hormonal assay for her including a sonography. My suspicions proved right when she was diagnosed with

PCOS (Poly Cystic Ovarian Syndrome). After cross consultation with an endocrinologist and gynaecologist, she was put on treatment which included a planned diet and a gym routine. In a couple of months, she lost oodles of weight, the acne cleared like magic and the coarse chin hair had vanished. Nivedita is now much sought after in the hospitality sector. Nivedita's experience taught me that often, acne is a mask for something lurking deeper.

The most sought after treatment is, no prizes for guessing, a magic potion to make you *fair*, man or woman. Absurd, but true, and as an aesthetic dermatologist, this is the reality I had to live with. Being fair in India is a culturally and socially-driven criterion to succeed in any walk of life, be it career, marriage, dating or even hanging out with a peer group. Every new day, I gawk in shock at the numbers who flock to our clinic for laser treatments, fairness peels and even injections. Steroid abuse is rampant. But my firm policy is not to treat any such requests unless the dark pigmentation is of medical origin.

My dermatological practice includes what I call "General Dermatology" which is the treatment of various types of clinical skin diseases, including chronic ones. But I have also gained credibility and reputation as an Aesthetic Dermatologist over the years. Here are my secrets.

BRIDAL SKIN, HAIR AND BODY CARE

Do you have six months, a year in advance? Then:

- Find the right doctor, nutritionist, masseuse and gym.
- Start your daily workout which includes cardio exercises, strength training and yoga. This dumps endorphins in your system and sends the blood rushing, giving you that enviable glow.
- Right nutrition is vital. So remember to have a rainbow of colours on your plate. Eat a low-salt, low calorie and protein rich diet. Carry something from home so that you don't succumb to junk food while shopping.
- Include supplements like calcium, iron, antioxidants, Vitamins A, C and E and Coenzyme Q10.
- For those with acne, start treatment right away. Your dermatologist will recommend peels and other therapies which need time. Post-acne scars require treatment with considerable

downtime. So waiting till the last minute is not a good option.

- For those considering laser hair removal, start at least eight months in advance.

- Start oil massages alternating with regular skin exfoliations.

- Keep nails clipped short.

- Look for flaws in your hair and get suitably treated. Remember, 1mm of hair grows in a month.

- Get a minimum of six to eight hours of sleep every night.

- Remember your sunscreen is your best friend. Avoid sun exposure and use a gel sunscreen with SPF 50. Apply it at least twenty minutes before you step out in the sun.

You have just a month to go? And all of the above hasn't quite worked? Here are some quickies:

- Microdermabrasion is a quick, safe and convenient treatment which removes dead cells from any part of the body leaving behind a smooth and supple skin.

- Photo-facials or photo rejuvenation. A laser or an intense pulse light (IPL) is used. This tightens the skin and closes the open pores. Warning: get this done only by a qualified professional.

- Oxygen therapy with mesoporation. Oxygen is delivered to the skin under pressure which stimulates the skin. A mesoporation device helps the skin to absorb the nutrients which are applied to the skin. Voila! Smooth skin with closed pores.

- Fillers. For deep hollows under the eyes and to plump up lips.

- Botox. For those suffering from excessive perspiration.

Phew! A week to go?

- Do not start anything new. Things can go awfully wrong and there might be no recovery time.

While I was busy honing up my career as a dermatologist, I was also developing as a committed animal activist. To begin with, my children and I started feeding the community stray dogs. Feeding strays made them friendly with us humans and helped us plug into the Animal Birth Control Programme (ABC) which involves spay-neutering. Initially, I took the dogs to the only shelter, which is a wonderful animal welfare organization. But before long I realized that Jaipur needed another shelter to take care of the multitude of problems encountered by animals. And thus Aashray was born. I joined the large network of animal welfare organisations in India and abroad. Rescue calls to Aashray have increased over the years. We now have a van to rescue small and medium-sized animals, two vets and staff to take calls 24/7.

My work with animals have convinced me that they can suffer just like us. They must have rights too, like all other oppressed groups. We need to make humane food choices, give up the use of other animal products, speak up against animal cruelty, acknowledge the misery of captive animals and see the world from their perspective too.

What have I learnt from my experience as a dermatologist and animal activist? Beauty comes from within. No amount of makeup can camouflage a malicious heart. Be the kindest person you know. Gratitude reflects on the skin. Stress and lack of compassion destroys it.

If I could leave you with a last bit of advice, be kind to all, humans and non-humans; strive for excellence and live in gratitude. Make your life a life of beauty. Take this from a Dermatologist who believes in aesthetics...... including that of the heart.

About Dr. Geraldine

Dr. Geraldine Jain has been practicing Dermatology, Aesthetic Dermatology and Laser surgery since 1992. She strives to offer her patients the best available treatments while differentiating what really works from the "hype" in the many, never-ending new technologies available in Cosmetic Dermatology, Anti-ageing medicine and Laser surgery. She takes great pride in providing her patients with the safest and most effective techniques to enhance their natural beauty. She is committed to providing highly-personalized and compassionate care during all stages of treatment. While patient safety is the top priority, every attempt is also made to make the experience as comfortable and simple as possible.

Dr. Geraldine Jain has conducted workshops in aesthetic dermatology, worked in clinical trials in skin of colour for pharma and personal care industries, including safety and efficacy trials on laser devices, clinical investigations involving neuromodulators and filling agents for skin rejuvenation. Her career goal is to pursue the highest expertise in both clinical and aesthetic dermatology with ample time devoted to academic pursuits as well.

This combination of extensive clinical and research experience along with over two decades in dermatologic practice make her uniquely qualified to customise skin care regimens for wide range of ages and skin types. Her desire to offer the latest and most expert skincare and cosmetic procedures carries her all over the globe, exchanging experience with other authorities, enabling her to bring back what is best for her patients at home.

Effectively putting into practice the adage of *Thinking Globally and Acting Locally*, she has picked, chosen and invented various types of treatments and procedures to suit Indian skin. She has the backing of International panels from AAAM, ASLMS, who frequently advise her on advances in wrinkle removal, laser techniques, botulinum toxins and filler injections.

Dr. Geraldine Jain has been associated with premier institutes of the highest standards throughout her medical career. She is the Director of Punarnawah Medical & Research Centre. She is invited as faculty and speaker at various national and international conferences. She is also pleased to be able to educate not only her patients, but people interested in her expertise worldwide by maintaining a healthy presence on the Internet through social media sites.

Dr. Geraldine Jain is also the Founder Director of Aashray, a rescue and relief shelter for injured and abandoned animals. She works relentlessly for the welfare of animals and animal causes.

Her latest activity is to stop the spread of botulism in Rajasthan, India.

Connect with her at:
www.punarnawah.com
www.facebook.com/punarnawah
www.twitter.com/punarnawah
www.aashrayjaipur.com
www.facebook.com/aashrayjaipur
geraldine.jain@gmail.com

CHAPTER 20

RESTORING HEALTH WITH CHIROPRACTIC

BY DR. JANINE BREMER

Are we in the middle of a health care crisis? Huge medical facilities costing trillions of dollars are being constructed in hopes to cure disease. Yet the numbers of people facing catastrophic illnesses continue to rise despite our best efforts and research. Health costs are spiking to their highest levels even though our government scrambles to control them. Is there any solution to this seemingly out-of-control situation? I am blessed to have been a Chiropractor for almost thirty years. I have seen amazing results with so-called "incurable" problems when we give up control and let the body do the healing. Quantity and quality of life are both attainable with healthy life choices.

NOT JUST FOR BACKS ANYMORE

Chiropractic is frequently associated with back pain after slipping and falling, or after a car accident. These are excellent times to get adjusted, but is that the extent of why we should be calling for an appointment? The purpose of manipulations or adjusting is to restore joint mobility. This can be accomplished by manually applying a controlled force into joints that have become hypomobile – or restricted in their movement. All joints of the body including the arms, legs, hands, and feet can be adjusted. These joints can be damaged and have minor dislocations or subluxations that require mobilization. I frequently see golfers that have sprain/strain injuries to the rotator cuff. They quickly return to their game after implementing a customized plan of treatment, using mobilization of joints, strengthening exercises and application of ice.

One of my recent patients had unsuccessfully been treated by specialists for her foot pain over eight months. After adjusting her foot five times to redistribute her weight on the foot she no longer experienced any pain. This is just one example of how Chiropractic treatment can allow the body to heal itself naturally.

Neck pain is also a frequent complaint, but nerve dysfunction often leads to many other problems that we do not associate with the neck. Some of these symptoms are: dizziness, migraines, interrupted sleep patterns, increased stress, high blood pressure and arm and leg pain or numbness. Pinched nerves interfere with normal nerve function causing pain, reduced movement, and muscle spasms. Adjusting the subluxation relieves the nerve pressure and the symptoms. To solve these problems, we are lead to believe through advertising that taking a pill will make us feel better. The truth is the medications treat the symptoms, not the cause. Additionally, the side-effects are often worse than the problems they are treating. Nutritional supplementation, especially the B vitamins, help reduce nerve pain and improve regeneration without causing more problems.

Are joint and muscle pain the only symptoms that can be treated with an adjustment? Each vertebra of the spine has a nerve that innervates a corresponding internal organ. When the vertebrae are adjusted, nerve pressure is relieved and normal function of the organs is restored. Through the reduction of nerve pain and proper alignment the corresponding symptoms are reduced or eliminated.

I worked with a patient who had stomach pain and digestive upset. He had been tested for ulcers and gastritis, and was prescribed acid-reducing medications. Spinal manipulation to the restricted vertebrae allowed normal nerve function and healing of the stomach. Gradually he reduced his medications and the symptoms were relieved. Healthy on the outside means healthy on the inside!

ADULTS ONLY? CHILDREN WELCOME

"What? Adjust my baby?" I hear this all the time from waiting patients when they see parents leave with their kids after an adjustment. Most of us assume our children are immune to problems of the spine. However, they have more falls and are susceptible to more sicknesses than most adults. Why not get them adjusted right away to give them a healthy start?

Research indicates that the release of cells produced by the immune system is boosted after a spinal manipulation and proper nutrition. These cells improve the healing of infants and children who have ear infections, colds, allergies, asthma, and flu symptoms but also protect them from being infected. From babies to adults who are adjusted experience fewer incidences of colds and flu, take fewer prescriptions, and heal faster than those who do not get adjusted regularly. Vitamins and minerals including: vitamins A, D, C, B, and zinc are found in organic food and whole food supplements. They will improve the results and increase the body's resistance.

Colic is another common condition I treat in young children. Presently I have been treating a six week-old baby that had been sleeping only two hours at night before waking up crying. Her doctor has diagnosed colic, and suggested diet changes which weren't a long term solution. The nerves from the lower back and pelvis control the function of the large intestine. When these nerves are pinched or have pressure on them they can create symptoms related to digestion. The vertebrae in these areas are adjusted allowing normal breakdown of food and motility of the colon. The gas and cramping associated with colic is relieved and the baby's symptoms improve. After her last visit for an adjustment she was sleeping six to seven hours per night. Now everyone is getting much better rest!

What about older kids?" Asthma and allergies are also common with the young generations. Mobilization of the nerves to the lungs, upper back, and neck improves their breathing by allowing more expansion of the alveoli of the lungs. Stimulation of the immune system prevents the allergic reactions and infections they often face.

Kids in their teens, especially young women start developing scoliosis or curvature of the spine. Analysis of the spine, adjustments, and specific back-straightening exercises can help reduce and eliminate the curvature. Many schools have discontinued scoliosis screenings due to budget cuts so it becomes imperative that they get evaluated by a Chiropractor. Children with a curvature can be detected early by parents through evaluation of their posture. They will have uneven shoulders, hips, or neck which can be noticed on pictures, uneven hems of clothes, and when getting a haircut. Scoliosis can be hereditary, caused by an injury, or carrying a heavy backpack incorrectly. Diet also has a significant impact on reducing the incidence and improvement of scoliosis. Sugar found in processed foods made of white flour and sugar take calcium out of bones, tendons, and ligaments. Diets that are deficient in minerals found in whole grains, green leafy vegetables, and fresh fruits also contribute to the problem. The bones and surrounding tissues are weakened. The results are musculoskeletal injuries, worsening of a scoliosis, and subluxations occur.

I did a scoliosis screening of a young girl who was starting to show symptoms of scoliosis. She was consistent on getting adjustments as she grew. Last year she was sixteen and her medical doctor took x-rays to evaluate the severity of her scoliosis. The radiology report confirmed that the previous curvature had been resolved and there was no medical treatment needed. Chiropractic works for everyone; it takes away nerve interference, allows the body to heal itself, and helps you stay healthy.

PRESCRIPTION OVERLOAD

I ask new patients a variety of questions before treatment including a list of their current medications. I am amazed at the number of prescriptions that many of them are taking at the same time. I often discover they have been prescribed two or three medications by different specialists without considering other prescriptions. Each drug has its own side-effects but when taken with other medications there are many unknown interactions causing a multitude of symptoms. Certain specific medications used sparingly for life- threatening conditions can be necessary and helpful, but their abuse is addictive, expensive, and out-of control.

After heart surgery, a middle-aged lady complained of middle back pain, she was unable to lay flat due to pain and muscle spasms. After reviewing her history, I discovered she was prescribed a cholesterol-lowering medication. She was experiencing many side effects that could have been caused by this drug. Lab results indicated normal blood levels of cholesterol. She immediately contacted her medical doctor and quit the medication. Three days later she returned, her pain was almost gone, and she was able to lie on her stomach completely flat. Providers often lack the time to completely research a patient's total list of medications. This can result in over-prescribing and unwanted drug interactions for the patient. Pharmaceutical companies pushing to sell more drugs to increase their revenue is another reason for the problem. Specialists often overlook medications prescribed for a different area of the body. Overwhelmed patients become prey to drug overdoses and prescription drug abuse.

The body can and will heal itself when it is given the opportunity. You should be aware of what doctors are asking you to take. Before filling a prescription, learn a few details like: Is it absolutely necessary? How long do you have to take it? . . . and what are the side effects? If there are negative consequences after taking it, call the doctor and let them know. Do not continue! There are safer alternatives to the traditional medical approach. The medical profession has not admitted that many of the problems that they treat can be helped by other methods. I have explained how Chiropractic keeps the nervous system healthy both inside and out. Chiropractic care is a very important part of your health plan both in prevention and treatment. Consistent spinal adjustments are mandatory to maintain a healthy nervous system, prevent disease, and preserve musculoskeletal integrity. Nutritional supplements also have a necessary role in maintaining a strong body.

Most food that we buy and consume is depleted of nutrients and contaminated by chemicals and hormones. Over-consumption of processed foods adds calories and fat but not essential vitamins and minerals. Supplementation is one way to feed our body nutrients which is lacking in our diets. Good food choices are essential in maintaining a strong, healthy mind and body. Some of the benefits from a nutrient-rich diet are: faster healing, less sickness, stronger bones and muscles, better athletic performance, maintaining a healthy weight, and slowing the aging process. Acupuncture and various physical therapy modalities can balance your body's energy, speed the healing process, reduce the pain, and increase the body's strength and vitality. It is time to take back control of your body and do what is best for your health!

THE LIFE-CHANGING ADJUSTMENT

The spinal adjustment is a very specialized art of mobilizing the vertebrae of the spine. This allows the innate forces of the body to heal itself without nerve interference. It is accepted as treatment for a multitude of musculoskeletal conditions and internal disorders. Chiropractors have amazing results daily as they adjust subluxations of the spine. The body's innate healing energy has the ability to bring results that seem like miracles to our patients.

Medications frequently will interfere and inhibit our natural ability to heal, weaken our natural immune mechanisms, and harm our tissues and organs. We are told that pharmaceuticals are the answer, but the truth is they only treat the symptoms. Treating the cause of the problem with the appropriate alternative allows us to take back control of our body and live a longer, more productive life. Diane has been using Chiropractic care as her primary treatment for twenty-five years. She receives regular adjustments, exercises regularly, does Yoga and meditation. Nutritional testing and treatment with whole food supplements for specific nutritional deficiencies and weaknesses are essential in her regime of lifestyle choices. Her diet is carefully planned, organic, and gluten free, She feels she has never felt better since living the Chiropractic lifestyle. Chiropractic is about your life – not about your pain!

About Dr. Janine

Dr. Janine Bremer uses her talents as a Chiropractor to help heal patients complaining of musculoskeletal problems and various internal dysfunctions. She has a family practice treating all ages including infants, pregnant moms, athletes, and the elderly. Her experience of nearly thirty years gives her the expertise to understand and treat multiple conditions. She has adjusted thousands of patients giving her insight into the most effective form of treatment. Designing specific treatment protocols for each person allows her to utilize various techniques and modalities for the best results.

Dr. Bremer graduated from National College of Chiropractic specializing in nutrition and acupuncture. She is the CEO of Gravon's Natural Chiropractic Center operating under the philosophy that "Chiropractic treats the cause not the symptoms." She is known for her success in using acupuncture in conjunction with spinal manipulations to balance the body's energy and overcome the neurologic interferences. Nutritional consultations are used in her clinic to eliminate chemical imbalances by utilizing hair analysis, saliva tests, and Contact Reflex Analysis. Weight management and cleansing protocols improve patient's health but also speed recovery time and stabilize the body's musculoskeletal system for long-term relief.

Currently, Dr. Bremer runs her own practice in Worthington, Minnesota where she helps a diverse clientele. Janine does various speaking engagements and public events to educate the public on the benefits of Chiropractic care. She is a co-author along with Brian Tracy for the upcoming book, *Beat The Curve*.

When Janine is not working, she enjoys spending time with her family and pursuing hobbies that include gardening, fishing, and hiking.

You can contact Dr. Bremer at:
www.gravonnaturalchiro.com
www.facebook/gravonsnaturalchiro

CHAPTER 21

WHAT YOU DON'T KNOW IS COSTING YOU A FORTUNE!
— EXECUTIVE SECRETS REVEALED FOR GENERATING EXTRAORDINARY RESULTS

BY JEFFREY H. WATTS, THE CATALYST

You've probably had these thoughts:

- *If only* things were better, I wouldn't have all this stress.
- *If only* I had <u>more</u> money.
- *If only* I had a <u>better</u> education.
- *If only* I had a <u>different</u> spouse.
- *If only* I had <u>more</u> customers.
- *If only* I had a <u>better</u> product.
- *If only* I had a <u>different</u> territory.

This vicious cycle of "more, better, different" is a dead-end street. It is frustrating, humiliating and there never seems to be enough. You've probably taken classes, attended seminars and read books to improve yourself, but never got the results they promised. You can "if-only" yourself to death.

You are now faced with a choice. You can either keep trying to do it on your own, spending countless hours and thousands of dollars, or you can master the four phases described in this chapter and save yourself from much pain and suffering.

How do successful people generate extraordinary results on a consistent basis, year-after-year? What are their secrets? What catapulted them to the next level?

As a top corporate advisor and a Certified High Performance Coach™, I have spent over 20 years coaching executives and entrepreneurs in Asia, Europe, and the Americas to be the very BEST in their field. Based on those experiences and extensive research, I created a system that is easy to learn and implement so you too can be #1.

Think of Clark Kent hearing a cry for help and running to the nearest telephone booth to jump into his costume, emerging moments later as Superman, ready to save the world. Clark has all the super powers of Superman – even when he is in his suit, tie, and dark glasses. Clark Kent is Superman. Nothing magical happens in the phone booth.

The executives I coach possess talent, skill, and vision, but don't consistently tap into their "super powers." *They get stuck in the phone booth, waiting for something magical to happen, just waiting...instead of being true to their vision and accessing their power.*

I have great news for you. You ARE a Superhero! What will your life be like when you access all your "super powers" to achieve the wealth, health, and success that you desire? You can have it all when you live in the world of High Performance.

High Performance is a state of being; a way of living that yields extraordinary results and personal fulfillment. The path to extraordinary results is clear: BE – DO – HAVE. You must BE who you are, DO act with courage and commitment, connect with people and your passion, and you will HAVE your vision or dream come true. This is accomplished by taking charge of the direction of your energy to continuously employ the four phases of the High Performer Cycle.

Diagram. 1. The Four Phases Of The High Performance Cycle

PHASE 1: CLARITY

Clarity is the difference between living an OK life and an extraordinary one. It is the difference between "I'm fine" and "Wow! This is fantastic!"

Most of us are unsure of how to bridge the gap from where we are now to where we want to be. That bridge you seek is made out of "clarity." Clarity relies on the quality of your questions. If you want to have better answers in your life, you have to ask better questions.

Begin by asking these three:

a) *Identity: Who are you?*

Psychology is clear: problems come from *not being* who you really are. Are you authentic? What character traits are consistently evident in your life? What roles are you playing that prevent others from seeing all of you? Does who you think you are match with who others say you are? Ask ten people you know to describe you in five words to find out.

b) *Influence: How do you engage others?*

Are you crystal clear on what you want to accomplish in your life? Do you enroll others into your vision and dreams? The quality of your life experiences is directly related to the quality of your personal and professional relationships. The traits you exhibit today may not be working for you, or others may experience you in a negative way. No worries—you have the power to create what you want. Decide what three traits that you would like to declare for your relationships today.

c) Impact: What makes you successful?

Remember your greatest success: How did you feel? How did you behave? How did others experience you? Analyze what works for you now. Be clear on your strengths and qualities.

I was a psychologist in private practice for ten years. I spent my days discussing what patients didn't like about themselves or the difficult people in their lives. I learned something significant in those sessions— if I shared my diagnosis with a patient, they often exhibited more traits of that disorder. When I did not "label" them or focus on their flaws, their behavior usually normalized and they improved. You see, humans have the amazing ability to bring things into existence. If a patient studied their disorder, read books, watched videos, or talked about their specific problems, then they became a perfect example of that disorder. The opposite is also true. This fact caused me to change my career and become a consultant and coach, where I could be the catalyst that led people to discover what was right in their life and guide them to apply their strengths to conquer any area of difficulty.

Now you get to choose how you "show up" in the world. You are the creator. You get to establish your empire and declare yourself King! You can accentuate the positive attributes of your personality, apply your influence and use your personal power to overcome any challenge.

Power Boosters:

1. *Make a list of your greatest strengths and rank them in order with strongest at the top.*

2. *Remember your greatest victories and biggest wins. What are their common traits?*

3. *If you could achieve extraordinary results in only one area of your life, where would it be?*

4. *Make a "bucket list" of everything you would like to do and have in your life.*

5. *Choose the top three items you want to "create" in your life now.*

PHASE 2: COURAGEOUS ACTIONS

What is the *compelling* vision or dream for your life? No Plan = No Power. Extraordinary results only appear when you have a clear plan and *all* of your actions are directed toward bringing that plan to fruition. Ask for feedback from your advisors and analyze your performance? Declare your vision to the world every day to remind yourself what is in it for you.

What are you afraid of? What stops you? High Performers are committed to acting courageously in spite of their feelings. They are not deterred by threats of danger, pain, ridicule, or fear. Fear is always present: fear of the unknown, fear of what others will think or say, fear of failure, and maybe even fear of success. They push through and toward their dreams. Choice conquers fear. Choose bold actions, do them consistently and fear will dramatically diminish.

Every adventure movie examines the flaws or "Achilles heel" of the Superhero and how they choose to use their powers in the world. It becomes clear that super powers can overcome weaknesses, fears, and shortcomings. Seeing, acting, relating and determination are the natural responses of both the Superhero and the High Performer. Access your inner Superhero and use the areas that you are confident and courageous in to strengthen all the other areas of your life.

It bears repeating: "Fixing" anything you think is wrong with you will not generate extraordinary results. There is much more to be gained, more success is imminent, and you will go farther when you magnify your strengths and talents instead of focusing on fixing your perceived flaws. Embrace your strengths now.

Power Boosters:

1. *What is your personal definition of Courage? Study the times you have been courageous.*

2. *What do you really want to conquer in your life? Clearly state your vision.*

3. *Create your master plan based on the top three priorities you have.*

4. *Schedule a consistent time each day to plan your steps and review accomplishments based on your master plan.*

PHASE 3: COMMITMENT

Commitment and consistent effort require energy, planning, and intention. High Performers dedicate themselves to being *who they are* in all situations. They tell the truth. They keep their promises as though their life depends on it.

High Performers avoid drama in their life...in fact; they actively fight against anyone who generates drama. They are so committed to their chosen path that they don't have time for distractions.

Research shows that High Performers practice their craft more than ordinary people. Their mantra is: "If it is to be, it is up to me!" They commit to their master plan and break it down into daily, attainable goals. The best examples are professional athletes like a PGA golfer. Being average is not an option. They spend their entire career practicing, perfecting their techniques, looking for any edge. They have a coach in the good and the bad times. They practice in a specific, planned way every day. Practice makes permanent, so they strive to focus and only spend time on activities that support their master plan and make their vision a reality.

By now you realize that leading a fulfilling, powerful, and exciting life is not a passive endeavor. You must increase and maintain your energy. In fact, High Performers create their own energy! Are you physically healthy? Do you eat a healthy diet? How do you exercise? Do you take supplements? How many hours of sleep do you get a night? You must be healthy to generate the energy required to focus, engage and pursue your dreams.

Power Boosters:

1. *What does it mean to "keep your word?" How important are promises to you?*

2. *Describe the last time in your life where you were focused, productive and passionate.*

3. *What in your life is so important that you are willing to die to make it happen?*

4. *Rate your health, fitness, energy level, and ability to focus on a scale of 1 to 5.*

5. *Commit to take only one step to improve your lowest scoring area.*

PHASE 4: CONNECTION

Connection is simply a relationship in which a person, thing, or idea is linked or associated with another. Most people struggle with being connected to their strengths, passions, and dreams, yet are intimate with their struggles, pain, and disappointments. They are also bewildered by personal relationships at home and at work. To enjoy an extraordinary life, one must discover a deeper love of connection – connection to their vision and to all the amazing people around them.

Connection is not about having a work/life balance. Balance is a myth. You don't have a work life and a personal life…you have only ONE life. Are you intentionally connecting with the lives you encounter every day? Are you passionately connected to your vision and dream in the now?

A major role in connection is to learn how to remove or limit distractions. Today, we are glued to our smartphones, are bombarded by endless information, hundreds of emails, and other interruptions (I have even seen people sitting at the same table texting one another!) If you don't control your agenda, lots of others are ready to do it for you. High Performers know how to take charge of these situations. Limiting the "daily chatter" is mandatory in order for you to stay connected to your life purpose and intimately connect to the people in your life now. What activities or social media take you away from *true connection*?

None of us want to "do life" alone. Connection is life. High Performers are connected on as many levels and in as many ways as they can generate. They understand that fulfillment, success and intimacy come from using their influence to enroll others into their dream or life vision.

Power Boosters:

1. *Rate your level of emotional connection to your vision or dream. What could you do to be more connected?*

2. *What teams have you been a member of and what was your typical role on the team?*

3. *What areas of your life vision or dream would you would like to enroll others in?*

4. *How do you attract or enroll the people you desire to be connected to?*

5. *What are the personal and professional benefits of having these people enrolled in your life vision?*

WARNING: YOU WILL MAKE MISTAKES

You may struggle when analyzing your own results (or lack of thereof). What if you have gaps in your clarity? What do you do when you lack courage? What is the process to enroll resistant people in your purpose? Who will give you honest, direct feedback, brainstorm with you, discuss possibilities and share techniques that will shorten your learning curve? The fact is that High Performers have coaches: sports trainers, a spiritual advisor, a doctor, a yoga instructor, a nutritionist, a marketing executive, a supervisor, a teacher, a consultant or a guru with an online course. It will become obvious where you require guidance or assistance as you gain clarity in your vision or dream, take courageous actions consistently, and connect with others.

A word of encouragement – whatever happens is perfect. Whatever struggle you may face is simply your teacher or coach. Honor the struggle. What you resist persists, so don't fight your results. Results are merely feedback to determine if you are fulfilling your purpose. For different results, modify your strategies to align more fully with your master plan.

Extraordinary results are the natural outcome for those who consistently follow the High Performance cycle. When you live the life of a High Performer, your clarity, courage, and commitment ensure that you are not consumed by busy work and that your efforts further your Life Work.

HAVE IT ALL

Continuously implementing the High Performer cycle will create extraordinary results. You can now perform at higher levels because the highway has already been paved for you. Develop your plan to experience a rich, connected life now! Hire a coach—or two or three—to assist in turning your breakdowns into breakthroughs. No more failures. Everything is possible. Face your day with courage. Limit distractions. Recommit daily to your purpose with clear intention and build connections with other winners.

Now is your time! Develop and use your Super Powers to create your Vision!

About Jeffrey

JEFFREY H. WATTS is a *Venture Catalyst, Executive Coach, Global Entrepreneur* and *Transformation Author.* He grew up in his family's jewelry businesses, yet chose his own path to become a psychologist. During ten years in private practice, Jeffrey found that focusing on a person's strengths, not their weaknesses or flaws, was the key to true, rapid transformation. Inspired by this discovery, he shifted his career to become an executive coach and corporate trainer. Twenty years later, hundreds of clients and companies have been revolutionized by Jeffrey's leadership – they call him *"The Catalyst."*

Today he is known in the following roles:

VENTURE CATALYST

The combination of leader development and venture advising is a real "power booster" for any business. Jeffrey Watts is the "go-to" guy for executives intent on revolutionizing their entire organization by combining his coaching and consulting. Jeffrey becomes *The Catalyst* within the team and guides them to leverage their greatest strengths to achieve the greatest results. As an operations specialist, Jeffrey's initiatives are proven to increase profitability, enhance employee retention, and expand market share for Fortune 100 and Mid-Cap companies.

EXECUTIVE COACH & MENTOR

Successful executives and leaders seek out Jeffrey Watts as their coach. He has a proven track record of "creating #1's", propelling clients to the top of their company or field of endeavor. Jeffrey is a Certified High Performance Coach™ and a Certified Practitioner of Neuro-linguistic Programming. He has trained thousands from the stage, one-on-one, and online.

GLOBAL ENTREPRENEUR

A successful entrepreneur, Jeffrey Watts has advised, operated and owned businesses in Asia, Europe, and the Americas. His experience is as diverse as the industries: automotive, beauty and cosmetics, finance, insurance, marketing and media, technology and trading. These companies benefited from Jeffrey's ability to envision new possibilities and enroll people into what can be achieved in today's Global economy.

TRANSFORMATION AUTHOR

In 2015, Jeffrey Watts was recognized as one of America's Premier Experts® for his contributions in the area of High Performance. Jeffrey's writing and courses illuminate concepts and strategies drawn from the fields of business, psychology, spirituality and history. His three decades of transformational experience motivated him to formulate the High Performance Cycle discussed in these pages.

CHILD ADVOCATE

Caring for orphans and widows is Jeffrey's passion. He works with *Arms of Love International* in Nicaragua, supporting orphans as well as building homes there for single mothers. His service in South Florida includes *His House* and *Kids in Distress*, two organizations dedicated to meeting the physical and emotional needs of orphans and foster children.

FAMILY MAN

Jeffrey is committed to living a miraculous life overflowing with joy, possibility, prosperity and adventure. He is married to his sweetheart, Nelly, and lives in South Florida. They travel frequently, enjoying outdoor activities such as canyoneering, hiking and spending time on any beach to recharge their batteries! Jeffrey is committed to passing on his family legacy of faith, love and service to his three sons.

WANT MORE?

Discover what Jeffrey Watts, *The Catalyst*, can do for you and your organization at these two websites: www.JeffreyHWatts.com and www.WattsCatalyst.com

CHAPTER 22

CHANGE: DEALING WITH THE INEVITABLE

BY ANKIT SHUKLA

One of the definitions of change is to form to a new situation; whether it is mentally, emotionally and/or physically. Change literally happens when what actually occurs is different from what was intended. People face this in all facets of life and at completely unpredictable times. Whether people like it or not, and are ready or not, they will have to adjust to certain situations. It is unnerving, but also unavoidable. I've learned throughout my whole life, with everything I've done, that change will occur and you can choose to adapt and progress, or choose to be left behind. Those are basically the only two options. Let's compare water to a brick. Water flows and is able to adapt. If you put water into anything, it will re-form and adapt to it. A brick, on the other hand, is solid, rigid and very difficult to reshape. In order to do so, it will have to break itself, or the container it's trying to form to. It is better to be like water.

In reality, we start experiencing change from the moment we are born. On a daily basis, we live life learning new ideas and the change is often so minute, we may not notice it for weeks or even years down the line. Think about seeing a photo from a few years ago, and how many changes have occurred. Sometimes, change is much more abrupt and noticeable. A toddler may touch something hot and immediately learn a painful lesson. This was a learning and growing experience for the toddler and he or she will have many of these throughout their life. How many times do you self-reflect, then suddenly realize that things are much different than they were a year ago. We immediately begin growing physically, learning subconsciously through events and also experiencing many new emotions.

As a traveling nurse, every few months I am in a completely new environment. No matter what I knew in the past or what I had accomplished, it really didn't matter when I went somewhere new. I had to adapt to this change very fast as I had to get used to the new environment, learn their policies and work well with the new staff. I also had to show them that I knew what I was doing. If I did not adapt quickly to the change, I would basically have to take my ball and go home. Having lived and worked in many different places, and with so many different types of people, I have become quite adept at dealing with change.

Furthermore, while working to become a successful entrepreneur, I have had to learn very fast that ways to market yourself, to run a business and taking care of financial matters evolve very quickly. If you do not have good computer and Internet skills, you are way behind the curve. I was never a huge fan of technology, but I understand that being tech savvy is a must. To succeed in the business world, or the professional world in general, we must keep up with new technology. A good website is a must; and if you only accept cash payments, while others are able to use their smart phones in all sorts of ways to accept funds, you will be missing out on a lot of revenue. Gone are the days when you can only accept cash, now that so many different ways of doing online payroll exist. These are just some of the changes I have had to deal with in the professional world.

Lucky for me, I love and embrace change. I get very excited about getting new experiences and actually get anxious when I fall into too much of a routine and life becomes stagnant. This is one of the reasons I've always held multiple jobs or businesses, sometimes to my own detriment, because I was not properly prepared. Nonetheless, I need the changing environments, even if it burns me out. Despite this, change is still very scary, especially the anticipation of it. I've had to embrace it at every turn, or I would never have succeeded at anything I have done. I haven't always liked the new directions I have had to go, but I understood the necessity of it just to keep up with everyone else.

Many people do not like change, however, it is inevitable no matter how much we try to avoid it. At some point in life, change will occur, whether it is at our work or with our personal lives. The more that people are willing to get ahead, the more change they will have to deal with. In order for a person to improve the current situation in one's life, both professional and personal, he or she will have to deal with change. We live in a fast-moving world and we must learn to adapt, or we will be left behind. If we are to progress in any way, we have to experience change and overcome it. This is why we must all learn to adapt to change.

People who are successful in their careers know how to adapt to change, even if they don't like it. One example is a doctor. A doctor must be willing to learn the numerous advances that take place regularly in medicine. This can be a new, less invasive, method for performing a complex procedure, or switching to a computer versus a paper-charting system. If the doctor refuses to learn and adapt to these new changes, he or she will not be able to advance in their profession. I recall a number of times while working at the hospital, listening to doctors and other healthcare professionals complain about the new computer-charting system. It was a difficult transition, and came with some disadvantages, but we all had to change with the times. With this new technology came improved ways of transferring and keeping up with patients' health information. It is nearly impossible for a medical facility these days to keep up without some sort of computer-charting system.

A business person must continue to adapt to new and changing circumstances. They must familiarize themselves with new technology in order to make things more efficient and economical. Is it better to fly everyone to a certain location to have a meeting, or to host a webinar? Certainly, using a webinar system when possible can cut down on so many expenses and peoples energy. Clients would also appreciate the saving of time and resources in having a webinar versus the other option. If the business person refuses to adapt to the influx of technology, then much revenue, time and resources will be lost, and business will suffer . . . or even end completely.

What will happen to these two different professionals mentioned in the last two paragraphs if they refuse to reshape themselves? They will get left in the dust by those who keep reinventing themselves and how they do things. Don't let this happen to you because you refuse to move forward. Change is a constant process, but worth it if it gets you to where you need to be.

How do we adapt to change? The first thing we must do is accept it, because it will happen. No matter how much we try for things to remain the same, change will occur. Remember that the one thing predictable about life is its unpredictability. Embrace the idea of change and keep an open mind to learning new things. Even though it can be very scary, what is on the other side can be so much better. Accept that change will occur, and it will be much easier to deal with.

When you are a team player, others are more willing to help you ease into a changing situation. When you are willing to help others, work well with others and allow yourself to be easy to work with, more people will be eager to help you. With the support of other people, change can be easier to accept, or can even be welcoming. How do we become team players? First, learn to take the initiative. If you see a task needing to be done and you know how to do it, then do it. Second, if you see a co-worker struggling, help them the best that you can. They will appreciate it and if you do it enough, your kindness will not go unnoticed. Even just a simple, "Let me know if you need help," can go a long way. If your helpfulness is not appreciated, that is a problem within the other person. Don't let this stop you from giving a helping hand. Furthermore, be willing to take on some extra work when reasonable. This shows your bosses that you are willing to help the team. Remember, if others like you, they will help you ease into change. Be a team player and they will like you.

Remember to always set goals and work hard. With hard work, we improve ourselves. With self-improvement, the change in our lives is generally something we want. It is much easier to adapt to change when it is a change in direction towards something we desire to have. A promotion at work, for example, brings about many new situations: a new environment, new co-workers, new pay scale and new responsibilities, etc. If this promotion steers us towards our goals, then it will be much easier to adapt to, because it's something we want.

When setting a goal, make sure it is realistic and solid. A goal such as, "I am going to write a book someday," is not a solid goal. Change this statement to, "I will write a 200-page mystery novel by November of this year." This is a good, solid goal with a specific outcome and timeline. A little off topic, however, when going after a goal we will have to reform ourselves, and having solid plans will make this a little easier to predict and we will be willing to accept this change towards something we want.

Finally, be prepared for life as much as you can. We cannot be ready for everything that life may throw at us, but through careful preparation we are less likely to be blind-sided. Learn many different skills, from new business ideas to different vocations and job skills. Educate yourself on the basics of dealing with an emergency. Read and learn new information regularly, set up safety nets and have as many back up plans as you can. Why is this important? We never know when a change in our situation will occur. Many times, change, such as a job loss or illness, can completely devastate us financially, mentally, emotionally and physically. Being as prepared as we can with the aforementioned ways can lessen the negative impact of these changes and help us get back on our feet quicker. Though we do not want to get into an accident, we can take precautions like wearing a seatbelt and having good insurance, both of which will lessen the possible pain and suffering if we do get into one. Also, when we feel more prepared for life, we fear change less. Think about it, aren't you less nervous living day to day when you have a nice financial cushion to fall back on? Find as many ways as possible to prepare for life, and then enjoy the ride.

I may have repeated myself a few times, but it is imperative to understand the importance of adapting to change. No matter what people set out to do in life, they have to constantly reshape themselves and their ways of thinking. Otherwise, they will be left completely behind. Change is inevitable and we must adapt to it. Many times, change is actually a great thing for our lives. The fear of change is often worse than the change itself. Some people say the devil you know is better than the devil you don't. I prefer to get to know the devil I don't. Usually, they are not a devil at all. Either way, you will meet these so-called devils throughout your life. So, embrace them, be prepared for them and work hard to adapt to them. We all have it in us to adapt to life's ever-evolving situations.

One thing I have noticed is that people often fear change; however, they are generally much happier after the fact.

~ Ankit Shukla

About Ankit

Ankit Shukla was born in India, but he moved with his parents to Sparks, NV when he was only a year old. His parents were hardworking Indian immigrants who wanted a better life for their two sons, and they succeeded. He watched his parents struggle daily, but continue to work hard to create a comfortable life for themselves. Their struggle gave him the motivation and work ethic to continue to create a better life for himself. Ankit attended Sparks High school and then went on to obtain his Bachelor of Science (Nursing) Degree from the University of Nevada, Reno in 2006. He has one older brother.

After college, Ankit left Nevada to explore other areas of the country. He states: "It is one of the best decisions I have ever made." He started travel nursing in 2010, which he still does to this day, having lived in eight different states. He has lived life, learned from life and has had several different careers and businesses. Along with nursing, Ankit is pursuing additional careers in motivational speaking, writing, CPR instructing and teaching. He currently owns a home with his wife, Virginia, in Aurora, CO. They both enjoy the city life of nearby Denver, as well as the beautiful Colorado scenery. His hobbies include traveling, writing, hiking, reading, riding his bike and trying out different restaurants.

He has dealt with many different situations, both personally and professionally. He learned almost immediately after entering the workforce, just how important it is to be able to adapt to new situations and circumstances. As a traveling nurse, he has worked all over the country. In addition, he has worked in many different settings with all types of people through various companies and businesses. He has never been shy about trying new things. He believes he has learned equally from both his successes and his failures in life. Ankit is well-versed on dealing with change and what it takes to adapt to a rapidly moving and ever-changing world. In addition to his life experiences, Ankit has written many articles and blogs about dealing with change; along with many other topics. He has a genuine passion for helping people.

Follow Ankit on his Blogs and websites:
- www.theevenbetterlife.com
- www.rapidactioncpr.com
- EzineArticles.com/?expert=Ankit S
- www.facebook.com/TheEvenBetterLife
- www.twitter.com/ankitonur

Also feel free to contact him via email: ankitonur6@gmail.com. He would love to help you.

CHAPTER 23

TODAY'S SMART ESTATE PLANNING FOR TOMORROW'S UNKNOWNS: YOUR BEST STRATEGIES

BY BRIAN M. DOUGLAS, ESQ.

You've just entered the working world and are thinking about all the exciting change and growth you are experiencing. *Then all of a sudden people are talking about estate planning, asset protection, and wealth strategies.* You're thinking: *Slow down; I have a long time to go before I have to worry about those things.* You put it off until…you realize that time has flown by. You have all these amazing things—a family, a great career, a retirement account—but you do not have a plan. **Where you were once ahead, you are now behind.**

Staying ahead of the curve with what you've accumulated seems like a daunting feat, especially when you factor in how much our world changes at such a fast pace. Admittedly, it gets confusing, because there is so much information out there. And, as Confucius said, "A confused mind says no." You're stuck at no, but you don't have to be. Helping people transition from "confused" to "clear" through smart strategies that lead to the right actions is what I do as an Estate Planning Attorney. Need some motivation? Consider this: over 120 million Americans do not have proper estate planning in place. *Do you have a solid plan in place, if you even have a plan in place?*

YOUR "BASIC 3" MUST HAVES.

Crises do not give advanced notice, but you can still be prepared for them.

A lot of paperwork and planning can be overwhelming, making it easier to procrastinate. Where do you start? Although it's only the beginning of a truly effective plan, you should have the "Basic 3" in place.

1. Durable Power of Attorney

This allows someone you trust to make general and specific business and legal decisions on your behalf in case you are unable to do so due to disability, illness or incompetency. It will give your family access to your bank accounts, allow them to pay your bills, and make financial and legal decisions for you if you are hospitalized or otherwise incapacitated.

2. A Healthcare Proxy

With a healthcare proxy, we are telling others what we want to take place, should we ever become physically or mentally incapacitated. With this document, our specific requests and desires are laid out, providing us peace of mind while also alleviating tough decisions for those we love, such as removal from life support. This is another document that parents may want to consider for their adult children. Imagine. . . your child is 18 and they are in an accident. They're an adult so you can't get any information on them in regards to their condition or how to approach their care. A healthcare proxy prevents you from being cut out of the decision-making process.

3. A Will

This is the foundation of all your assets and specific instructions that you may have after you pass away. It's the document that courts and family members will look to for guidance in fulfilling those requests. It will also establish the guardian for your minor children. As a word of caution, this is not a "one-and-done" document; it is meant to be reviewed as your life changes from year to year, maybe even more frequently, depending on your circumstances. As life changes for you, your Will should, too.

ESTATE PLANNING IS FOR EVERYONE, NOT JUST THE WEALTHY.

You plan for the moment. Why not plan for what is really important?

I want to share a situation with you that most every parent can relate to. You have your first child and you're likely on overdrive with excitement, caution, some second guessing, and a bit of fear. Then it happens—it's time for your first outing without your baby. Let's say it's date night. You and your spouse start planning and preparing, using just about as much effort as you've ever put into anything in your entire life. *After all, you've never done this before and your baby is your treasure.*

You're making notes for the babysitter, looking around the house, creating a list of ICE numbers (in case of emergency), and think you are prepared. **But you double check again, and then again—just to make sure.** The babysitter arrives and you go through a forty-five-minute orientation with them—even though you've already thoroughly vetted them (because the babysitter is your wife's sister). Then you're off.

As you nervously chat away about how excited you are for date night, your hand is on your phone—just in case—and your mind is only half in the moment, because you're worried. Scenarios flash through your head. But you go through with the date and although it's pretty short, you did it! When you get home, you're relieved that all is in order and your plan paid off. Success!

Why don't we plan for everything in our lives the way we plan for moments like that? Without that planning, there definitely wouldn't have been peace of mind, right? In addition to those date nights, why not give your attention to:

- *What happens as you age?* Where do you want to go? What are your options?

- *What happens when you do pass on?* Do you want to control what happens with what you've worked so hard to earn, or are you good with someone else controlling it?

Most of us have grown up in a culture where we're taught to save money, contribute to our 401(k), and accumulate "wealth for the well-being of ourselves and those we love." It is comforting to have these things in place. However, **it is only half the equation!** *That is the truth, and it* *shocks many people when they find that out. They have no idea that there is more, but there is.*

PUT THE SECOND HALF OF THE EQUATION INTO ACTION!

The best thought-out plans will fail if they don't factor in the whole equation.

I've never met someone who said, "I love paying taxes!" Most of us dislike paying taxes, believing they are too excessive, and try to minimize how much we have to pay. Let me ask you, **if you don't want to pay taxes when you're alive, do you really want to pay them when you're dead?** If you don't properly plan, you will. *The tax man still cometh while you are in your eternal resting place.* You can ignore it and hope for the best, or you can make a point to know what you can do to protect your assets from the "tax man" and plan accordingly.

Your estate planning is like a recipe. You can have all the ingredients for the best plan in the world, but if they are not working together—for you—you are going to find that your plan flopped—just like bread without yeast falls flat. Your wishes for your assets are going to fall flat if you don't factor in taxes, because addressing them closes the loopholes that leave you vulnerable.

Estate planning isn't a rich man's game. It's for everyone, especially those that have worked hard to get what they have and need to make sure that they don't lose it. People have said, "My estate isn't big enough for a death tax." But what about the taxes that will apply to all transactions:

- *Capital Gains taxes.* All depending, you could be giving 20+% to the government from your residence when your heirs sell it. This is unavoidable, but can be minimized.

- *Taxes on investments.* If your heirs cash out on your investments they will pay some pretty big taxes. You likely paid tax on them, but that was just for you—not them, too!

A small number of people go through life thinking, I don't care if my last check bounces; however, most people are motivated by the desire to leave a legacy. It'll be a much smaller one when taxes are not factored in to the plan.

Estate planning handles what happens after you're gone, but also what will happen when you are still alive. None of us are immune from getting health problems that force us into a nursing home or Assisted Living Facility. Knowing this, it makes sense to understand how our finances are going to work for us if an undesirable situation arises.

Thinking about what we "could have done" will never be comforting when we are in a situation where our ability to make our own decisions has been taken away, or we find that we don't really have everything as organized as we thought. Are you looking to avoid going down that path? I bet you are, which means you're going to embrace what come next.

FIVE WAYS TO CREATE AN EFFECTIVE ESTATE PLAN.

Estate planning…for when you don't want to be fed to the wolves.

On average, we live longer today than we ever did before. This is why we should plan for our life, as well as for what happens after we are gone. *If you like to be in control, think of this as your last great act!* And if you don't care about control, think about how great it is to be ahead of the curve—because that's what you'll be if you handle your estate planning properly. Here are five actions you should take:

1. Have a Living Trust (Revocable Trust).

This way of organizing an estate started gaining popularity in the 70s and it is still on the rise. By doing this, you are doing two highly appealing things:

- *You will avoid probate court.* When you pass away and don't have the proper legal documents in place, the laws of your state will control what happens to your estate. This is done through a probate court and could take years to complete, depending on how complex it is.

- *You are addressing matters of incapacity.* Wills only address what happens after you pass away, whereas Living Trusts address what happens when you are alive, as well as when you pass away. A Power of Attorney is not always enough. Certain policies and guidelines exist today—many in banking—that make it difficult to conduct business even with a legitimate Power of Attorney. This takes loved ones away from you and forces them to deal with institutions and frustration in stressful times.

2. Estate planning is a team approach.

While I understand all the nuances that come with being an estate planning attorney, I do not know every section of the Internal Revenue Code. And likewise, just because someone is a tax expert doesn't mean that they know financial planning or insurance. That is why a team approach is the most effective. One individual cannot wear "every hat." When you build a team, you want:

- Them to work effectively together for your benefit.

- A group of experts in specific areas.

- Their combined efforts to create a more ideal situation.

Your team makes up the pieces of your estate puzzle. Put them together and you'll see the big picture. Can you control everything? No, because you don't make the laws that dictate what may happen with your money. However, you can have a team that understands the best ways to maximize your situation for your benefit and make adjustments as laws change.

3. Understand the difference between "Cost" and "Value".

If there is one specific thing I wish for you, it is to not focus on how much it costs to effectively plan your estate. Knowing that you are paying today for security tomorrow brings a level of comfort that you cannot put a price on. No one wants to throw money away, but if you are struggling with the concept of cost versus value, these scenarios should help put it into perspective:

- Would you buy a discounted parachute if it was only guaranteed to work 80% of the time? No way! You'd pay full price for a better guarantee, right?

- Are you going to trust your future to an expert or to some website where you download some "forms" that were prepared by some attorney you have never even met...if they were even prepared by an attorney? Or are you going to get advice and information from the professionals whose job it is to create a better financial picture for you and are in it for the long haul.

- What if creating an estate plan could save you 15% in taxes, and you have one million dollars in your estate? You would be saving a lot of money through your planning, right? $150,000.00, to be exact. That savings far exceeds the cost to set up the estate plan. *So the question becomes, can you afford not to plan?*

4. Your plan should be customized, not a template.

We've all been to the doctor with an illness or ailment and it always goes the same way; you fill out the paperwork listing your symptoms, they put it in your chart, the doctor reviews your chart and then conducts an examination of you in order to diagnose you properly. Why don't they just have you email your symptoms and they email you back a prescription or treatment recommendation? Because some things are so important that they should be subjectively examined every time the need arises. Estate planning is no different. We may have the same "outward" appearance as someone else—similar income, same number of kids, etc., but that doesn't mean we will get the same protections. Our goals may be different, not to mention our lifestyle, habits, and expectations. Filling in the blanks never works. *No two financial pictures or stories are alike, making customized planning the only solution.*

5. Set up ongoing measures for reviewing your estate planning.

If we have something wrong in our estate planning, we can go back and fix it after we realize the problem, which is great, but making sure we fix errors or loopholes proactively is even better! *Reacting to a situation is always more stressful and difficult than it is to evaluate if we're on the right path before we get lost.*

HAVE YOU CLOSED YOUR ESTATE LOOPHOLES?

You've made smart financial decisions your entire life. Don't stop until you've gone full circle.

Sometimes it takes less than we think to beat the curve and stay ahead of the game; especially in our estate planning. Good information combined with effective strategies can help us sustain a better quality of life while we are alive and leave a better situation once we move on. **Regardless of age or where you are in life, make sure you pay attention to what you have now, and grow comfortable with estate planning.**

Seek out the people who can customize your plan to the life you live today, as well as the one you are going to grow into.

About Brian

Brian M. Douglas, Esq. has always been committed to the belief that a person's legal needs are personal and not just business. This is a cornerstone in Brian's approach to law and how he serves his clients. In 2003, when he founded Brian M. Douglas & Associates, LLC, his vision was to create an entire culture that embraced this same powerful concept. And he has.

Brian received his Bachelor of Science degree from Marquette University in Milwaukee, Wisconsin, where he studied Mechanical Engineering while working full time as a manufacturing supervisor for a Fortune 100 Corporation. Upon graduation, he moved to Atlanta to attend John Marshall Law School, where he graduated *cum laude* and as *class valedictorian*. Brian was initially drawn from engineering to law because of his gifts for reasoning and logic—two qualities that are essential for a successful attorney. And he hasn't looked back since.

Today, Brian is a highly respected attorney with a solid reputation with his clients, colleagues, opposing counsel, and within the court system throughout the state of Georgia. Through his firm, he has taken on very diverse cases, working with bankruptcy, real estate law, civil/business litigation, foreclosure, criminal law, and what Brian is highly acclaimed for—estate planning and asset protection. According to Brian, "Establishing my own practice has allowed me the freedom to cover many areas of law. This fits my diverse range of interests and benefits the clients we serve."

A unique approach to business is a driving force behind Brian's success. Valuing the relationship with his clients and knowing that he is a trusted advisor for life's most important decisions, Brian stands out through offering concierge style services for his clients and having a no voicemail policy at the firm. When someone calls, they get a live person answering the phone and from that moment on, the relationship with a potential client has begun. He is also a contributor on Fox, ABC, CBS, and NBC, as well as contributor for *Star Tribune, Small Business Trendsetters, Worth*, and *The Miami Herald*. Recently, Brian appeared on the television show, *Time Square Today*. And now, Brian is an author, enabling him to reach out to more people about life's most important legal topics.

Brian reflects on his life's journey with genuine joy and how it brought him to Atlanta, and the practice that he loves. From day one, he's enjoyed the area for its people, the weather, and how conducive it is to enjoy some of his favorite activities, such as golf and tennis. Today, Brian is married to a wonderful woman, Tess. They have two small children who make life a daily adventure, and are passionate about animal rescue and fostering, along with all causes that help promote it. Now three Chihuahuas are also a part of the Douglas family. According to Brian, "Life is busy, but it's never been greater. I wouldn't have it any other way."

CHAPTER 24

THE FUTURE OF ENERGY MEDICINE IS HERE!

BY BRYANT MEYERS

INSIDE THE GROUNDBREAKING SCIENCE OF PULSED ELECTROMAGNETIC FIELD THERAPY (PEMF)

Because the science of Pulsed Electromagnetic Field Therapy (PEMF) can be an unfamiliar, sometimes intimidating topic for those who haven't spent their lives studying Energy Medicine, I think a familiar slice of pop culture via *Star Trek* makes the ideal introduction to this fascinating world.

I'm sure Trekkies everywhere remember the *tricorder*, a multi-function hand-held device used for sensor scanning, data analysis and recording data. There were three primary variants issued by the fictional organization, *Starfleet*. The medical version was used by doctors to help diagnose diseases and collect bodily information about a patient. It could scan the body and use energy frequencies to detect and heal. On the original TV series and through subsequent TV and film incarnations, the tricorder was a useful device in the 23rd and 24th Centuries and beyond. But as I detail in my bestselling 2013 book P*EMF: The Fifth Element of Health*, we don't have to wait that long to tap into and align ourselves with these frequencies to improve our lives and heal ourselves. The technology is here now!

THE OTHER LIFE ESSENTIAL

Let's start with the basics: PEMF is an FDA-approved reparative technique used in everything from pain reduction, tissue and wound healing and bone regeneration to the orthopedic treatment of non-union fractures and failed fusions and depression. In the case of bone healing, PEMF uses directed pulsed magnetic fields through injured tissue, believed to stimulate cellular repair.

I subtitled my book *Learn Why Pulsed Electromagnetic Field (PEMF) Therapy Supercharges Your Health Like Nothing Else!* for a good reason - because it does! Drawing on substantial research, I explain that the modern allopathic medical model is based on treatments rooted in the outdated, mechanistic reductionist science of Newtonian physics. Not to bash Sir Isaac's 17th Century breakthroughs, but I believe that a modern concept called Quantum Field Theory could possibly shatter the brittle glass separating our subjective experience from outward objective reality.

It's really mind-blowing to realize that the earth's magnetic field and its corresponding PEMFs are as important to our health as food, water, sunlight and oxygen. It's like this hidden dimension helping us sustain life. In fact, the Schumann and Geomagnetic frequencies, the two main components of Earth's PEMFs, are so essential that NASA and the Russian space program equip their spacecrafts with devices that replicate them! These frequencies are absolutely necessary for the body's circadian rhythms, energy production and – most people love this best – keeping the body free from pain.

While certainly not intended as a substitute for the recommendations of physicians or other health care providers, I want to share some of the practical applications of PEMF therapy.

One of the most exciting aspects of my book is what I call the body-mind-earth connection. The Earth's magnetic field, and the Schumann and Geomagnetic frequencies are roughly in the range of 0-30 Hz. Likewise, human brainwaves, as established by electroencephalograms, are also roughly 0-30 Hz (from delta, to theta, to alpha, to beta). And guess what range the tissues and the healing response in the body (those frequencies that the tissues in your body respond to)? Yep. The cells in your body also respond to 0-30 – and the energies that your body emits are also 0-30 Hz.

We talk about the body-mind connection, but really it's the body-mind-earth connection! In other words, our tissues, cells, brain, and our bodies are intimately connected to the Earth's frequencies and magnetic field. In my world, those kinds of realizations give us goose bumps!

PEMF RESEARCH AND FDA APPROVAL

When people first hear about PEMF, they're naturally skeptical. It sounds 'new agey', pretty magical, right? The good news is, there's nothing supernatural about it – and we have a lot of research and support in our corner. PEMF therapy was featured on the Dr. Oz TV show in 2011 as the most important breakthrough in pain management. Pain management is probably the #1 reason that people purchase a PEMF therapy device like the one my company Energy Ways distributes, the iMRS 2000 (Intelligent Magnetic Resonance Stimulation). It uses earth-based Schumann Frequencies and has a built-in intelligent biorhythm clock.

A NEW VIEW OF THE HUMAN BODY

To help you understand why I believe that the field of energy medicine is the future of health and wellness, I want you to think of the human body as you never have before. We have over 100 trillion cells, and there are around 500 billion chemical reactions happening every second in our bodies. That's mind-boggling. Those mainstream models explaining us as mechanistic or biological machines are insufficient to describe our body's majesty and complexity.

Energy medicine, quantum biology and the new understandings in biophysics are giving a whole new picture of the human body as primarily an energetic, holographic field of energy information which communicates via bio-photons. The PEMF therapy actually goes along with this new understanding of the human body and can assist the body energetically in healing itself.

My passion for this stems from my desire to help people take responsibility for improving their health, rather than letting themselves go through bad living habits and running to medical professionals to solve all their problems. I want to empower people to take their health into their own hands by embracing simple concepts like proper diet and hydration, full spectrum sunlight, proper exercise and sleep, and finding ways to connect with the natural energy fields of the earth.

ENERGIZING

Now that we've established that our bodies and minds are intimately connected to planet Earth, we can get into one of the coolest aspects of PEMF: *it's a whole body battery recharger!* The Energizer Bunny's got nothing on us. Our cells are actually miniature batteries – and we've got 100 trillion of them! In fact, did you know that the word "battery" is, by definition, a collection of two or more cells? When we get sick, our cellular voltage will diminish. There's a direct connection between your health and your cellular voltage. Dr. Otto Warburg did some pioneering research on the connection between cellular voltage and health. He found that healthy cells range between 70 mV to 100 mV. If you have chronic illness or disease, the voltage starts to plummet. Many chronic illnesses can have cellular voltages as low as 30-60 mV, and cancer 20 mV or below. Don't you find it interesting that we never hear about heart cancer? That is because the heart is the most energetic organ in our body, with 120 mV of voltage. That's a lot of power! Here's something to think about: scientific research has detected that the field from our body extends 15 feet out into space. Not surprisingly, the heart field is going out the farthest.

Here are five ways in which PEMF recharges our cells:

- PEMF recharges the trans-membrane potential (TMP). That's basically the voltage across the cell membrane.

- It also increases ATP production in the mitochondria. The TMP and ATP are the two primary ways that the cells store energy.

- PEMF enhances the sodium potassium pump. So it gives a net positive charge on the outside of the cell.

- It increases cellular pH. pH is a direct measure of the voltage of your cells. If you have healthy cells, you're going to be slightly alkaline.

- PEMF helps to oxygenate the cells and helps to lower blood viscosity and improve circulation and microcirculation.

Here's another word you might enjoy – electroporation! It means "using electricity or magnetism to make cells more porous." PEMF creates a healthy level of this, which allows nutrients to go in the cells more effectively, and waste products to go out. I'm proud to say that I have personally helped thousands of people with energy medicine and PEMF therapy devices to achieve pain relief, better sleep and overall better health.

GOOD AND BAD FREQUENCIES IN OUR DAY-TO-DAY LIVES

In the modern digital age, we have a two-fold problem: we are not getting enough of the good frequencies of the earth, and we are getting too much of the bad man-made ones.

One of the reasons we're not getting the good frequencies is that the earth's magnetic field has naturally declined more than 50 percent over the past 300 years – and it continues to decline in intensity or strength. We can't do much about that. But part of the problem is our lifestyle and things we use every day. We spend a lot of time indoors. We drive in cars with rubber tires. We walk in shoes with rubber soles. We sleep in insulated beds. We spend the majority of our time in concrete and steel structures. All these factors limit our exposure from the Earth's natural magnetic fields. How to solve this? Spending more time outside (weather permitting, of course) is a great start!

The second half of our two-fold problem is that we're getting too much of what I call "electrosmog." One main component of electrosmog is dirty electricity: 60 Hz. power line frequencies. You guessed it! The appliances in your house operate at that frequency. Certain modern technologies contribute to this, primarily microwave frequencies. 4G networks and the other technology we use, including cordless phones, Bluetooth, Wi-Fi, and smart power meters, operate at microwave frequencies. In fact, the 4G network is almost identical to the frequencies used by microwave ovens. Just because you can't see something doesn't mean it can't harm you.

Some action steps you can take to clear your house of electrosmog:

- Get rid of cordless phones. Use only wired or corded phones.
- Minimize cell phone usage as much as possible.
- Turn Wi-Fi off when you're not using it. Consider connecting directly to the Internet using an Ethernet cable.
- Get rid of all compact fluorescent light bulbs in your home.
- Avoid high EMF appliances; keep a safe distance from them.

- Don't use cordless baby alarms or monitors.

- Avoid water beds, electric blankets, and alarm clocks.

- Try not to live near a cell phone tower. Check locations of towers and antennas near you, using the website: www.antennasearch.com.

- Opt out of smart power meter installations.

- And, of course, invest in an earth-based PEMF device.

In my book, I talk about how earth-based PEMF devices can cleanse our body of all the static electricity you can accumulate from electrosmog.

PEMF – THE SOLUTION

So what can you do to reverse and solve this twofold problem? The future of medicine is here! Natural Earth-Inspired PEMF devices are the solution in that they give the body these much needed and ESSENTIAL Earth frequencies and energies. Not only that, but PEMF therapy has a great many benefits, including the following:

- PEMF helps to eliminate pain and inflammation naturally.

- It will help you get deep, rejuvenating sleep.

- It will increase your energy and vitality.

- PEMF will help you to feel younger, stronger, and more flexible.

- It will keep your bones strong and healthy.

- It will help your body with healing and regeneration.

- PEMF will help to improve circulation and heart health.

Action Steps to Better Health

Finally, let's go over some action steps based on the five essential elements you can take to change your life:

1. Earth/Food – Buy only organic and non-GMO whole foods. Avoid fast food and processed food.

2. Water – Drink clean and energized water like good quality spring or ionized water. Also invest in a shower filter. Avoid soft drinks and sugary drinks at all costs.

3. Fire – Use full spectrum light in your house. Also invest in a good

infrared sauna.

4. Air – Look into getting a good air purification system indoors.

5. Ether/PEMF – Invest in a Natural, Earth-based PEMF therapy device.

Additionally, get plenty of exercise and sleep (PEMF therapy helps with better sleep), stay positive, meditate and love and laugh more!

EMBRACING THE MISSION

One of the beautiful takeaways from all of my studies is the opportunity to understand the many ways science shows us the interconnectedness of all life. This has profound implications on our physical health, our spiritual development and relationships. Educating people on the reality that we literally extend beyond our physical body is for many a stepping stone to a higher spiritual understanding.

It feels good to help people with their health and alleviate their pain in ways they may have never considered. I want to encourage you to go beyond this chapter and investigate the value of PEMF Therapy further. In my book I go into further detail about how it can literally change your life starting on the cellular level. And if PEMF fascinates you as much as I think it will, check out the ways that earth-inspired PEMF devices like the IMRS 2000 can help you implement this therapy to help you achieve optimal health.

For more information on PEMF, please visit my website:
www.pemfbook.com

About Bryant

Bryant Meyers, B.S., M.A. (Physics) is a bestselling author and leading expert in the field of PEMF (Pulsed Electromagnetic Field) therapy and energy medicine. Bryant is a former TV show host and former Physics/Math Professor at Central Michigan. For over 18 years, he has researched, tested, tried, and investigated over $500,000 worth of energy medicine devices, studying with many of the world's experts. Bryant has personally helped thousands of people with energy medicine and PEMF therapy devices to achieve pain relief, better sleep, and overall better health.

During the past seven years, Bryant has dedicated his research to PEMF therapy because he feels it is THE most effective and best researched energy medicine device available today. Bryant's book, *PEMF - The Fifth Element of Health* was featured on the *Brian Tracy Show* that aired on ABC, NBC, CBS and Fox affiliates across the country. He has also been featured on GaiamTV, Hayhouse Radio, and has given many lectures and classes on PEMF Therapy.

Most recently, Bryant was an Associate Producer of the upcoming documentary *The Connected Universe* and is featured in the soon-to-be-released *Supercharged* documentary.

His book is available on Amazon and many other leading booksellers.

CHAPTER 25

TOOLS FOR SELF DISCOVERY

BY CATHIE RODGERS

It takes more than intelligence to be successful in your career. It takes purpose and passion, skills and interests, talents and gifts as well. How does one go about discovering all of these things about oneself? Do you really know who you are and what your purpose, passion, skills, interests, talents and gifts are? If you do, good for you. I am sure you have done a lot of inner work on yourself. If you don't, I have good news for you. You don't have to look any further than your own body.

Do you know that you carry with you a map of who you are, how you are wired and what your purpose, life lessons, talents and gifts are? Yes, that map can be found in the repeating patterns in your eyes, skin, hands and feet. All you need to do is learn how to interpret this information or find someone who does to know on a conscious level how you are wired. The study of *Scientific Hand Analysis* is one such form of reading these patterns that are found on your body.

MY STORY

I loved my childhood. It was wonderful until my mother became terminally ill. I was sixteen at the time. Since my mother could no longer coordinate the activities at home, my father brought in a caretaker to run the house and watch over us—myself and my three younger siblings. My older brother was off to college. The caretaker only lasted a couple of months. I don't know for sure but I think her leaving had to do with when my younger brother brought out Igor the iguana one afternoon. You see we grew up in Florida and had several reptiles come and go in our home. My brother bought Igor a leash and collar and loved to walk him around the block scaring all the little girls along the way. I learned at an early age to pretend I wasn't afraid of Igor. It worked for me but I guess the caretaker did not know that trick.

After the caretaker left, the chaos that built up in the house and family was unbearable for me. I couldn't stand it any more so, without asking permission, I took charge of running the house along with taking care of my younger siblings, finishing high school and attending college. My father was there most of the time but travelled on business a couple of times each month. When he was travelling, and my mother was in the hospital, I was the oldest person in the house. I learned many years later that my father prayed that none of the neighbors called the social workers about our situation otherwise we might have been sent to foster homes.

The month I turned twenty-three, my sister turned sixteen, and a week later on April 1, my mother died. I had told myself I would stay home until my mother died and my sister was sixteen, the age I was when I starting running the house. Now, it was time for me to leave home and start my own life. Getting married and having children was the last thing I wanted to do at this time. I needed to figure out who I was and what I wanted to do in life.

The year my mother died would have been my senior year of college but I dropped out to be with her during her final months. After she died I was too upset to return to college just then. While on my own I needed to work and support myself and since I didn't have my college degree yet, I thought to myself, what can I do? I said to myself: I just ran a household of six people so I might be good at practical office administration. I moved three thousand miles away to California so I would not be called back home to help out.

When friends asked me where I would live, I said: "I will let you know when I know." I first stopped in Monterey, California and later settled in the greater San Francisco Bay Area. I started working as a secretary, then an administrative assistant. From there I became a legal assistant. During my career as a legal assistant, the attorney I supported said to me: "You are very bright, you could be an attorney." I said "thank you" and went back to my desk. I thought about what he said, but knew intuitively that I was doing what I was meant to do.

In 2001, I finally became an executive assistant and in 2005, I attended the Professional Business Women's Conference at the Moscone Center in San Francisco. I was wandering the exhibit hall looking at the booths when I saw a booth with a banner that said "Scientific Hand Analysis." I was very curious but didn't want my colleagues see me go inside. I looked both ways and when the coast was clear I entered the booth. There were two women in the booth offering mini-scientific hand analysis readings for a minimal charge. I said yes and paid the amount for the reading. In twenty minutes of looking at my hands this stranger told me things about myself that take others years to learn about me. I was amazed at what I heard and wanted to know how she did this.

Five months later, I met with this stranger in her townhouse and had a full reading. In this hour-long reading she told me many things I either knew consciously or intuitively. The most important information I received that day was an understanding of my life-purpose. I didn't grasp the meaning of this information until days and months later, as I reflected on what she said and revisited my life work up to that point. It became clear to me why I ran the household at sixteen and why I choose to be an administrative assistant even though I have the intelligence to do many other occupations. You see my life purpose is the Matriarch: The person who holds groups and communities together and who inspires and empowers those within her community.

I had to admit that what she said made sense and wanted to know how she came to this conclusion about my life purpose. I bought the few books that were available at the time on the subject of *Scientific Hand Analysis*, and the more I learned the more interested I became on the subject.

At the same time I was thinking about what I wanted to do next in my career and hired a career coach to help me figure this out. After weeks of assessments on my strengths, weaknesses, talents, and skills, I finally came to the conclusion that I wanted to do what she was doing, I wanted to coach. After all, this is what I had been doing unofficially as an administrative assistant all these years. Now, I want to be officially known and paid for my coaching.

In 2009, I studied career coaching. The program I was taking included several weeks of self-discovery on one's talents, interests, skills, etc. As

I was practicing on my volunteer client I noticed that he was not happy with this process and thought to myself there must be a faster way to zero in on how a person is wired. At that moment I said to myself: of course, scientific hand analysis.

With that realization, I decided to take my study of hand analysis to the next level and become a certified Scientific Hand Analyst. As part of the year-long certification process, I had to read one hundred hands and do a special interest project that was to be presented to the class. My project was on "Vocational Indicators and Scientific Hand Analysis." From this special project, the Director added this course specialty to the school's curriculum.

TEACHING MOMENT

Scientific Hand Analysis by Richard Unger teaches that the fingerprints hold the information of our purpose, life lesson and life school. The lines in our hands are etched there from the neurons in our brain and when interpreted tell us how we are wired emotionally, mentally, and physically along with our talents and gifts.

I believe that this information makes for a quick assessment tool for self-discovery, rediscovery, and reconnection to who we are. We already know this information on many levels: consciously, subconsciously and intuitively. By having a hand reading and listening to what is said, this information is brought to the conscious level so you can use the information in your daily decision making.

That is why as a Career Coach I use *Scientific Hand Analysis* as an assessment tool for my clients. It saves them several weeks of taking exercises and assessments to gain insight into what their strengths and weaknesses are and what there talents and skills are. It also helps clarify what their purpose is.

Individuals can use the information from their hand analysis reading in:

- Understanding the student and master path of their purpose
- Looking at their current career through the perspective of their purpose, seeing if it gives them the opportunity to do every day what they do best and live out their purpose in their career
- If it does not, then they can consider what career might best fit with their purpose, gifts and natural talents

- They can observe how they are emotionally wired:

  ° Earth energy – needs alone time to feel and process information and feelings

  ° Air energy – needs opportunities to speak with others in deep meaningful ways

  ° Fire energy – needs to express passion and love of the work with others

  ° Water energy – needs a safe protective environment to be in touch with their sensitive self

- They can also discover if they are wired to be an entrepreneur or employee

Some uses for *Scientific Hand Analysis* in coaching career transitions are:

- **Career planning** - *Scientific Hand Analysis* is helpful as you think about what you are best suited to do at work and in which kind of environment

- **Relationships** – how you best relate and work together with others when you understand your individual emotional makeup – this also improves your emotional intelligence

- **Improving work performance** – the more you understand your purpose and strengths, the more you are able to focus on getting your job done more effectively

- **Interview preparation** – understanding how you are wired gives you clarity in answering interview questions

Embracing my purpose and applying it to my career of executive assistant shifted my mindset from task-oriented to people-oriented. Being aware that I am in the School of Love and School of Service shifted my attitude toward my work to being in loving service to others. It also helped me become more grounded and anchored.

I also learned that my Life Lesson is to be emotionally authentic in my dealings with others vs. hiding out and not revealing much about myself. Once I started to take the risk of sharing things about myself with others I learned a very important lesson. I learned that strength, not weakness, comes with being vulnerable.

In the palm of the hand lies the heartline (how we are emotionally wired), the headline (how we are mentally wired), and the life line (how we use our energy and how grounded we are or not in our body and life). All of this information is important for one to know in considering what kind of work you want to do, what kind of environment you want to work in and how being grounded or not grounded plays a role in your career. Even the sections of your fingers provide clues as to the best line of work for you – where you feel in sync with your natural aptitudes and potential.

Also, in the hands lie gift markings that bring extra energy to different areas of your life. For example: do you have extra artistic energy that will support you in your creative work or do you have courageous energy which will support you to be an advocate for a cause close to your heart. And what happens if you have these gifts and are not sharing them with the world?

SUCCESS TIP

I have learned that the better I understand myself the easier life becomes. Especially with the daily decision making process. When making a decision I ask myself the following question: "Does this opportunity help me to move forward on my path or take me backwards or off my path?"

CONCLUSION

Once I understood my purpose, passion and gifts, I realized that the attorney I knew many years ago was only looking at one aspect of my make up…my intelligence. Given who I believe I am from the information in my hands, I have to say that I was intuitively doing exactly what I am wired to do. I was working where I could be in loving service and share my gifts of intuition and compassion while inspiring and holding groups together in a well-organized home and office.

It is my hope and wish that you will someday know and understand your purpose and passions, gifts and talents as well as I have had the privilege to know mine.

Best wishes and Bon Voyage.

Cathie

About Cathie

Cathie Rodgers is a Professional Business Woman, a Career Coach and Certified Scientific Hand Analyst. Cathie is an executive assistant at a Fortune 500 company in the San Francisco Bay Area. In this role she is responsible for supporting the Vice President of Finance, Corporate Controller and Chief Accounting Officer. She is also a Career Coach.

Cathie began studying professional coaching in 2008 and decided to focus on Career Coaching in 2009. The death of her mother, when Cathie was 23, ignited a quest to explore the deeper meanings of life and an understanding of her role in this life. This quest continued throughout her years in school and work as she pursued personal and spiritual growth. It wasn't until she discovered Coaching that she found a venue in which to share the wisdom she had learned over the years. Now she uses this gift in all aspects of her life, including the corporate environment

As Cathie studied and practiced coaching, she noticed that many of the clients coming to her were going through major life transitions. Wanting to help them through their transitions as quickly as possible, Cathie became a Certified Scientific Hand Analyst. Now she enjoys combining Career Coaching with the self-discovery tool of *Scientific Hand Analysis*. She believes that the best way to live a happy and abundant life is through self-discovery.

Cathie is a co-contributor to the book: *Successful Life Story Transformations: Using the ROADMAP System to Change Mind, Brain and Behavior* with David Krueger, M.D.

You can connect with Cathie at:
LiveALifeOnPurpose@gmail.com

Empowerment through Self-Discovery

CHAPTER 26

THE FUTURE SCENARIO STRATEGIST – CONNECTING GREAT PEOPLE AND STRONG IDEAS

BY DAVID CAMPBELL

Outside-the-box thinking leads to outside-the-box results.

I have always felt this intense connection to be a part of an environment where I could help people make the transition from worried to wow. **Being a part of a culture like that excited me in a way that few other things did.** I sensed its importance and I wanted to experience it, too. Yes, I was fortunate to realize this from a young age and I gravitated toward it—sometimes despite myself.

After high school, I chose college right away; but without precise goals and a honed-in passion, I felt out of place, chose to find my own way and entered into the work force, eager to make money and a name for myself. I went into information technology support and professional services, knowing that I was confident in that area and comfortable talking with people. Through this, I became the person that others refer to as, "that guy" or "the guy who knows a guy." *Feeling inspired, I took it upon myself to be the person that others went to for solutions to their problems, knowing that if I delivered solutions we'd all be winning.* Yet, I wanted more…

231

In a bold move, I decided to enlist in the US Navy, where I found myself immersed in an experience that offered me more than I'd imagined. And it laid the foundation for me to learn life-changing things, including:

- Basic concepts of strategy and tactics
- The role of a strategist
- The role of a tactician
- How strategy and tactics vary from each other
- How to implement a strategy and the corresponding tactic that goes with it
- The advantages of experiencing practical examples and applications that I could apply to management accounting and strategic advisory services

To some, these important points of awareness may seem like jargon, but I assure you, they are much more than that. I saw how they applied to the military, of course, but I also recognized something meaningful in these concepts for "civilian life" as well. These principles and actions hold the power to impact all of our lives on a considerably more personal level. *And never being someone to be comfortable inside the lines, upon my time serving in the Navy coming to a close, my mind opened up to how I could use all this great information to help the world around me, and in particular, veterans and women trying to show the world that their skills are a highly valuable asset.* This inspired me! Contributing to an individual being better was a way to build up to a better world, and I haven't looked back since. For me, the concepts of strategy and tactics have helped me chart a course where I can serve as an inspiring catalyst for the changes others wish to see.

STRATEGY VERSUS TACTICS: USING MILITARY CONCEPTS IN THE BUSINESS WORLD

Successful businesses implement tactics that lend to their organizational vision.

The military refers to strategy as the full utilization of all their forces, regardless of whether in war-time or peace-time, to ensure ongoing security through comprehensive, long-term planning and development. Tactics, however, refers specifically to securing the objective set forth by the strategies, and involves maneuvers that eliminate or reduce enemies or a potential threat. I think of this and I get so excited, because I see how these very specific, intense concepts are so applicable in our business world. When business strategies and tactics are well thought out and designed and implemented properly, they are effective, and can change people's lives – both personally and professionally – in this profoundly incredible way.

When small businesses and entrepreneurs begin realizing that strategy and tactics are separate yet equally important tasks they will find success. Really, it's not strategy versus tactics, as much as it is a cooperation of the two for a stellar end result.

A great way to process this is to think about how you would enter an address into your car's GPS and select the *satellite* view so you get an aerial image of your destination, which will include terrain, 3D buildings, and other topographical features. Then you enter your starting point and select the *route*, receiving step-by-step directions that should take you to your final destination. This same concept can be applied to business.

- **The satellite is your strategy:** you can get a birds-eye view of your overall operation, including present and future obstacles and opportunities. This allows you to identify comprehensive objectives—something a successful business demands.

- **The route is your tactic:** you have access to a clearly defined set of instructions that take you toward the realization of your strategic objectives.

I've been asked, "Is it possible to have strategy without tactics, David?" Honestly, it is, but do know this: if you do, you'd best be content with aimlessly ambling in the general direction of your goals without a very specific purpose or mission. *This is actually the point most people are at when I connect with them and together we start to create the catalyst for positive change that leads to a fruitful outcome.*

The merger of strategy and tactics is centered on these concepts:

- Strategists point your business in the right direction and steer toward a long-range destination while tacticians chart the way with step-by-step directions.

- Strategists think in "big picture" abstractions while tacticians think in concrete details.

- Strategists determine which resources are necessary, while tacticians utilize the resources to transform goals into outcomes.

- Strategists are responsible for a business's comprehensive success, while tacticians are responsible for a specific set of outcomes.

- Strategists are focused on long-term steady approaches, while tacticians focus on short-term flexible approaches.

- Strategists rely on research, analysis, critical thinking, and communication, while tacticians rely on experience, planning, process, and resources.

- Strategists set objectives and benchmarks for success, while tacticians produce firm deliverables and measurable outcomes.

Together, the relationship between the strategist and tactician is what I have focused on as I've created this dynamic, innovative, unique approach to being a catalyst, coach, and future scenario strategist through my fractional CFO consultancy, Tier One Services.

UP CLOSE AND PERSONAL WITH THE STRATEGIST

By nature, true strategists look beyond the day-to-day details and focus on establishing a long-term business perspective.

Steve Jobs. Bill Gates. Mark Zuckerberg. These three names are known to almost everyone on this planet for what they've created. Where did it all start? With them becoming strategists and that is what we should really celebrate about them, much more so than their wealth or even their product. **Strategy comes before the results, before the money, and often before we ever know who highly successful people are.**

When we focus on articulating our business trajectory, it is best accomplished through using a strategist mindset. Strategists are known for confidently making high-level decisions that relate to positioning and direction. I remember when I was first in the Navy, I was constantly amazed at the confidence and insight from those I was learning from and there was no greater compliment to me than when I was able to recognize that I'd become that confident, insightful person to others. I saw the big picture and all the details of which the picture was made.

How did this happen? I knew the questions that needed to be asked.

Questions that a strategist is likely to ask include:

- How will the industry look in one year, five years, or even ten years?
- How will emerging and future changes in the industry affect the business over time?
- How will the global economy look in one year, five years, or even ten years?
- How will emerging and future changes in the global economy affect the business over time?
- What is the optimal future positioning for your business or brand?
- How will your business and brand need to adapt and evolve to reach the long-term goals?

A serious discussion needs to take place, along with the pertinent research to reach these answers, if you want to adapt a strategist approach toward success. There is no make-or-break formula to answer all those questions with absolute certainty; however, there are four abilities and attributes that must be displayed.

These are:

1. Find an unobstructed view.
Strategists have a thorough and unwavering understanding of and commitment to the vision, values, and missions of an organization.

2. Give attention to the "what if(s)."
Understanding the current reality is necessary, of course, but strategists also comprehend the optimal direction in which to face in the future.

3. Measure your results.
Winston Churchill said, "However beautiful the strategy, you should occasionally look at the results." This is exactly what strategists do, because they know that a strategy without benchmarks will result in failure; however, with intense benchmarking, failure can result in victory for a strategist!

4. Develop the art of communication.

Whether it's a formal discussion or a casual conversation, a strategist will find an appropriate way to reinforce company objectives and further integrate them into the fibers of the organization.

Strategists offer the innovation, along with the ability to convey their vision to a capable team, which is led by another vital part of the organization: the detail-oriented tactician that will take the vision and create a successful outcome with it.

UP CLOSE AND PERSONAL WITH THE TACTICIAN

Tacticians are what separate the dreamers from the doers.

Tacticians are masters of taking strategic goals and converting them into actionable plans. They do this by having the insight into the strategy and understanding it, while also having the ability to hone in on the daily work that needs to be done and by using the resources at hand. **They know who needs to do what, when, and with what resource.** Ultimately, this leads to an efficient marriage of goals with resources to accomplish the objectives. And, they ask the right questions!

- What immediate problems and challenges are standing in the way of business objectives?

- What are some realistic and unrealistic potential solutions for these challenges?

- What are the costs and benefits associated with each of the alternatives?

- What qualification factors influence the feasibility and benefits of each alternative?

- Which alternative will yield the overall greatest results?

An impressive skillset is involved with being a tactician and it usually has to be learned. Few people are able to naturally fill this position without some type of training, which is something that, combined with my innate ability, is a large focus for me when I work with businesses and organizations to create the follow-through on the ideas that lead to their success. A tactician must have three attributes to really distinguish themselves.

1. Commitment to the plan.

Growing restless with a plan is not a part of the tactician's personality. They understand that 'Rome wasn't built in a day', and that their overall objectives cannot be reached in a day, either.

2. A propensity for fifth gear.

Some people subscribe to the adage that "slow and steady wins the race." Tacticians realize that it's often a sprint right out of the gate that makes the difference. Why is this? It's because our best chance of success is through sheer momentum and it's hard to gain that type of power at a turtle's pace.

3. The ability to "role" with it.

In classic heist movies, they usually have a very specific set of characters and roles. There's the central character—the mastermind—that hand picks a team to help him/her coordinate the undertaking. They each have specific skills and areas of expertise, and the team's success is reliant upon each of these people using their skills to their greatest potential. A tactician can do this same thing with their team, using all the members' best strengths to achieve the ultimate outcome.

The right strategies will lead to success for a business. However, it's the battles that are fought in the trenches and won by shared, implementable tactics that lead to success.

STRATEGY AND TACTICS EXAMPLES

Strategy without tactics is all ideas and no execution.
Tactics without strategies is chaos.

When I work with businesses, it's important to relay that the merger between the strategy and the tactics make a goal achievable, because that is what is necessary to create a successful, healthy business. When these two things are in alignment, company-wide objectives are met and exciting things happen—things that I love seeing because they constantly remind me of the rewards of my career as the future scenario strategist. These examples give you an idea of how this works:

Example #1:

Strategy: Achieve brand visibility within your industry.

Tactics: Implement a marketing campaign to engage customers

through a mix of online advertising, social media, and real world events.

Example #2:

Strategy: Connect with consumers in a more meaningful way.

Tactics: Design a mobile-friendly website and branded mobile app to foster faster and more fulfilling consumer experiences.

Example #3:

Strategy: Increase profitability by predetermined percentage.

Tactics: Reduce operational costs, restructure jobs to enhance workflow, and eliminate redundancies; source materials from lower-cost suppliers.

Example #4:

Strategy: Gain a greater market share in your industry.

Tactics: Temporarily reduce prices (penetration pricing), to encourage consumers to try your product or service.

Example #5:

Strategy: Improve quality control by reducing waste and minimizing mistakes.

Tactics: Reevaluate job-training programs and expand or improve as necessary; set and stick to firm standards for materials, inventory, and suppliers.

Example #6:

Strategy: Improve employee retention for top performers.

Tactics: Offer employees incentives such as competitive compensation packages and improved benefits, including sabbaticals and trips; offer more "buy-in" by soliciting employee ideas.

All these examples are noteworthy goals that most organizations embrace. As you can see, the strategies make sense, but without the tactics to achieve them, they are nothing more than ideas—ideas that will grow stagnant if they are not acted upon.

A FUSION OF STRATEGY AND TACTICS
IS THE CATALYST FOR CHANGE

*The skills required for strategy and tactics are specific and deep,
and few consultants simultaneously master both.*

I've taken it upon myself, with great excitement and joy for learning and knowledge, to become a master of strategy and to partner with masterful tacticians. It's the heart of my business and what sets us apart. Helping individuals grow into strong business leaders is complicated, to be certain—but it is not impossible! *It's a matter of taking the right steps using a better approach.* For me, that's so exciting. Ideas become "show time," because we are not talking about results, we're delivering them. This is how my dreams to transform the prosperity of a nation, one veteran at a time, one entrepreneur at a time, are coming true. It's truly rewarding and the energy that it ignites in me is something that I hope is contagious for many, as it has the potential to spark great ideas in great minds.

About David

David Campbell is a skilled problem solver, entrepreneur and Future Scenario Strategist. He served as a *Cryptologic Technician* for the U.S. Navy, where he learned the invaluable role *strategy* and *tactics* play in the creation of success. From there he graduated from Rutgers University with a degree in Information Technology and Informatics.

As *Technical Services Manager* for BusinessWeek.com, David helped launch the Technical Services Department and developed his expertise in both technical services and strategic support.

David then attended courses at a global personal development company. After much training, he stepped up to provide private coaching for up-and-coming entrepreneurs. David purposed to help veterans, like himself, redefine their roles in the workforce and in their communities at large.

As part of his effort to positively impact the lives of veterans, David moved on to strategic advisory services.

He wanted to transform the economic prosperity of the nation by giving businesses the foundation and systems they need to create jobs in the communities they serve. This vision is what motivated David to create *Tier One Services*, a growing fractional CFO services consultancy on the East coast.

Through *Tier One*, David offers his clients strategic advisory services and management accounting. The original mission of *Tier One* was to serve the underserved, providing strategic and tactical management services to businesses that need it the most.

In 2013, Jaime Campbell, David's wife and a Certified Public Accountant with 12 years of accounting experience, joined forces with Tier One. David knew that Jaime's prodigious skill set would be an asset to Tier One, and he was correct.

Together, with David's strategic management insight and Jaime's forward-looking financial services, *Tier One* offers its clients world-class expertise and is now able to meet the needs of an entirely different class of clientele.

Without abandoning its original altruistic mission to serve veterans and women entrepreneurs, *Tier One* now focuses on the clients it serves best. Whether that's providing independence solutions to audit firms or partnering with corporate attorneys, private equity, and venture capital companies, David and Jaime are committed to the success of every organization.

As a Future Scenario Strategist, David is focused on one central tenet: *mastery brings freedom and opportunity.* From his time in the Navy to his work with veterans and independent entrepreneurs to his role as CEO of *Tier One Services*, David's career has been a reflection of the truth that every person connected to *Tier One Services* is treated to a premier experience as a person of prestige worthy of dignity and respect.

To relax, connect, and contribute, David enjoys singing in community choirs. He sang in the Collegiate Chorale with Bob Bass at Carnegie Hall and most recently sang tenor for Karl Jenkins Stabbat Mater performed in Princeton, New Jersey. David loves listening to barber shop and he is obsessed with personal and human development.

While fans of coloring inside the lines may be challenged by David's relentless pursuit of the Next Big Thing, those looking for transformative change are in exceptionally good hands with David at the helm.

CHAPTER 27

HAPPY MARRIAGE – HAPPY LIFE

BY JOHN R. VOGT, PH.D.

Men and women are different. Now after you have quit laughing, rolling your eyes or just saying "duh" I am talking about more than the physical differences. If you are unhappy at home, it affects everything you do, including your professional live. When something fantastic happens, you want to be able to share that with someone. The reverse is also true. When something bad happens, you need to be able to have someone to help you understand and move through it. Communication is the key that unlocks the barriers to most of the problems you will encounter.

The communication problem arose early in our relationship. I was in the Air Force when I met Kathy and we fell in love. For a wedding present, the Air Force gave me orders for Okinawa, Japan. So, just after three months of marriage, I packed up and headed halfway around the world with Kathy joining me two months later. There, in a foreign land, away from family and friends, we started our new lives together. Being two very independent and strong-willed people, it didn't take long for us to lock horns. One evening it came to a head about who was going to carry out the trash. Never mind that the trash cans were only fifteen feet away from our front door and on the way to where the car was parked, it was the principle of the thing. She was home all day and I was working a twelve-on and twelve-off shift.

During the shouting match, Kathy threw her wedding ring at me, I left and drove around for a while when it came to me that this was ridiculous. Our wedding vows kept going through my head "Love, honor and cherish." The next day we sat down and talked about it. First thing I apologized and asked for forgiveness for my actions and my attitude. Next was that we don't believe in divorce and life is too short to go through it being unhappy. Then, "I want you to tell me one thing that I can do at a time to show you that I love, honor and appreciate you. Please don't give me a list (I think it would have been long – at least two or three pages), but one thing at a time and I will do the same." We started to have deeper conversations on what each of us needed and wanted out of life. We found out that our needs and expectations were different—not wrong, just different.

After leaving the Air Force, we started working with teenagers. Several years later, those teenagers grew up and married. We happened to run across one of those couples in a store. She said you guys have been married for over twenty years and are still holding hands and snuggling in public yet we have been married just a few years and are having major problems. What are we doing wrong? We stated sharing what we had learned and now we would like to share some of it with you.

For this to work, you need to create a safe environment in which you can freely share what is on your mind. This can be difficult to do, especially if you are used to heated arguments or one of you walks away without resolving the issue. Notice the first things I did, I took responsibility and ask for forgiveness for my actions. Next we stated our intentions. We are not going to split up. We are going to work this out no matter how long it takes. What we have found is that when you set these parameters, most problems can be worked out.

Next is to work on is your ability to really listen to what your spouse is saying. We started using a formula called "the floor." One of you is the speaker and has the floor. We use a piece of tile to help, but anything can be used to represent the person speaking. That person is to speak how they feel about whatever is bothering them in a short paragraph or thought. **This is not a time to mount an attack on the listener, but to express how the speaker feels, such as when you do this in a situation, it makes me feel this way.** The listener has to honestly listen to what the speaker said and repeat the meaning back. The listener cannot add their own comments to what the speaker said. If the listener is correct then the speaker moves on. If not, the speaker will rephrase what was said until the listener understands the correct meaning.

After a little while, you reverse roles. This may feel mechanical, but it will help you get your feelings across to your spouse in a safe environment. Then hopefully you can find a win/win solution to the problem. To insure the best outcome, the time needs to be set when you are both rested, calm and have the time it takes to talk it out.

Another thing we explain to the ladies is that men are not mind-readers. Most women are used to sharing with their girlfriends and they pick up on subtle hints and body movements. Most men do not understand them. One evening I could see that Kathy was very upset with me. I asked her what was wrong and she replied, "You know." I told her I didn't know but she insisted that I did. After convincing her that I would never do anything to upset her on purpose and if I don't know what I have done, how will I know not to do it again? That finally made sense so she told me what I had done. We learned a valuable lesson. Now if I do something or say something that hurts her, we have a catch phrase: "Thank you for ruining my day." She will tell me this when we are alone. That allows me to ask what I have done and then she feels safe in telling me what I did or what she heard me say. I can make it right and move on to have a great day. Otherwise she might be mad at me for a long period of time before I picked up on the hints.

Ladies, what you say to other people about your husband or how you act toward them in front of others matter too. He must be able to let you know what you did or said bothers him without fear of retaliation. Sometime what was heard is processed differently than what was actually said. Men speak and hear through a blue filter and women speak and hear through a pink filter. Each has their own language. For instance, if a man says he doesn't have anything to wear, that means that he doesn't have anything clean to put on. When a woman says that, it's off to the store for a new outfit. To fully explain this would take up another chapter so I will have to leave it at that.

Men, if you see that she is visibly upset and she says nothing is wrong, do not stop there. Women have a need to know that you are really interested in them, so it may take a few questions before she feels safe to open up. What's wrong? Is it the kids? Is it me? Is it work? Before long she will tell you what is on her mind. I have found that a lot of the time women just need to vent or talk out a problem and most men are designed to fix things. When she wants to talk it out and the husband is in the "fix-it mode" it causes her to get upset with him. She just wants him to listen. Now when Kathy wants to talk out a problem; she tells me I just need to talk, so I can shut down the desire to fix the situation, sit back and empathize with her. When she is finished venting, she feels better and I didn't have to think of how or what to do next to fix the problem.

Ladies, the opposite is most likely the way your husband will react. If you see that he is upset, you will ask him what's wrong and he'll say nothing. You can see and sense something is not right, so you start to question him and he ends up getting upset. A man is wired differently. He may not know how to verbalize it or is still working the solution in his head. The best thing to do is to let him work it out and then later ask him, "I noticed earlier that you seemed upset. Can you share what's wrong with me now?" This allows him to work through the situation. Men, you can alleviate this problem by saying, "Not right now, do you mind if we talk about it later?" Women care about their husbands and want to be a part of their lives.

That brings up the next item. Guys: professionals say that women need to talk about twenty-five thousand words a day and men only speak about eleven thousand. This means when a man gets home he is already talked out. Your wife wants to be a part of your life so you'll need to be able to listen to her and tell her about your day. After the tenth time of her getting upset because I told her nothing much happened at work, I decided to make a mental note of what I did the next day. So when Kathy asked, what did you do today, I spent forty-five minutes describing the building of a jet engine down to the seating the bearings and torqueing the nuts and bolts. She sat there and listened on the edge of her seat. It was exhausting for me, but she seemed to enjoy it. A few weeks later, we had my crew over for dinner and they started talking about another crew's engine failing engine run-up tests. Kathy popped up and made mention of the #2 bearing area problem I had described to her. She was really listening. I learned an important lesson that day; women need to hear about what we do so they feel a part of our lives. Now when she asks about my day, I try to give her more than just saying the normal stuff.

Next, women are better at multi-tasking than most men. When I arrived home one afternoon, I saw Kathy cooking supper, washing dishes, feeding our youngest in the highchair, helping our toddler with her coloring, and talking to her mother on the phone. If I had tried to do all that, I would most likely have dropped the phone into the dishwater, burned supper, or put the wash cloth into the baby's mouth. Reality is that most men can't multi-task. When a woman has a short gap between something she is doing, she can redirect her time to another task and men don't do that as well. Women are like a computer running Windows. They can slice their time to do several things at once. Men are like the old DOS system that has to stop one project and then open another. This is why some men get upset with their wives when they (wives) see their husbands have a few minutes before the next step in a project, and they want to redirect them onto starting the next thing. Men are not normally wired for that.

The last and the most important item is how you act and react with each other. I referred to it in the first paragraph. The greatest need a wife has from her husband is unconditional love, and what a husband need from his wife is unconditional respect. At our seminars and counseling sessions we have handed out a survey. All it says is, if you had to choose, would you rather be Loved or Respected? Second is: are you male or female? The overwhelming response for women is being loved, and for the men, it is respect. Many times I have been told by the wives: well, if he would just show me a little love then I could show him respect. Then the husband says that when she doesn't show him respect, it is difficult to respond in love.

When this happens and there is an argument, it starts a downward spiral that can get out of control quickly. He acts unlovingly to her and she responds with disrespect. That causes him to react unlovingly and causes her to react disrespectfully. If it continues, it adds up to an unhappy marriage and often times, it ends up in divorce court. At this point, we are asked who should make the first move to stop the spiral. The answer is simple: the one who is more mature and willing to say they were sorry.

So I want to leave you with this.

- Women: treat your husbands as if they were the best thing since sliced bread and be their personal cheerleader.
- Men: show your wife that you love her and she means more to you than anything in this world – including your job, car, hobby and anything else that might get in the way.

With this attitude and these suggestions, you too can have a long and happy marriage and "Beat the Curve!"

About John

Dr. John R. Vogt along with his wife Kathy, enjoy helping married couples find the happiness that lasts a lifetime. They have a unique difference in the marriage seminars that they conduct. Both are on the speaking platform together to share their own points of view. They poke fun at themselves by telling stories about their relationship, while showing that even when things go wrong you can turn them around. This engages the couples to see how a couple that have been married over forty years have overcome obstacles and trials, and still have a great and strong marriage. Their goal is to help couples find out what you need to make a poor relationship better and make a good relationship the best it can be. The main point is that communication is the key that opens the door to understanding, and that can lead to the best relationship you can have. They help you understand what your spouse's wants and needs are, and to truly get to know each other.

John has his Bachelors in Religious Education from Oklahoma Baptist University, Masters and Doctorate in Pastoral Psychology from Clarion Seminary and School of Ministry. His series, "Marriage Maintenance" is a post graduate course at Clarion Seminary. He has been a member of the American Association of Christian Counselors for many years. He is also president of Together ForEver Ministries and serves as an associate pastor of married couples and counseling at Christian Life Fellowship in Moore, Oklahoma. John also is a trained facilitator, a senior IT software trainer, and teaches the DiSK© profile assessments for supervisors and the workforce.

You can reach John at:
John@together-4ever.org

CHAPTER 28

FIND THE FIRE OF YOUR FOCUSED BURNING DESIRE

BY JOE L. DARDEN II, BSW, MBA

A lack of focus can kill your dreams. My dreams nearly died in the third grade. I was told I would have to repeat the third grade, and suddenly all my dreams of becoming the champion I had dreamed about exploded in my face. What was I going to do? What did I need to do? Accidently, I discovered that my success would depend primarily on my own ability to *"make it happen."* I was overwhelmed and the pain of failing trampled me in a panic. I questioned everything. I questioned myself and my motivation. I was hypnotized by failure. All I could focus on was failure. I even wondered if I was more afraid of succeeding than failing? "Maybe," said a small voice in me that raised the possibility that I deserved to fail. All kinds of distracting feelings and thoughts captured my attention. I had started playing football at the age of six and my attention turned to football. Due to my athletic ability, I would go to college. I was determined that football was going to be my way to "beat the curve." I was successful, but I continued to spiral down emotionally. It was football or bust. I was focused, at least on football. Little did I know how important having the right focus and persistence would become. Persistent focus was becoming one of my keys to success.

During my teenage years, peer pressure threatened to derail my dreams again. I was suspended, earned bad grades, and went to jail. Outside of football, you name something bad and I experienced it. And then again, someone told me I don't have what it takes to make my dreams come true. This time it was my high school guidance counselor. She told me that I wasn't college or university material. In an authoritative and knowing tone of voice, she said that I should focus on going to a trade school. Hurt, angry, and dejected, I lost focus. The counselor's words stripped my soul naked. I became emotionally distracted and the small nagging negative voices started up again. I began to wonder if I could ever "beat the curve."

Football allowed me to attend college despite what my high school counselor had advised me. Imagine spiraling downward in my heart of hearts while fighting with my only tool, football, to defeat the influence of my high school counselor and my past experiences of "missing the mark." Then some of my college professors prophesied that I would not graduate even with my football prowess. I had been thrown a curve by my study habits and less than focused courtship with my classes. Again, I was told if I didn't make satisfactory grades for the remainder of the year, my race to overcome a poor start even with football would come to an end. What a daunting task, because I hadn't taken college seriously up to that point in my life.

The providence of God is a wonder to behold. I experienced a defining moment in life. I met a man who would become my mentor. He was a nationally-known and well-respected expert in sports psychology and a mental coach, "Dr. Nick." Dr. Nicholas Cooper-Lewter saw greatness in me. He helped me reset my focus on my dream. He also told me I was dreaming too small a dream.

Dr. Nick advised me to study success and successful people. He recommended that I start reading certain books like *Think and Grow Rich* by Napoleon Hill, *Success Principles* by Jack Canfield and Janet Switzer, *Psycho-cybernetics* by Maxwell Maltz, and *As a Man Thinketh* by James Allen. Dr. Nick encouraged me to work on my communication skills, listen to influential people like Zig Ziglar, Anthony Robbins, and Les Brown on audio. He talked about dressing for success. I began to focus on my dreams again, but this time my dreams began to grow. I began to dress professionally and focus on what my mentor suggested. His promise was that I could have or be anything I wanted, if with persistent focus I would conceive, believe and 'beat the curves' thrown me to date. Those words have had a profound effect on me finding my focus.

Challenged by someone who clearly saw something in me, I decided to take full responsibility for maintaining my focus and habitually taking the necessary steps and completing the required actions daily to realize my dreams. I experienced the "fire of a focused burning desire to succeed and help others."

I took this experience, the "fire of a focused burning desire" into my new profession of sales. I became one of the top sales representatives at Pitney Bowes where I achieved entrance into the "Conquest Club." The invitation and acceptance into the "Conquest Club" was reserved for an elite group of individuals who exhibited exceptional performance in the area of competitive displacements. Then, while still at Pitney Bowes, I reached the highest percentage of quota solutions at 130% - which made me their Number 1 Sales Representative in South Carolina.

Apparently beating the odds attracts the attention of others who want champions on their team. So I was recruited into the pharmaceutical industry. Filled with the "fire of focused burning desire", I achieved the level of "Master's Club Earner" my first year. The "Master's Club Earner" remains one of the most prestigious awards given in the industry of pharmaceutical sales. I can only imagine the consternation of those who downgraded me and my dreams. At this place in time, and not on a football field, I was in the top 20 out of 148 representatives in the company for final incentive plan payout rankings.

Throughout the years, I have worked to keep the "fire of a focused burning desire" aflame. As a result, I have built a respected reputation and distinguish sales career in the medical and business service industry that exceeded my earliest dreams. With all of these accomplishments, I have wondered what else was possible. In a few words, I decided that I would like to gift to other "Joes" who have been told they could not overcome the odds or 'beat the curves' life throws in their way, this recommendation. *Find a mentor who can see greatness in you and seek the experience of an intense "fire of a focused burning desire."* Do so and expect to explore "the world of no limits and infinite possibilities."

In the midst of my experiences, the words of one of my ancestors rushed out of my heart and into my mind. I would like to share their story. Once there were two wolves, one represented darkness and defeat and the other one represented light and infinite possibilities. Their advice was that the one you feed is the one that will grow. Personally, I recommend feeding the one that represents light and infinite possibilities a steady diet of the "fire of a focused burning desire" to be unstuck, unstoppable, unleashed, and unlimited.

I graduated from Webster University with my M.B.A. in 2006 with a GPA of over 3.0. I also hold a Bachelor of Science degree in Social Work from Benedict College. In my free time, I enjoy spending time with my wife and two children, going on movie dates with my daughter, working out, and of course, reading books.

In 2013, I left Pharmaceutical sales to start my own company called Healthy Environment Solutions. Healthy Environment Solutions is a commercial cleaning company dedicated to serving the community.

In my CEO capacity with Healthy Environment, I developed and implemented strategic business plans leading to substantial revenue and profit growth. With a burning desire to reach back and set on fire those for whom the fire has been drowned in negativity, darkness, and defeat, I am venturing forward as a motivational speaker, entrepreneur, best selling author and success expert. My mission is to help others find their fire and focused burning desire, and become the champions they were intended to be.

To sum up it all up, I offer the following recommendations:

1. Decide which wolf you plan to feed a "fire of focused burning desire." And feed that wolf regardless of what others might recommend or advise.

2. Find a mentor who sees greatness in you and has the expertise and desire to bring it out of you.

3. We all need... "Key people at key times with key information who intentionally fan the flames of our God-given potential long enough and strong enough until we can embrace it as real. ~ Dr. Nick."

4. Take 100 percent responsibility for your own dreams coming true by staying focused daily on possibilities even if others believe your dreams are improbable.

5. Dare to have the courage to embrace the uncertainty of excellence which, in the words of Napoleon Hill, is Definiteness of Purpose.

Our inner wolf brings either success or failure depending on which wolf we allow to dominate our focus.

6. Remember Purpose without Focus and Persistence is dead. Take action, find your focus and become the champion you were intended to be.

Note: Being a "Champion by Choice" is a matter of an intense "fire of focused burning desire." It is an unlimited, unstoppable, unleashed heart in action.

About Joe

Joe L. Darden II, BSW, MBA is an Entrepreneur, Motivational Speaker, Sales Leader and Author. He has been on a journey "from ordinary to extraordinary." His commitment to "applied character" is expressed through intentionally refining a pleasing personality, insisting on a strong work ethic, fueling a persistent strong desire to win, becoming a 'fired up' and intensely motivated self-starter, demonstrating a giving spirit, cultivating a willingness to learn, becoming a believer in the power of a positive mental attitude and the right circle of friends, embracing a strong spiritual tradition, and insisting on being a serious husband and family man.

Joe, on his journey from a resource-deprived beginning has applied his character in consultative and solution sales, new business development, contract negotiations, B2B sales, key account management, and network and relationship building. His ability to identify needs and provide solutions working independently or as part of a team, has helped him exceed company expectations. His awards and recognition include earning the rank of Top Sales Rep/Highest % of Quota Solutions – 138% in 1st Quarter 2010. Meter leader of the month December 2008, Meter leader of the month November 2008, Order leader of the month December 2008, Master's Club Earner in his first year in Pharmaceutical Sales, Top Rep based on Bonus Dollars per district, Final Incentive Plan payout Rankings for 2011 – #20 out of 148 reps.

Joe, your maturity and quickly gathered appreciation for our business, and an obvious ability to sell, will form a strong basis for quality marketing to gain and maintain referral sources. ~ Century Financial Services

Joe Darden lists as his top ten accomplishments: getting married to his wife, having two beautiful children, Haile and Hanson, getting his own new house corner lot and being youngest in his sub division, getting saved, earning "Master's Club in Pharma" the first year in industry, reaching the Top 20 out 148 reps in his company in the pharmaceutical industry, receiving an MBA, earning a top award for Pitney Bowes with 138% of quota, for being a solution leader and making him the Number 1 Sales Rep. in SC, embarking on becoming a best selling author, and starting and growing a successful cleaning company.

Joe believes and is a living example that we can all grow from ordinary to extraordinary if we "choose to apply the character" required.

Joe Darden is available for speaking and motivational engagements and trainings, and can be reached at: (803) 479-7388, joedarden2003@yahoo.com

CHAPTER 29

A MOMENT OF CLARITY

BY ANTHONY MONTOYA

The odds were stacked against me the moment I inhaled my first breath of life. My mother had me when she was barely legal to drive; my father turned into a magician and vanished. As I grew up, negativity slithered into my mind. It was difficult to let the past go. After spending the first two few decades of my life developing resentment towards the world, I soon realized I needed help. I used to think asking for help was a sign of weakness – one of many misconceptions in my own mind.

My turning point came after I disappointed my future wife. It all began when a client decided to dismantle all of the hard work we had been pursuing for months, despite data proving our new system was outperforming the old. However, the client went with their gut and decided that the new system was a bust. This was the first time in many years I felt as rejected as my father made me feel as a young boy. At the time, the only way I knew how to handle this type of emotion was to have a drink. One quickly turned into a half-dozen, which increased my likelihood to make more shameful decisions. That night, I made it home but my future wife arrived home later only to be completely locked out without a way in. There was nothing that could have awakened me from the 'state' I was in. As the sun rose and crept into my room, I soon realized the one I loved wasn't there. After leaping out of bed and frantically looking for my phone, I finally found it and discovered a full-page text message about how she wasn't mad – just disappointed.

That is when I realized that disappointing the person I was about to spend the rest of my life with did not align with my ultimate life goal –

to be a good father.

It was my *Moment of Clarity*.

Since that moment every decision moving forward in my life and in my business has been based on: "Will this help me become a good father, yes or no?" If there is any hesitation, I do not participate. I no longer engage in something that doesn't align with my core beliefs. This lifestyle change wasn't easy, and I had to take massive actions including: *altering my diet, rethinking family and friends, approaching my business differently,* and *finding new daily routines and habits.*

Even though I don't have any kids yet, I feel that after they arrive the most important thing will be for me to be there for them as long as possible. This starts with having a healthy mind and body. Eating fast food and drinking everyday will not cut it. My (now) wife and I started to meal prep every Sunday. We cook our lunches and dinners for the week and have everything pre-portioned, which saves us a tremendous amount of time and money. . . and calories.

ALTERING MY DIET:
COOKING AT HOME TO BE HEALTHIER

- Eating out leads to more fried food, more oil/butter, and added salt and sugar. Ingredients aren't as fresh.

- Cooking at home allows you to be in control of what is going into your food and allows you to use healthier alternatives.

- Prepping food at home is cheaper. To food prep lunches and dinners for 5+ days costs us less than $100, about half as much as eating out, and it's better tasting, healthier food!

- Cooking with your significant other is a great opportunity to do something creative together, problem solve, bounce ideas off each other, complete a task with company, and just plain be together without a smartphone or a monitor or screen of any kind.

- Food prepping forces us to prioritize ourselves and will benefit our kids when they come. Including grocery shopping and clean up, the entire system takes us anywhere from five to eight hours a week— a very reasonable commitment considering the benefit you gain in return.

You feel better and are more energized when you are eating better food. Fast food is attractive mainly because you think it's more convenient when you're running late or racing from point A to point B. But having food prepared ahead is actually faster and easier when you have it all ready to go in the fridge at your office or in your cooler in the car. You don't have to spend time finding a restaurant, waiting in line, etc.

Prioritizing my health is important! It requires conscious effort and decision making and forming new habits. But if I don't make it a priority, it very easily slips to the back burner because there are always other things to do besides eating properly and working out. It's never too late to start habits that will benefit you in the future. I'm doing it for myself so I'll be that better father and a great husband, too.

Prioritizing my health also meant I had to quit drinking. This was a tricky one. After my Moment of Clarity, I reached out to someone who was in a recovery program. They had planted the seed in me a long time ago that if I ever thought my drinking would be a problem I should contact them. I found out after attending a few meetings, that the key was not to think about quitting forever. Their mindset was "no drinking today no matter what." This was such a simple concept for my brain to understand that it became my daily incantation.

RETHINKING FAMILY AND FRIENDS

Overcoming cravings has a lot to do with removing yourself from negative environments. Sometimes you need to let go of your negative family members and friends.

I know I need to align myself with people who have common beliefs, goals and drive. I suggest being around people who can teach you and help you grow. In sports you might say, "Always play up," meaning you should try to find people who are better than you so you can strive to be better. Also, ask yourself, "Do they bring something to the table?" Avoid those who bring you down and just want to hang out and do nothing.

Keep in mind you always need a replacement behavior when removing something in your life. Now, instead of me going to undesirable places, I do yoga and meditation.

APPROACHING MY BUSINESS DIFFERENTLY

Once I started to physically feel better, the next indicated step was to eliminate the things in my business that were creating unnecessary stress:

- Ending a partnership
- Providing too many services
- Changing cash flow strategies
- Letting go of undesirable clients and having options for those clients when I needed to let them go

Habits in our business and personal life are hard to break, plain and simple. But good habits are just as hard to break... and I decided having good habits made more sense than hanging on to the nasty ones that made me feel bad every day, and gave me a "no" answer to that question up there about being a better father. With my goals in mind of becoming a good dad, I have started running my company with renewed focus on values like honesty and integrity. We treat our clients and staff with courtesy, and take them into consideration when making big decisions. It's never "our way or the highway."

We don't approach our business in a cutthroat way, and heading down that path almost always leads to misery. You should not sacrifice your happiness and health for pure profits. You need to create a positive lifestyle that supports your growth both personally and professionally. I'm not very old, but now I'm a lot happier, and I hope my decision to change can help you change, too.

FINDING NEW DAILY ROUTINES AND HABITS

I have found that there are three categories of ways to pull yourself up and give the answer to this question, "If you were to die today, would you be happy?" a resounding YES! The categories are: Thinking, Speaking and Doing.

1. Thinking

- Stop feeling sorry for yourself
- Avoid hanging around people who have negative thoughts

- Learn to live in the moment... Today will be gone by tomorrow.
- Focus on how you can make better decisions starting today.

2. Speaking

- Open up and share what's going on in your life
- Learn to keep quiet and really listen to other people's experiences
- Discover solutions to your own problems by listening to others
- Find someone you can openly talk to
- Learn to say "no"

3. Doing

- Avoid self-destructive habits
- Help others before they ask you for help
- Stop exposing yourself to negative people in the wrong places

As my life starts to take off like a rocket, it seems that so many more opportunities are arising, and I'm becoming aware of every action around me. Become the best person you can be today for it will be gone by tomorrow. Make sure you set yourself up to succeed and not to fail. My Moment of Clarity came when I was young, and I know I am going to be a good father because I'm starting early. So whatever it is that you want from your life. . .

. . . Believe you can do this before you do it!

About Anthony

Anthony Montoya has been designing websites professionally since before he was old enough to drive. Anthony also built his first computer by age twelve from which he developed a passion for technology.

Anthony sold his first computer repair company back in 2014 and now focuses his time on developing corporate websites. His designs are on the cutting-edge in graphically stylish formats as well as functionality. His website responsive features help maximize your results in your call-to-action.

Anthony Montoya's secret to keeping a work-life balance is by giving back to the community. He coaches Little League baseball and spends quality time with his family.

CHAPTER 30

LIVE BY DESIGN, NOT BY DESTINY

BY AZIZAN OSMAN, PhD

"My life was not meant to be this difficult."

Raised in a small town in Pontian, Johor and later, Melaka (Malaysia), I grew up trying to understand why life was so difficult. My father was a government servant and we could not afford a lot of things. But after years of struggling to save, my parents got me a college education.

I completed my college diploma in Investment Analysis, and pursued a career in a stock-broking firm before quitting two years later. I tried sales to earn more money. Some days were good, but most days I could not even sustain a meal. With a one-thousand-five-hundred-ringgit salary, I would spend it in less than three days. I was broke for the rest of the month till pay day.

To survive, I lived on my credit cards. My debts grew deep. I attempted several quick-scheme businesses, but I failed and failed. I was almost a bankrupt. At the end of 1999, I persuaded my parents to mortgage our home to invest in a get-rich-quick scam and I lost the money. My biggest mistake was seeking loans from loan-sharks. I was pursued day and night to repay my debts.

I attempted approaching several successful millionaires for guidance to rebuild my business, but my attempts failed. None of these individuals could make time to meet. I was frustrated, but I grew determined.

I finally met an elderly Chinese businessman, Peter, owner of a small trading company. Though he had minimal formal education, he was savvy in business. He made average monthly sales of half-a-million ringgit. His wisdom and success became my inspiration.

Peter's advice was simple. He was crude but frank. He said, "Azizan, you are stupid. Your university degree does not guarantee your success in business. Go find a mentor who is able to not only teach you, but someone who has been in business for awhile with proven results." Though my fragile ego was bruised, I valued his honesty to help me, unlike the rest. Peter admitted he was no mentor though he was financially successful.

I continued pursuing knowledge and mentors over time.

In early 2001, I secured a corporate door-to-door sales job to sustain my debts. Over a short period, I was able to climb the career ladder to the top and was appointed as the Project Manager. Not only that, I was given the chance to run my own advertising and marketing firm supported by my principal company. What a sudden change of destiny, I thought.

In 2006, I made my first million at the age of thirty-two. I worked practically twenty hours every day. I managed to clear my debts but I had no life balance, and was faced with a bitter divorce. I had financial success but not happiness. I was not at peace with myself. And I felt lost and mostly miserable.

I reflected hard on my circumstances. I kept asking **why** repeatedly: "Why me?". . . "Why is my life fated this way?". . . "Why can't I have total success in every area of my life?"

In the early part of 2008, my marriage got worse and we were divorced. I then embarked on a four-month self-discovery journey. I knew one thing for sure. In pursuit of financial success, I had faltered in my spiritual faith. I failed to care for my family and led a life that only benefited myself. It was during this period that I discovered and truly understood the Laws of the Universe. Nothing happens by chance. Every word, every thought, every feeling and every action has a consequence. . . "We reap what we sow."

In every waking moment, we are creating and altering our lives and destiny. Our present surroundings and future is and will be a product of our thoughts, our visualizations, our words, our emotions, our beliefs, our attitudes, our expectations, our deeds and what we will or will not allow ourselves to experience that will shape our lives. I continued my search for answers during these hard times.

In June 2008, I terminated my contract with my principal and started my own advertising agency. I began consulting with several multinational companies in addition to countless small business owners and my success increased.

Harnessing my corporate and business expertise along with my personal self-discovery experiences for total success, I was resolute in helping more individuals build their lives and businesses. I ventured into training and coaching – a stepping stone for building a future corporation. People from all walks of life and circumstances began attending my self-discovery and business-mastery seminars. From a classroom size of nine individuals, I have been privileged to train thousands of people today to be high achievers on a personal and professional level.

Within eight years, we became the largest personal development and corporate training company in Malaysia, apart from my running my advertising and marketing firm. We ventured into diversified industries like real estate investment; we built our own business college, a corporate advisory business, and we are building a technology platform among many others.

Here are the lessons I learned and the steps I took to rebuild my life, from being a "trouble-maker" kid to becoming a respected and successful businessman, a loving father of six, and enjoying a successful second marriage since 2010, a balanced and fulfilling life emotionally and spiritually, supporting the charities I love, and most importantly, giving back to my family and the community.

You'll be able to use my experiences to empower your life in the same way I benefited from my mentors and from the consistent pursuit of knowledge. These lessons that I've coined into an acronym in my native Malay language, will take you from where you are to where you want to be. But knowledge alone without action makes no difference. It remains as knowledge. The truth is, you can have the power to create your circumstances and reality with the right knowledge and persistent actions.

What is M.E.S.T.I? It's a combination formula that must be applied together to rebuild one's life for success.

The meaning of the acronym M.E.S.T.I is *must* in English. The acronym stands for:

• **M** – Mentor

• **E** – Emotions with Right Knowledge

• **S** – System

• **T** – Take Massive Determined Actions Consistently . . . and

• **I** – Identify Your Direction and Vision

1. MENTOR

Mentorship can be life-changing and extremely valuable to your personal development and business. It empowers you and drastically increases your chance of succeeding. Mentors have invaluable experiences and knowledge. They have insights into building a business and they can help you through your life-changing journey. Many of the most successful entrepreneurs around the world credit much of their success to their mentors. Even the wealthiest billionaires like Bill Gates and Mark Zuckerberg had mentors that guided them to success.

2. EMOTIONS WITH RIGHT KNOWLEDGE

The Law of Attraction (another Law of the Universe) simply responds to how you feel about what you say and what you think. Therefore, it is fundamental that you have the right knowledge of what you would precisely want to attract into your life – as thoughts and emotions are energy. If you use it wisely to choose positive thoughts and emotions, everything you desire will start to move your way until it materializes in your surroundings.

3. SYSTEM

Life without a system is chaos. For anything to be achieved, you must have a system that you can focus and follow till you achieve your desired results. Having a system is beneficial in helping you plan and organize your daily life and in business. When systems are in place, it provides clear concise guidelines. It is easily replicated and it limits our scope of deviating from the defined processes. It helps you to stay on track.

4. TAKE MASSIVE DETERMINED ACTIONS CONSISTENTLY

What we do consistently shapes our lives today. To achieve great results, we must commit to taking massive determined actions consistently. We must focus and take conscious responsibility for our consistent actions in order to design the lives of our dreams. Taking big action steps can help bring big results in return. And taking fast action will bring about fast results. The most crucial part in taking massive determined actions consistently is to define your goals clearly and to know your biggest "why". By identifying and understanding your biggest "why", you will be constantly motivated to achieve your goals. Does having success gives you the ability to provide a good, comfortable and worry-free life for your family? Does it give you freedom of time and money? What does success gives you?

5. IDENTIFYING YOUR DIRECTION AND VISION

One of the biggest challenges people face today is the lack of purpose and meaning in life. Each of us must find our own direction, a vision for our lives. Otherwise, nothing we do means anything. The Creator has blessed each one of us with a set of talents and uniqueness for us to discover our own greatness. Only when we realize our true potential and that we were created for a good purpose in this life, are we able to achieve abundance of wealth, success, health, happiness and a blessed spiritual connection with the Creator.

6. HAVE FAITH IN YOUR SOURCE

No matter what you call your Source – Creator, God or Universal Intelligence – you must have faith and complete confidence in this higher power to help you with your given abilities and powers to shape your own destiny. You must build a strong connection with this Source and have ultimate faith in this higher power and yourself to achieve the life of your design. This faith must persist in both good and challenging times.

Faith is an inner source that speaks to you about goodness, greatness and appreciation for all creation and how this entire universe works. We need to step out of our own unbelief by trusting the Creator as He wants us to trust Him, along with what the Creator can do when we choose to believe—irrespective of how perplexing our situation may be.

What usually happens is that people are consumed with their issues of life as a result of focusing too much on the severity of their problems, rather than what the Creator can do if they're willing to have faith. With man, many things are impossible, but with the Creator, all things are possible.

7. THE POWER OF PRAYER

Prayer is one of the greatest privileges that the Creator has accorded to mankind in order for us to be able to relate to Him in such a powerful way. A prayer is a conversation we have with the Creator concerning our daily needs, to express our gratitude as a result of His many blessings bestowed upon us, and to seek the Creator's will and purpose for our lives. It's a means of communicating by inviting the Creator to intervene on our behalf in our problems, challenges, trials, and circumstances that we are facing on a regular basis in the life we are to live by. We should never underestimate the power of prayer. Prayer is a matter of humility. It implies acknowledgement of our human dependence on the infinite greatness and power of the Creator.

8. ACTIVATE YOUR GOODNESS

The value of doing good, including caring for nature and animals and helping others, as well as activating our own goodness, character, feelings and thoughts can make extraordinary things happen. It can lead you to a life filled with opportunities. It has the power to liberate you from your past to find your place in this world, in a way that is most inspiring, empowering and life-enriching.

9. THE MORE YOU GIVE, THE MORE YOU GET

Believe it or not, you can get rich and successful by giving. This is one of the greatest money-attracting and life-enhancing secrets of the universe. Like energy, the more energy you use, the more energy you would need to replenish. The same with wealth, love, happiness, and all the good things in life. The more giving you are, the more you will have to receive in return to maintain your life force balance. Personally, being able to give to my family and the causes I support, and seeing the difference it makes in their lives drives me to create more, earn more, and make my money work harder. But the only way to know if "giving" really works is to actually do it yourself with the right intentions.

I believe that every individual has the power to bring about significant changes, good or bad. Whether we choose to use that power bestowed on us for the benefit of all and for what purposes, defines the life we can have, the destiny we create and the legacy we leave behind for generations to come. May you always be blessed with the goodness the Creator has willed for you, for this is the essence of having an Extraordinary Life!

To Your Wealth & Success!

Azizan Osman, PhD
Success Coach & Asia's No.1 Marketing Maestro

About Azizan

Azizan Osman, PhD is a Social Entrepreneur, Best-Selling Author, Business & Marketing Strategist, Success Coach and Philanthropist.

Azizan has been a serial entrepreneur all his life. He started as a teenager selling food, books and just about anything from his dormitory during his campus days. He had two formal educations, one in a Chinese school and the second in a Muslim religious school. Both educations set the very foundation for Azizan's business acumen and the core values in his life today.

His first experience in the corporate world was with a stock-broking firm. Two years later, he pursued a career in sales. He pursued several unsuccessful business ventures and eventually was betrayed by his business partner. He ended up with hundreds of thousands in personal debt.

Picking himself up in 2001, he worked as a trainee executive in a UK-based marketing company called The Cobra Group PLC, one of the largest and most successful global sales and marketing companies. He shot to meteoric success with his great track record and exceptional marketing talent.

During his tenure under the London-based organization, Azizan received fourteen personal accolades for his outstanding performance in the fields of leadership, management, human resource management, advertising and marketing -- for which he holds a strong passion.

He then took his credibility to another level when he was awarded the *Chairman's International Platinum Award*—the highest accolade to be handed out by the organization, after only two years of service. As an international marketer, Azizan is a certified Guerrilla-Marketer mentored by Jay Conrad Levinson.

In 2008, Azizan made a bold move to pursue his life-long dream of owning his own company. He brought on board his vast experiences to be shared with those in need of his expertise. His experiences with hardship and failure made him one not to be defeated. He began to reflect on the fundamental laws governing success and failure. His theories and experiences became the stepping stone for his next multimillion dollar business which brought him huge financial success and ultimate fulfilment.

Azizan, who champions life-long learning, has multiple international certifications in human and mind-science development, marketing and business besides attaining an MBA in 2009. Not long later in 2013, he obtained his PhD in Management.

As a coach and best-selling author, Azizan has trained over 650,000 people, empowering them with priceless knowledge to succeed in life and business. He has helped countless small business owners and multinationals generate revenues reaching millions in annual sales. To the masses, he is renowned as a Success Coach and Asia's No.1 Marketing Maestro.

Azizan's success has been well documented by the local media for his desire and sheer determination to help individuals and business owners to achieve their full potential. His aid comes in various forms including talks, seminars, personal coaching, online training, blogs, books, videos, social media, his frequent columns in leading newspapers, and appearances on television and radio programs.

Currently, Azizan is the Founder and Chairman of a conglomerate comprising of twenty-seven subsidiaries under the Richworks Group of Companies flagship in various trades besides coaching and training.

If you would like to learn how to grow your business, contact us at:

Richworks International Sdn Bhd
Tel: +603 5519 1260
Email: inquiries@richworks.com.my
Website: www.azizanosman.com
YouTube: Dr Azizan Osman
Facebook: Azizan Osman Official Page
Blog: www.azizanosman.com/blog
Twitter & Instagram: @drazizanosman

CHAPTER 31

MARINE-STYLE MARKETING
— 3 STEPS TO GET PRE-QUALIFIED PROSPECTS TO CALL YOU AFTER THEY'RE ALREADY PREDISPOSED TO BUY

BY DON LOVATO

I am going to teach you my 3-step process to quickly and easily position your business with tremendous authority in your marketplace. Your new position will attract more great clients to you, so you can create a more predictable and repeatable flow of leads and income that will allow you the lifestyle you deserve, giving you the freedom to take more time off to enjoy the things and people you enjoy most.

Sounds like a tall order, doesn't it? Well it's certainly possible.

What if someone almost begged you to sell them something, would that strike you as common in your daily routine? Probably not — at least — not for most people. If someone would have said any of this to me eight years ago, I would have thought they were smoking something and written them off as a lunatic.

You may be thinking that right now about me too. I undoubtedly wish I had known of and definitely implemented this 3-step formula before the

271

economy crashed. It would have saved me years of pain and suffering, as well as hardship. I want that for you too, and this is why I will be teaching you my 3-step process.

It's no secret, that the most desirable way to sell your products or services to a prospective client is when they come to you and then ask you to help them buy the right solution for them, like a trusted advisor, right?

It's just more comfortable. There's no need to knock on doors, cold call or hard sell anyone. In our businesses, we've actually had prospects ask various members of our sales staff, "How much do I make the check out for?" before they were even shown a product and within moments of meeting them – no joke!

The primary reason the prospects were so convinced is a concept called preeminence. They can be sold before they even meet you or see your product. They envision themselves experiencing their desired outcome from hearing or reading a story of the experience someone else had with you or your company. Imagine, hundreds of your clients saying great things about you and your company so enthusiastically and convincingly, others immediately come to you for the same experience. They didn't even consider buying from anyone else; they want exactly what their friend just described to them.

Remember the famous scene with Meg Ryan in that diner scene from that 80's film *When Harry Met Sally*? She faked an 'O' so well that the lady sitting right next to her thought it was the meal she was enjoying which had given her such jubilation, that she practically shouted a command to the waitress "I'll have what she's having." There was no sales resistance; that's the type of unbridled request you want to get from your next prospect, right?

These happy and enthusiastic "disciples," your clients, can share their experience with others by word-of-mouth, or simply leaving a video or written review – and the good news is – it can all be done by automation if set up properly. These verbal, video and written online "testimonials" are called your proof elements, they can be so convincing and authentic that you never even need to talk about how great your company is. It never even comes up because they already know it. It's so much more believable when someone else says you're great versus when you say it.

It's much more tasteful, and certainly not seen as a puffery statement or simply a platitude.

You too can make this happen, it just takes two things on your part, commitment and desire. That's what all business success takes. Luckily for you, with today's 'drag and drop' or 'plug and play' technology, it can take less than an hour to set up the whole process and the results will blow you away. The rewards will come in the form of financial compensation as well as the natural, effortless promotion of your stellar reputation. This phenomenon, which I've witnessed first hand, can perpetuate for a lifetime.

Let me ask you an unusual question, I'll get to why I'm asking it in just a moment. What's the first thing that comes to mind when I mention the U.S. Marines? Clearly Marines have a global reputation that precedes them for Strength, Courage and Patriotism – an Elite Corps of men and women that serve not only our nation, but also are often the first to come to the rescue and defend any nation in the world from tyranny where there is despair, without hesitation. They have an obligation to be the most ready, when our nation needs them the most.

As a former U.S. Marine, what comes to mind for me is all the above and more—much more. The very first thing that comes to mind when I think of the Marines is certainly not marketing – not even close.

In fact, the first time I saw an ad for the Marines, I was a sophomore in high school, enrolled in the JROTC program, it was a poster of a Marine Sniper hidden in his Ghillie suit, totally camouflaged and barely, if at all, noticeable – I got goose bumps – I still do, actually.

I'm reminded specifically of the Marine recruiting commercial called "Toward The Sound Of Chaos." It goes like this, "Where chaos looms, the Few emerge. Marines move toward the sounds of tyranny, injustice and despair—with the courage and resolve to silence them." And in that scene, everyone else is running away from the chaos.

Here's why I asked the question earlier. It's not often, if ever, that you hear the references of Marines and Marketing, let alone both words used in the same sentence. I am bringing this unusual example to you, primarily because my service in the Marines allows me to convey to you a more complete understanding of why they do it, and also as a real world illustration of the way they pre-screen and pre-qualify the potential recruit (or prospect) before they even call or visit a recruiting office in their local area. And why starry-eyed hopefuls beg the Marines to physically, and mentally challenge them to the very core of their existence in the grueling twelve weeks of hardcore U.S. Marine Corps Boot-Camp.

Think about how that commercial can evoke a sense of patriotism and pride, the desire to be one of them, as well as simultaneously and automatically filter (pre-qualify) out a potential Marine candidate or prospect that would not have confidence to apply be one of: *The Few. The Proud. The Marines.*

Good marketing does exactly that. It sifts, sorts and screens out the good prospects from the bad, all the while compelling the good prospects to automatically pre-qualify themselves, allowing all the 'heavy lifting' to be done by automation.

If executed properly, the system will then take pre-motivated, qualified prospects that are already predisposed to buy your products or service, allow them to raise their hand and identify themselves as being interested in giving you money to help them with their problem.

Imagine having an ad that drives prospects to your website where they find hundreds of credible and influential third parties verifying that all of the reviews are made by real people. The key here is to have a badge or logo that mentions that these reviews are third party verified. Ultimately, your site will educate them on all the things they didn't know they didn't know, and how to be a well-informed consumer, all done simultaneously. It's almost an "Invisible Close" – your prospects are closing or convincing themselves before they even meet you.

Now, I'm going to teach you step-by-step, and in detail, my simple 3-step process for getting you to your next level of success. It'll be easier than you think and performs better than you can imagine, I promise. It's so simple, you'll wonder why you didn't think of it yourself. Here is the 3-step process:

    I. The first step will be to get a quality, reputable online-scheduling system if you meet people for sales calls or if they come to you for a booked appointment. If you don't and they come to you randomly, there is another one out there that I use in conjunction with it – the more the merrier in my book – and it allows you to email a request for review to your clients. Also, if you don't have the time, the system will call the client for you and get the verbal review via telephone transcribed and placed on your site. This is key and crucial; it is the place to start for surefire and fast results.

II. The second step is to claim and confirm your Google and Bing business profile; chances are both companies have already started one for you. All you need to do is claim and confirm it, then complete the profile 100%, and correct any errors they may have made. It happens, since it's all generated by automation – no biggie – just edit the profile and move on. Google and Bing reviews are verified, but there's no one to call for help, since it's a free service. That's part of why I didn't make them the first step. The other part is because the reviews may or may not appear on your business profile page for either Google or Bing.

You may be thinking, this is so simple, and asking yourself why something this easy isn't implemented more often by your competitors. You may be even questioning why this is so effective. I'll tell you the answers to both in just a moment. First off, I get emails from people all the time telling me they can't believe the results they've gotten with such a simple idea, how much easier it is to help people buy their products or services after they have seen the reviews. The reason they never set it up is that they believed it was a complicated set up – which is why they never started an automated review process.

III. The third step is just as simple. The video is engaging, and people resonate with it in a way that can only be matched with live interaction – that's how powerful it is. So, your next step is to create a list of questions that people ask you over and over again; these are obviously FAQ's.

The next part is even more simple and it's the things you are thinking while they're asking you those FAQ's; I know I think it and you most likely do to. Here's what I think while people are asking me FAQ's. It's "I wish they'd ask me _x_? Because if they did, it would make them a more informed and smart buyer; more importantly, it would be very hard for someone to take advantage of them."

I personally have close to fifty FAQ and SAQ videos on one of our websites that tell people what they didn't know they didn't know – thereby making them a knowledgeable and informed buyer, while simultaneously building trust with them. The other interesting benefit is that people look at you as an expert.

I want to say that we test everything; I mean everything, as you should. We find the videos with myself or one of our staff members versus a professional actor gets more completed views. That goes to show you that the super-duper polished and over-produced videos are not worth the investment. Now, I'm not saying you can get away with bad audio or lighting in your video; just make it look good and the authenticity you project on camera will win them over – *as long as the content is relevant and useful!*

Content is king, no doubt. Don't start your videos with a long elaborate logo reveal and think that'll carry the video or replace poor, or irrelevant content, because it won't. Believe me, I've tried, because I used to be very camera shy and a perfectionist. Perfection is the enemy of progress – and Money loves Movement. Don't over think it, your own idea of how you look on camera is irrelevant, and do not 'nit pick' your video to death.

Your viewers won't, I promise. They're more interested in the content, and if they aren't, you don't want them for clients because they'll just 'nit pick' everything you do too. I am reminded of my buddy Mike Koenigs – who taught me that you can only provide two out of three of the following things: your company can be Good, Fast or Cheap, but not all three and still remain in business. You can't afford to.

The more relevant thing I took away in my experience with his equation is that people who want all three of those and won't relent are usually picky, crazy and cheap. . . and you certainly don't want to attract those folks either.

Why am I mentioning this to you? Well, let's just say that I have a lot of experience trying to be all three of those things for over twenty years. The moment I stopped being "that company," my profits, complaints and call backs – as well as joy for life – improved; and I mean a lot.

I'm going to leave you with this to think about if you've been in business for any length of time and have paid attention. When you get a really great client that's easy to work with, compensates you fairly because they see the benefit in your value proposition, and maybe send you a referral, they're almost always the same high caliber of client, aren't they?

Well, that's the secret sauce of this automated referral system. Great clients leave great reviews, and great clients are typically attracted to those reviews. So, this becomes a referral and lead generating system that is unmatched by anything I've ever seen in my twenty-five years in business.

Moreover, the reason for the effectiveness is that we are all hard-wired to believe someone else's account of their experience with you versus your version. Who hasn't been lied to or bought something they regret because it doesn't do what they claimed it would? People have natural sales resistance, because they've gotten burned, some more than others. Don't fight human nature, just harness its strength and use it to your advantage.

Go now and get started today, before your competition does. Besides, no one is going to do it for you or have the same commitment and desire that you do. Let me know how it's working for you and send me a success story. I'd love to hear about your successes, it gives me great pleasure to hear stories from those who implement what I teach – that's my most gratifying reward.

About Don

Don Lovato is a decorated former U.S. Marine and serial entrepreneur from Albuquerque, who has been in the Flooring Industry for 20+ years. He has also founded an online Follow Along Fitness System called *Wake The Fork Up*, along with a Marketing Agency that helps local business owners around the world. Most recently, Don and his wife became partners with an Anti-Aging and Acne Clinic with clients across the globe.

Eight years ago, Don found himself caught in a downward spiral when several life challenges occurred within a very short period of time, starting with an IRS Audit, a divorce, a Trade Name lawsuit, a brain aneurysm, and complications from brain surgery that resulted in emergency open-heart surgery due to a major infection. The compounding of these events decimated his life's savings, retirement and business cash-flow, after returning to work nearly a year later, he found the economy had turned around globally.

Don has acquired nearly every book, product and piece of teaching material on the subject of Direct Response marketing from his contemporaries, including Frank Kern, Mike Koenigs, and Joe Polish. He learned, mastered and implemented these direct response concepts, along with the idea of preeminence – as taught by his now friend and mentor Jay Abraham. He also studied the copywriting techniques and strategies from classic mentors like Claude Hopkins, David Ogilvy, Al Lasker, John Caples as well as the legendary Robert Collier.

Don's new and existing businesses quickly began to see fantastic results, the revenue in one business alone rose from $1 million to nearly $3.1 million annually consistently over the next seven years. At the request of his friends and colleagues who witnessed all of this, he opened a marketing agency where he offers consulting, business growth strategies, as well as marketing strategy.

In addition, in his newly-acquired Direct Response Marketing abilities, he opened an ABQ Skin Care & Acne Clinic four years ago with his new wife; the clinic experienced zero to multiple six-figure growth revenues annually in less than four years, and is booked out at least two to three months. He was also selected as one of America's Premier Experts™.

Don is now a two-time #1 Best Selling author, passive income business owner and mentor to many. He enjoys travelling the globe with his wife and children.

CHAPTER 32

BEAT THE CURVE IN REAL ESTATE AND FINANCE — FOLLOW A WELL-CLEARED PATH TO A SECURE RETIREMENT

BY JOE DORNER

The Great American Dream of *'Work hard during your Earning Years and put something away to enjoy your Golden Years'* is elusive. It's hidden in plain sight, yet for many it is on the verge of becoming the **Great American Myth**.

This is the short story version of a long journey and series of stories that led to the discovery of "How to Beat the Curve" in real estate and finance and follow a well-cleared path to a Secure Retirement – cutting years off the process without the hard lessons, while avoiding the common mistakes that can set you back.

The solution that enables the dream and allows you to follow the well-cleared path to a secure retirement will be revealed in a brilliantly simple manner in just **Three Magic Words**.

As a baby boomer born B.C. (Before Calculator and Computer) into a hard-working family with strong farming roots and plenty of family depression-era memories, I naturally developed a strong work ethic. As the oldest of 4 children I also developed what my parents identified as an above average case of the 'I wants'. I was fortunate enough to learn from the example of the strong family work ethic and started learning to earn at an early age with a paper route, by cutting grass and shoveling snow, and by various other enterprising activities fueled by my imagination.

I was also fortunate enough to pick up a strong desire for reading, learning, and discovering how things work at an early age, which helped me develop a strong drive for self education, which translated into a low tolerance for the conformity of the school system and subjects where I didn't see the immediate practical value, which led to an early interest in real estate and finance that was fueled by books I read as a youth on real estate by Bill Nickerson & Tyler G. Hicks, and later by a high school marketing teacher. I started learning and working in the mortgage business in the late 60's.

My good fortune was compounded by timing which, as I later learned, can be a huge difference maker. I grew up with the prime rate ranging from 3% to 5% before inching up and down to no more than 7%. Home prices were very low but inflation was starting to rear it's ugly head, and my ultimate good fortune was joining the core of our cadre in the mid 70's not realizing at the time we were in for the roller coaster ride of our life, as prime would get up to 12% then settle back down in the 6's, 7's, and 8's before the hell that broke loose over the next couple of years, culminating in a prime rate that hit 20% on April 2, 1980, and conditions never before seen that wreaked havoc on real estate and the economy for a couple of years.

Knowledge is power, or more accurately put: *Strategic Action based on specialized knowledge is power*; and that's what we used to survive during those times, and then went on to thrive in the face of adversity and some pretty daunting challenges. We were fortunate that real estate prices were low, with a nice house costing less than $20,000 – which required strategic planning and strategic marketing to generate enough volume for any meaningful revenues. Even at under $20K, an important part of real estate was to know where the money is, and what it takes to get it, so our application of strategic specialized knowledge (especially marketing) made the difference and led to the creation of our own mortgage company and several of our Core Programs.

There are far too many stories to detail all the struggles we faced, our survival, the birth of our Core Programs, and our going on to prosper in the face of adversity. It would take at least a trilogy to even begin to lay the foundation of the main story lines, but in the end we not only survived, but went on to thrive, putting well over 10,000 deals worth billions under our belts in the process before our pre 9/11 retirement from the business, but not from doing deals, and our subsequent post-mortgage meltdown rebirth.

We saw the mortgage meltdown coming long before it happened, and it wreaked havoc when it hit – reminiscent of when prime was high double digits. We planned our rebirth to create access to our House of Programs and Private Deal Platform in the process for the next generation of Clients and Associates to capitalize on, without having to learn the lessons or pay the price we paid.

The Great American Dream of work hard during your earning years, and put something way for your Golden Years is an elusive dream at best. I remember in the 60's hearing Earl Nightingale state that only 5% make it, and in 2015 the statistics aren't any better.

A recent Report about the returns investors have been getting in the stock market over the last 30 years paints a picture that is not very pretty . . . According to DALBAR, Inc., the well-respected research firm, the average investor in asset allocation mutual funds (spreading your money in a blend of equities and fixed-income funds) earned only 1.76% per year over the last 30 years!

These investors didn't even come close to beating inflation, which averaged 2.7% per year. The average investor in equity mutual funds averaged only 3.79% per year – beating inflation by only 1% per year.

And the news gets worse: The 3.69% return investors in equity funds got over the last 30 years was almost two thirds less than the return of the S&P 500 index over that period! Pity those who invested in fixed-income funds. They only managed to eke out a 0.72% annual return, significantly trailing inflation, and reducing purchasing power.

Investing in a tax-deferred account like a 401(k), IRA, or 403(b), you also pay hefty fees, plus you'll have to pay taxes when you start taking income, which can wipe out another 30 to 50% of the meager returns you managed to eke out.

All of which makes it abundantly clear that if you're invested in the market, you're playing in the Wall Street Casino and only fooling yourself instead of growing real wealth, where the reality is that you may be digging yourself deeper and deeper into a hole you may never be able to climb out of.

Just who is the "average investor"? The Dalbar 2015 Quantitative Analysis of Investor Behavior states "average investor" refers to "the universe of all mutual fund investors whose actions and financial results are restated to represent a single investor." This universe would include small and large investors as well as professionally-advised and self-advised investors.

The Conclusion of this New Report is that...

"The results consistently show that the average investor earns less – in many cases, much less – than mutual fund performance reports would suggest."

After decades of analyzing investor behavior in good times and bad, DALBAR concludes that, "Investor behavior is not simply buying and selling at the wrong time, it is the psychological traps, triggers and misconceptions that cause investors to behave irrationally."

Among those psychological traps and triggers, they cite:

- **"Herding"** – copying the behavior of others even in the face of unfavorable outcomes
- **Optimism** – belief that good things happen to you and bad things happen to others
- **Loss Aversion** – expecting to find high returns with low risk (... yeah – and I've got a gold Rolex watch I'll sell you for $100 ...)

Knowledge is power, or more accurately put: *Strategic Action based on specialized knowledge is power.* For Real Estate as an asset class: Investors in real estate own tangible assets – buildings that can appreciate and generate cash flow whose value cannot drop to zero.

With strategic use of our Programs, some of what makes it possible for our Clients and Associates to *Beat the Curve* are the ability to:

- **Get the result, but skip the lesson,** saving time in the process.

- **Get the property but forget the bank,** cutting out the red tape.
- **Do two things at the same time with the same money,** and get 1½ to 5 times the results to accumulate safely.

Our Programs and Platform are an exclusive, 'members only country club' that without an invitation from an existing Client or Associate, you can't join or come through the gates. Once you come through the gates, apply, and are granted membership, you gain access to our House of Programs. Six Core Programs make up the Anchor House of Programs.

The **foundation** of our programs is our **Buy Me A House Program** where as a Client you can get the house or investment property, and forget the bank, it provides a very solid foundation under all of the other programs.

The Four Core Program Rooms Are:

1. The **Buy My House Program** for our Clients that want to sell their house or investment property as it is, at a fair price, on their schedule, and skip the real estate commission.

2. The **Save My House Program** for our Clients that want or need to preserve their property from any of a number of problems, and skip the hunt for the right solution and high fees.

3. The **Fix My Loan Program** for our Clients who do not have a loan that meets their current needs and requires some adjustment in order to make sense and meet their needs.

4. The **Fund My Deal Program** gives our Clients access to funding for their deals without bank red tape with review by seasoned deal-makers.

The **Roof** over the **Anchor House of Programs** is our **Secure My Retirement Program** which is the ultimate end goal we all consciously or unconsciously seek, but so many find to be elusive, but it is easier to find when following one of the paths plodded down by the many that have come before.

Just like in any house, there are ancillary rooms inside the **Anchor House of Programs**, some of which are: The **Associate Income Program**, the **Find Me A Deal Program**, and the **Make A Difference Program** among others. So we have programs that can be the solution to most any real estate or income problem.

The depth and breadth of our Programs is good news for our Clients, however the bad news is our founding fathers stopped accepting new Clients prior to 9/11. It is possible there can be some good news for potential clients, but only if they have an existing Associate willing to assist and vouch for them, and we have a program for that too.

The **Associate Income Program** is for people who want a supplemental income that can transition into a new financially – and emotionally – rewarding career and make a difference doing it helping people:

- **Grow funds using a 1 + 1 = 3 equation** utilizing a fix-the-problem strategy.
- Move swiftly to the point where they can **Be the Bank** to reduce work and effort while increasing stability and yield.

Those are the **Three Magic Words** that make the dream come true in a brilliantly simple manner, don't let their simplicity fool you. Yes, you can **Be the Bank!**

Starting from learning one of the first lessons in real estate where we got to know where the money is and what it takes to get it, we went through the other lessons and the ups and downs until we discovered how to Be the Bank, and once we did our marketing, expertise smoothed out the ups and downs.

We help our Clients get there more quickly than we did by skipping the hard lessons on the path to a Secure Retirement and Being the Bank helps beat the curve to get there.

Be the Bank: It's the best position to occupy in a real estate transaction, get there quickly with our Build Me A House Program. You have nothing to do other than deposit your checks. You do none of the work and you end up with the most benefits while you spend your time as you wish.

We have the Programs, the Platform, and the Solutions which we will continue to provide exclusively to our long time Clients unless and until any new potential clients are fortunate enough to secure an invitation from one of our existing Associates and are able to pass the screening of our Advisory Board to gain admission as a Client to enable access to the Platform, Programs resources and deal review.

About Joe

Joe Dorner helps his Clients and Associates plot a path to secure their retirement and helps them achieve it step-by-step with out-of-the-box thinking utilizing conventional assets in an unconventional manner, a unique proprietary process, six Core Programs, and a Private Deal Platform established by a cadre of successfully-retired Deal Makers enabling member only access to their Programs, Platform, and resources.

Joe the B.C. (Before Calculator and Computer) dinosaur retired from mortgage banking and real estate prior to 9/11 and stopped taking on new Clients (as did the cadre), but none of them stopped doing deals. In addition to utilizing their Platform to do deals for their long-time Clients the cadre engineered a virtual re-birth of their pre-retirement Associate and Advisor model for the next generation. Joe is a Sr. Advisor with the least seniority, having only joined the cadre as 'Joe the new guy' in the mid seventies, and was 'volunteered' as the 'gate keeper' for Program & Platform access, charged with screening new potential Clients and Associates for entry before submitting them to the Advisory Board for Membership approval.

Joe's Clients have an above average net worth and early retirement rate which some would have never obtained without Joe's counsel. Joe was always a quick study, an avid reader, and a lifelong 'young man in a hurry' who stayed ahead of the curve. He was an enterprising youth that first got interested in real estate in the 7th or 8th grade after reading a book by Bill Nickerson. He had little patience for school and was more interested in working and earning money ever since his first paper route at six years old. He quit high school twice and got kicked out once before the Marketing 101 course caught his attention and a good teacher made it make sense.

He started learning the mortgage business in his last year of high school, got to a level of competence, and moved into restaurant management doing real estate and financing on the side searching for the right niche and mentor until joining the cadre in the mid 70s where he got his marketing chops.

Joe is a graduate of the 'School of Hard Knocks' educated by reading, doing, making mistakes, getting knocked around pretty hard, and knocked down a few times in the process, but always getting back up, and always learning from the experience. Joe is the author of three books; *Consistent Winner Black Jack, Achieving the American Dream*, a *30 Day Blueprint for Success,* plus one he's embarrassed to mention. He has #4 and #5 in the works, and has been featured on radio and television a number of times including on: *Ask an Expert, The Market Basket Report,* and *Let's Talk About*

Money where he was a regular guest and was recently recognized as one of America's Premier Experts.

Joe prefers a quiet life with his family and wanted to turn down the assignment he was 'volunteered' for, but since he could not, he is the babysitter until the next generation of Associate leaders is found.

You can connect with Joe at:
Joe@AnchorAA.com
LinkedIn.com/JoeDorner
Facebook.com/JoeDorner

CHAPTER 33

ACHIEVING CAREER SUCCESS

BY SUZANNE RICCI

Success starts with . . . well, the start! Over the years I have come to figure out, when it comes to success, many people don't know where to start, how to start or sometimes even what to start. Why is that?

DEFINING SUCCESS

Throughout our childhoods we are told some form of "Grow Up and Become Successful," "Study Hard and You Will Succeed," or "Make Smart Choices." Very few people get the guidance they need to learn how to become successful, how to study hard or how to make smart choices.

Think about it . . . did anyone ever help you define success? We surely use the words "become successful" all the time. We see it in school advertisements, articles in magazines, and on the covers of books, but what definition of success is being used? The definition of success is different for every person. The definition of success also changes depending on the stage in life you are in.

What about teaching you how to study? In school you were probably told to "study hard," but did anyone ever teach you study techniques? We even have "study hall," but rarely are we taught study strategies. And when is the last time someone taught you how to make a smart choice? Many people learn these things through the school of hard knocks or by watching others. Sometimes we just "keep trying" because that is what we are told to do. However, most of the time, we have no real concept of what we are doing. Only a lucky few have stumbled upon really good guidance.

GUIDANCE STARTS HERE –
THE TIERED APPROACH TO SUCCESS

Luckily, it is now your turn. Over the years, I noticed the difference between people who were able to achieve success and people who just couldn't make it happen. Many were ordinary people, with the same education and the same opportunities and living situations – seemingly equal in just about every way. So what was the difference? To sum it up, the successful ones knew two things. First, they knew how to start. I'm going to share with you the basic steps to getting started on reaching your path to career success. Second, they had a realistic definition of what I call "tiered" success. Basically, this means that your definition of success has to change over time. If your definition of success doesn't change, you will either never reach your goal, or worse, you will start to move backwards.

My very first customer used the tiered approach to reach his ultimate career goal. He was a retired military professional who went back to school to get a bachelor's degree in Information Technology (IT); he had been laid off from a service company and decided to move to a new area. He took advantage of his layoff and decided to change careers. He had no formal IT experience; he was just what we call a "home hobbyist" with a degree. Together, we came up with a realistic tiered plan for success. First, he started off making less than what he eventually wanted to make. He continued to work his plan annually, being sure to change his definition of success as he went, until he was finally making the amount of money he ultimately desired in the industry he wanted to be in. It didn't happen overnight; he put in a lot of hard work. But he did reach his final career success goal because he had realistic definitions of success along the way and used the tiered approach until he achieved the level of career success he wanted.

One of the advantages to the tiered approach is that you have time to figure out what tactics and strategies are needed along the way, depending on the situation you are in at any given moment. By not taking advantage of the time that a tiered approach affords, you may find yourself setting unrealistic goals, like the truck driver that called me once about a program I was teaching. The average salary in this field was $50,000 a year and most of the graduates had experience. When I explained it was unrealistic to start in this industry with no experience at $50,000 a year, he hung up on me. He had an unrealistic definition of success and wasn't willing to take the tiered approach to reach his goals.

DO YOUR RESEARCH

If you are new to an industry, changing careers or just starting your first career, you may not know what is truly realistic or where to start. I suggest starting with online research. Just be sure you are using valid and reliable resources when online. It's important to differentiate between someone's biased opinion and facts. A reliable starting point for valuable career path information is the industry association in your field. The Department of Labor and your local workforce centers will also have information that will point you in the right direction.

Next, interview people in the industry you think you want to be in. Don't just interview the person in the ultimate position you want. Interview people all the way up the ladder. Learn from their experiences. Using social media, LinkedIn, and your own personal and professional networks, you will be surprised how many connections you will be able to make with people who will take the time to speak with you and share any information they have, including their career successes and failures. Remember, you can sometimes learn more from failure than from success.

When interviewing people, be sure you are considerate of their time. Interviews can be scheduled via online chat, Skype, traditional phone, email or in-person. Always keep your interview to the amount of time they agreed to. Have a list of preplanned and printed questions and take notes quickly, so you can get a lot covered. Ask about their education, their career path, what they would have done differently, and what their suggestions are for getting into a position like theirs. Keep in mind that times change. Depending on how long they've had their position, the path to that position may be very different now.

During the interview, be sure to ask about their daily tasks. Think about if those daily tasks interest you. I have had several clients come meet with me, tell me they want to do a particular job, but when I ask them what tasks a person in that job does, they are way off. I have had several clients over the years who have in-demand medical credentials. When I ask them why they don't want to work in the medical field, I hear things like, "I don't like blood," or "I am very introverted and I don't want to work with people." If they had done the two-step research phase, they would have uncovered that this was not a realistic career path. It would have saved them time and money.

If you receive conflicting information from your research, I suggest you look at why you received conflicting reports. Do the interviewees have up-to-date information? Are they out of touch with their industry? Was one of them just being nice and trying to sugar-coat the path to success? Ultimately your research from associations, the Department of Labor, and your local workforces should help you get a clear picture.

BREAKING IT DOWN AND PUTTING IT ON PAPER

Defining career success begins with breaking down your ultimate goal into smaller goals. Achieving smaller goals is always easier and you tend to stay motivated because you are actually achieving and having wins along the way. Start with clear, concise and realistic career goals and then move on to strategies and tactics to help you achieve them. If your ultimate goal is to make $80,000 a year, be sure you are being realistic. Your industry must present that opportunity, you must have a clear career path and you must be willing to invest in the education and skills training required to get to that level. Also be realistic about whether you are willing to work the hours and do the tasks required. Most often making more than $50,000 a year comes with long hours and hard work. If you know you want to spend ample amounts of time with friends and family and work forty hours per week, then make a realistic plan that accommodates this definition of success. I once had a customer move from New England to Tampa, Florida. He wanted to make the same salary for the same job in Tampa as he did in New England. This just isn't realistic, so he ultimately didn't achieve his first definition of success. We did work together to come up with a clear, concise and realistic career goal for his current situation, which I am happy to say he achieved.

Once you feel comfortable with the path to take and the skills you will need, it's critical to put your plan on paper. Remember the plan can change and it will need to change, but having it written down will make it easier for you to take the first step. Depending on where you are in your career, you can write out one-year, three-year, and five-year goals. If you are new to your career, then write out seven- and ten-year goals too. Your written goals should include approximate salaries and approximate job titles. If you know the company you would like to work for, write that down too. The more detailed the written plan is, the easier it will be to execute it.

SKILLS AND EDUCATION

Now that you have a written plan of where you want to be, it is time to be realistic about what it will take to get you there. Make a list of the skills you have today and the skills you will need to achieve at each milestone. Remember, you should be gathering skills along the way. For example, your seven-year plan should list all the skills you need to acquire to reach your seven-year goal. You're probably not going to have every skill or credential you need at the beginning. That's okay. Even if you have a college degree, you most likely will be missing some skills required or desired for the field you've chosen. Education and training is usually a major part in achieving career success.

You may need certain skills that aren't taught in high school or college to accomplish a certain task. Acquiring additional skills doesn't mean you need another degree, a new degree, or even any degree at all. Continuing education or training may be the missing link for you. Get all the information you need to make a decision regarding the training classes, seminars, degrees and educational opportunities that will allow you to obtain the skills you need for the opportunities outlined in your plan. Be sure the skills are in line with the research you have gathered and are needed to take the next step.

If you determine that you need additional education, taking the time to do additional research when selecting a school is key. Don't rely on the recommendation of a friend or family member. They may have different needs than you when it concerns education. This choice is important for reaching your goals. Go and visit all the schools, training centers, and seminar facilities in your area that teach the skills you seek. Take a list of questions to ask when you're meeting with the school representative.

School representatives should be familiar with the job opportunities you're pursuing and have some information about how the skills they teach will help you achieve your goals. You should never be asked to sign up on the same day, unless the class is starting that day. Take the information you gathered home, think about it, compare your options and make an informed decision.

If you have trouble making a choice, I suggest going with the school that seemed more knowledgeable in your field or will let you sit in on a class before signing up. Education is a very important decision and you shouldn't feel pressured. And finally, remember to reinvest in learning new skills every year, even if you are at the level of success you desire. Obtaining new skills every year will help you reach or keep you at your defined level of success.

FINAL ADVICE

We've covered a lot of ground but I want to share one final suggestion. Every January, write down the three or four goals you want to achieve that year. Share them with your friends and loved ones. And start implementing these goals immediately. Don't wait.

If you follow the steps above, you will have a clear road map. All you need to do now is to follow it.

About Suzanne

Creative, strategic, and hard-working, Suzanne Ricci's goal-oriented thinking and her desire to be the best are traits that have expressed themselves since she was a little girl. As a top badge holder in Girl Scout cookie sales and a consistent first place winner in both hula hooping and jumping rope, Suzanne's passion for success and leading the way started early on and became lifelong pursuits.

With a relentless drive to win, Suzanne learned to create and follow well-planned recipes for success in everything she set her mind to. Recognizing her abilities and the happiness she found in helping others, she then took the strategies she employs in her own life and started sharing them with individuals and companies. Through career advice, individual training plans, and corporate staff education programs, she has helped many others find their way to the top. And for Suzanne, who takes great pleasure in helping others reach their potential, seeing her clients succeed is 'the icing on the cake.'

As in every life, twists and turns have given Suzanne opportunities to explore and flourish. Believing every experience represents a chance to grow and learn, Suzanne draws on her life experiences and adventures to create unique plans for growth tailored to individuals and companies in all phases of development.

From idea girl to execution master, Suzanne's ability to make complex situations simple always exceeds her clients' expectations.

You can connect with Suzanne at:
Suzanne@SuzanneRicci.com
www.facebook.com/suzricci
www.twitter.com/suzricci

CHAPTER 34

THE INS AND OUTS OF GENERATING INTEREST

BY WAYNE D. HARRIS

In this chapter, I will discuss not only the theory of Generating Interest but I will share with you some of the tactical approaches you can take to transition through this phase. I will unlock how to identify by signals and sounds, a person in the Generating Interest phase. Remember: *The well-honed ability to recognize which phase a prospect is moving through determines how seamless the process will be.* There really is no point in having these phases if we can't recognize where people actually are in the decision-making process. I will also discuss where interested people come from, and your role as a sales professional in executing this phase of the process.

First, let's look at the appearance and behavior of a person in the phase of generating interest. When someone has entered this phase he displays a noticeable level of intrigue, unrest, concern, misery, or aggravation around certain types of events and trends that are either impacting him personally or on a business level. These events and trends will be the influencers that give him dissatisfaction. After all, change (a sale) is made at the intersection of dissatisfaction and hope. A person that is in the interest-generating phase will also exhibit a laser-like focus when issues, challenges, or opportunities come up that impact his comfort level. This general interest then turns into urgency to appraise the circumstances, the next phase of the decision-making process. If this person with a generated interest views you and your organization as accessible, reliable, and credible, the door will creep open allowing the two of you to transition into the next phase. The overall purpose of this phase is to identify those individuals that are not fully content, and have some evidence of dissatisfaction.

Generating interest has basically two components. These are the *creation of leads* and the *commitment* to enter into the decision-making process with you. People who have identified themselves to have interest should now be considered prospects. They have moved from one of the many fish in the sea to a catchable fish swimming around your boat. From the sales professional's point of view these prospects (people with a generated interest) come from two directions. The first direction is *from the company itself, in its marketing efforts.* These are the prospects that have responded to an external marketing source. The second direction prospects come from is *through your prospecting efforts.* I find that companies that employ salespeople use one of two approaches. They either market very well to create an abundance of inbound prospects through traditional methods, or they rely on the salespeople to be both the marketing and the sales departments. I will focus on the latter of the two approaches.

When it comes to sales people having to be the marketing department (unless they allocate to you a marketing budget to run effective print, mail, TV, radio, and Internet campaigns) you will more than likely be forced to develop your own personal prospecting plan. This usually translates into your taking the initiative to develop systems utilizing the phone, knocking on doors, and networking to gain prospects. What you must keep in mind is that *prospecting* isn't a function of sales, it is a function of marketing. If you are calling on a *warm prospect list*, your strategy should be totally different than cold calling on a random list that has not indicated interest. When calling on a warm list these people have already entered into the decision-making process. The goal is therefore to get an agreement to move to the next phase of the decision-making process, either immediately or by establishing an appointment to complete the transaction.

When it comes to working the cold list, those that have not shown interest:

1. Remember: ***Everyone isn't a prospect yet!*** Most will become a prospect at some point. By using the right frequency of contacts, we can be there for them when they are interested!

2. Remember: *Interest is created by the prospect and not by you*. Our role is simply to expose the interest and the interest must ignite the prospects mind! We then align ourselves with him in exploring a solution. With that in mind, the first step in prospecting is to select the best targeted list that we will use to call, to knock on doors, and to network.

Here is a scenario to consider: You are a software sales professional. The company you work for specializes in accounting software for veterinarians. The first qualification for any list you would want to call or door knock would have to be exclusively veterinarians. The next level of qualifications would need to focus on ideal veterinary types. Maybe your software is really only good for veterinary practices that do less than 500 transactions a month. Would it make sense for you to spend your time calling on vets that do 1000 transactions a month? Maybe another qualification is that you find your best clients also have company XYZ's software and the two are really compatible which makes for an easy transition. Would you want these vets identified and called upon regularly? Most prospecting efforts are wasted by a lack of preparation. The amount of energy and effort you put into identifying the most likely prospect types makes the rest become much simpler and effective. Think of it as a funnel with the most likely prospects coming through.

The next phase of prospecting, which is actually the interest generating part, is to gain knowledge of the challenges, opportunities, and subjects that will more than likely be on the prospect's mind and in the prospect's field of expertise. This knowledge should include an awareness of the potential prospect's job responsibilities and the vocabulary the prospect uses in his field.

For example a business owner might always be thinking about...

• Cash flow

• Revenue

• Hiring

• Customers

Your ability to know these generalized thoughts about business owners and the specific types of people you would be prospecting is how you will ultimately unlock their dissatisfaction. Simply stated the veterinarian's constant topics of thought about his business will be different than the individual's in the next scenario.

For instance, a homeowner might always have in his mind. . .

- Maintenance
- Security
- Home value
- Mortgage payments

These generalizations of thoughts are your ticket to getting in the door. The way you will use these generalized topics to move into generating interest is by first linking benefits to these topics. The easiest way to link benefits is to look at it as if you are either adding or deleting, increasing or decreasing, minimizing or maximizing, gaining or reversing to accomplish goals.

Benefit action words need to become ingrained in your vocabulary as highly important terms. We live in a complex society with ever-changing terminology, and we need to emphasize the terms that create action in the mind of the prospect.

Once the benefit statements are created and become a regular part of your daily communication, you will notice that as you use these benefit statements, such as "boost safety," potential prospects will start asking you how you do it. This response to the benefit action phrases is your indicator that you have found an initial interest point or dissatisfaction with current status. There is another level of communication you must master to transition into the second half of the generating interest phase. We will need to turn these benefit phrases into "how to" statements. It is the "how to" statement that gains credibility with the potential prospect and opens the door to transition to the next phase of the decision-making process.

While there is no set template for creating these statements, the statements will all start with one of the benefit action phrases and will end with an action phrase.

For Example:

- We maximize the effects of marketing dollars by applying proven formulas to boost ad effectiveness.
- We eliminate the expense of bad hires by applying a proprietary

screening method that quickly illuminates the best hiring opportunities.

- At XYZ Corp, we boost net profit by leveraging tools and resources that minimize company waste by up to 55%.

- We eliminate the expense of exterior home maintenance by applying a protective shield on the outside of your home that lowers energy bills while enhancing the beauty of your home.

I challenge you to come up with as many of these action phrase statements as possible. Create two or three around every concern, opportunity, challenge, or problem that could possibly be on the minds of your potential prospect. The more of these you have in your arsenal, the more likely you are to generate interest. Look at it this way: If a hurricane with 100 mph winds was coming and you were tasked with putting a tarp on your most prized possessions to protect them from the rain, the action phrases are the bungee cords and ropes that will enable you to have success securing the tarp. The more bungee cords and ropes you have, the more likely your tarp will sustain the storm. Create as many action phrases as you can. The creation of these action phrases and statements will allow you to generate interest with ease and secure you in the storm.

Once you have multiple action phrase statements around your typical prospect's top-of-mind topics, I recommend saying them over and over to anyone and everyone until you are well versed in saying them. I also encourage you to gauge people's response to the phrases as you use them. You will find that different action phrases and different ways of saying the same general topic will evoke several different types of responses particularly emotional responses. As you gain comfort with these phrases, you will begin to get predictable replies.

There is one more step we must take to effectively move through the decision-making process. We must transition immediately into the next phase of the decision-making process or into a future appointment. This will depend on the type of sale you are trying to make. Keep in mind this current step of the decision-making process is simply to identify any dissatisfaction so that you can transition to the next phase.

To begin the next phase we must do a little trial closing. The trial close is simply a test to see if enough interest has been displayed to move on to the next step of the decision-making process together.

We might say something such as:

> "Based on our ability to boost net profit by minimizing waste, when would you like to get together to talk more about how much wasted profit we can recover for you?"

What happens as we roll out a trial close like this is that we will instantly be able to know where we are within the step of generating interest. If there is interest at all, this question will force action. The prospect will either have to say "yes" and schedule a time or do a dance and tell you several reasons why he cannot schedule the time. Realize two things in the moment this happens. The first is that any objection here is likely a stall. It is a stall especially if you shot out a benefit statement, and the prospect responded with a "how-do-you-do-it" reply. So, if he stalls in this manner, I recommend asking the following question:

> "Is it finding the time to set aside, or are you confident that you are getting all the net profit that should be on the table?"

This response should either put a nail in the generate interest coffin or ignite a response that opens the door for a future appointment.

The second thing you must realize in setting appointments is that the potential prospect is not telling you "yes" or "no," but is in fact telling himself "yes" or "no." He is either saying, "<u>Yes,</u> my dissatisfaction level with net profit is great enough to look into it," or "<u>No</u>, I am content. My dissatisfaction level is not great enough to even consider any options." It is important and better to get him to say "no" to himself here than to invest your time chasing a content, satisfied individual around hoping he will consider a change. ***Content people do not take action.***

If we have the type of sale that takes less than 15-20 minutes to make a decision, we want to move right into the next phase of the decision-making process. The transition to the next phase is to trial close, to see if you and the potential prospect are aligned to move forward together. I might transition like this:

> "Based on our ability to boost net profit by minimizing waste, would you like to talk more about how much wasted profit we can recover for you?"

Or I might be somewhat assumptive and say something like this:

"Based on our ability to boost net profit by minimizing waste, how often does wasted profit jump into your mind?"

Both of these styles of transition phrases should give you an instant indicator of whether or not you should be moving forward. *The biggest mistake I see with sales professionals is racing to get into their presentation prematurely.* There are very few good things that result from being premature. Often the decision will be totally ignored simply because at this phase there isn't commitment to actually consider making a change. Dissatisfaction was not recognized by you or the potential prospect, leaving the door wide open for sales failure. It is hard to believe that all of this often happens in less than a two minute exchange of words.

That is enough about the tie down and transition portion for now. I will certainly revisit the topic as we look to transition in and out of every step of the decision making model. The good news from here is that yes, our efforts of utilizing action phrases, action phrase statements, tie downs, and transitions, is that we now have an appointment. There is still a transition that needs to be made. This transition reminds the prospect of why we are having a meeting and starts the appraisal of circumstances phase. I have come up with a handy little acronym for this transition. My acronym is B.R.E.A.C.H.E.R.

A BREACHER in the military is the soldier whose primary responsibility is to open the door or open the path. He will use whatever means necessary depending on the situation. This is a very important role that must be fulfilled on any mission. Otherwise none of the other soldiers will be able to get in to do his part of the mission. I would like you to always remember this term. Think of this transition as opening the door to fulfill the mission. The mission for the prospect is to end his dissatisfaction. On the next pages I will break down the steps of how a sales professional can be the BREACHER in the decision-making process.

B.R.E.A.C.H.E.R.

Begin with introduction

Reveal a bit about your company

Explain the purpose of the meeting

Advance the conversation

Correlate viewpoints

Harness direction

Enter Analyze the Circumstances Phase

Remove the tough exterior

The concept of breaching into the next phase of the decision-making process starts with an introduction and ends with the transition into the next phase of decision making, *Analyzing the Circumstances.*

The verbiage should look something like this...

1. **Begin with introduction**
   "Hello_____, I'm _____ I look forward to our time together."

2. **Reveal a bit about your company**
   "At XYZ Corp we boost net profit by leveraging tools and resources that minimize company waste by up to 55%."

3. **Explain the purpose of the meeting**
   "_____the purpose of the meeting today is to...
   – Learn about you and your company.
   – Uncover as many wasted resources as we can in our time allotted,
   – and see if a solution is necessary to capture the available net profit we uncover, or if you can capture it on your own."

This is critical. It says you are there if they need you but content if they don't need you. This relieves the pressure.

4. **Advance the conversation**
   "I know we are getting together today to discuss how we boost net profit by minimizing company waste. What was it about boosting net profit, or minimizing waste, that made you want to spend the time?"

**It is critical here to make sure you slow down and listen. Regardless of what they say, do not let it throw you off of the BREACHER game plan. It is quite possible you will encounter resistance at this point.*

5. Correlate viewpoints

"I can appreciate what you are saying about . . . *(their response to previous question)*. Many of the people we help tell me the same thing."

6. **H**arness direction

"If at any point in our conversation you have questions, feel free to ask. I will try to keep the focus on finding net profit and minimizing waste. That is the scope of our expertise."

What happens in BREACHER is that we are establishing a comfort level with the conversation as well as establishing a level of expertise.

7. **E**nter Analyze the Circumstances phase
   – "I have a roundabout idea of what you guys do as a company, what do you think are the most important things I should know about your company?
   – "What are some of your goals around retaining net profit over the next 3 to 6 months?"

Remember: *This is where the Analyze the Circumstances phase is in full swing. The ability not just to hear the words, but the ability to hear changes in the prospect's voice, tone, and cadence are actually more important than the words he chooses to respond with.*

8. **R**emove the tough exterior

Chances are you and the prospect will both become uncomfortable with the conversation at some point during the *Analyze the Circumstances* phase. It is important to realize that the better you are at truly listening to the prospect the easier it will be to remove the prospect's tough exterior.

The BREACHER strategy assists you with building a unified approach with the prospect to analyze the circumstances. There is a natural progression that occurs that allows an easy transition into the analyze phase. Develop your action phrases, hone your action phrase statements, become comfortable with the transitions, and master the BREACHER principle. You will find that defenses will come down and real conversations will take place.

About Wayne

Wayne Harris is known as a perceptive thinker. During a career that has spanned more than twenty years, he has shown an uncanny ability to stay at the forefront of thought and to be highly adaptive while performing in the sales, marketing, and business operations arena. He has led companies to great success with recognition on the Inc. 500 list and has received letters of recognition, numerous sales achievement awards, and personal service awards.

He believes that salesmanship can be ethical, powerful and personal all at the same time. He is now on a mission to share the abundance of knowledge gained through the study of sales techniques and through professional experiences. Through workshops and turnkey sales systems, Harris is out to change the negative public perception of salespeople. He firmly believes that public perception can be changed while increasing the effectiveness of salespeople.

The work he puts forth to educate and build true sales professionals has a greater purpose. He recognizes that we each have God-given talents that can truly be of benefit to others. He volunteers his talents while serving on the board of Armonia US, a non-profit organization that for over thirty years has worked diligently to break the poverty cycle of the indigenous people of Mexico.

Wayne is the author of the acclaimed book, *The Humble Salesman* and has most recently appeared on *Get Real with Kristi Frank* on ABC, NBC, CBS and Fox. He conducts conferences and leads seminars so that others can have the opportunity to make a large impact on the world we live in. It is his hope that laymen as well as sales professionals will benefit by becoming better decision-makers and facilitators of decision-making not only in business, but also in personal, family and community life.

For contact and further information, visit: www.WayneDHarris.com

CHAPTER 35

EDUCATE YOURSELF TO BEAT THE CURVE

BY SONPAL RATHOD

At times I felt that this chapter should be titled as "Stories of My Failures!" Learning from failure is one of the most important requirements to Beat the Curve.

In my teens and as a youth, I ranked in my schooling and college. I ranked in poetry and other open writing competitions in state and city, and then failures accompanied me for many years. That happened until there was nothing behind for me to fail in. . . !

"Help me please!" "Help me, I am a failure, everywhere and each-time!" I kept on praying for help from the Universe and it's live counterparts, i.e., humans, animals and plants that they are. . . !

For few months...somewhere between 8 to 9 months, there was just silence, no help and nothing turned around! I had to live with my depression and frustrations. I used to call my friends, and then their friends – girl friends used to listen to this telephonic conversation and they would ask my close friends . . . "Is this guy okay?" Why is he asking for advice all of the time, why is he not able to manage himself well?

Most painful was my relationship which was an international deal, and was expected to end up in lifelong living together, but it started weakening and was about to end during this difficult time. I never thought that the relationship would weaken, but the boss in the company was hard on me, and during this time of frustration I wrote some harsh words to her and it started killing our relationship; she was the greatest thing and person I have ever imagined until that time! Finally, I lost that person and the relationship for which I cared so much deep down in my heart to keep it up and alive. I had to carry that pain for a long time, and I was depressed until I learned some theories of time and memories and their relationship through the books of Einstein and J. Krishnamurti. I owe it to Einstein for defining time as a scientific phenomenon and to Krishnamurti for explaining psychological relations with time and memories.

I will get back later to show how, in that time, the hard treatment of my boss became the life-long stepping stone for me towards my dreams, those I saw in my childhood and forgot altogether – until the shock of ending that relationship hit me hard in my heart.

. . . When living things were unable to help me, I started figuring out the solutions on my own, because the frustration was quite unbearable. One day during my frustration, while seated quietly, a red-covered book with a white title attracted my attention, maybe it came through intuition. It was, *How to Get From Where You Are to Where You Want to Be*, by Jack Canfield. Before I started reading I counted the pages, because I was not sure whether I would finish it up in a particular passion period or if I would leave it half read as per my old habit. I calculated one page would take somewhere around seven minutes so the book would take about two and half months for me to read and understand it fully. Somehow I agreed to make this deal with myself. Actually it only took close to one month, about half the period that I calculated for reading and understanding this book fully. The book gave me solid systematic steps towards success, but the great benefit after completing this book was my own courage – that I was able to read the complete book within a much shorter time.

I went for the second book, It was *Goals* by Brian Tracy! Later on, Brian became one of my favorite authors. That book gave me the courage that I can read and finish books, but also the courage to know that with some steps I may recover something. The third book I got and I heard about, was a pretty popular book. But, since I hadn't read many books on self-help, I started reading it with a very little conviction. It was one of the world's top self-help books; that third book was *The Magic of Thinking Big* by David Schwartz. That book gave me the complete and true message, the fame the book promised. Before even completing the book, I started getting up my courage to recover most of my lost world. The book also gave me courage and some inner assurance, like: "I amount to something worthwhile and I truly deserve that, right after I am born. I have some skills already with me and I need to find out some areas in which to shine. Areas I may love and I may not be aware of!"

Later... I don't know why my intuition didn't push me towards academic education, but rather kept me reading about self-help, astrophysics, biographies of saints, scientists, world-known philosophers from East and West, peace and wisdom, relationship of time and memories, emotions and much more. It was about a five to six-year period I spent in reading – sometimes very seriously and sometimes just with normal interest.

WHAT THE BOOKS WANTED TO TELL ME: WHAT THEY HAD AND HADN'T

. . . While reading, sometimes I was getting into the books seriously and sometimes I was getting distracted. But again I was getting serious to read them or other ones! It was like books wanted to tell me something! Like they had some message. . . ! That may be the reason I was less serious at times!

Perhaps the books wanted to tell me, "We cover almost everything that life needs to be guided by, but not each and every important rule and principle. Everybody's life is different! There may be something of immense importance which might have not been covered. So find out what is not covered in the books. Check and remember the principles of the books and try them in everyday life; correct and change wherever it is required. Listen to the stories of the common people on the street passionately, and they will tell you some of the important principles or ways that books might have not covered. There can be better ways. . . those people can tell you some of the missed principles."

Books told me that everybody is unique! Everybody is a great one! Everybody has some very important story to tell you, to share with you. Every event has some message just to be loved or to be lived with – or how to improve yourself because there is a need and there is a cause.

I followed the rules and principles of the books as much as I could! Mainly about goals, how to achieve them, how to plan for them and how to move towards your dreams. But I noticed that in addition to the principles in books, some kind of self-monitoring points and self-correction are necessary on a day-to-day basis to help move towards goals and dreams. That correction can be through messages from others, lessons or learning from daily occurrences and daily events. It can be from your own thoughts and emotions based upon the analysis of these events, or it can be from new self-exploration. Sometimes it can be through inspiration from leading personalities we see and meet.

WHAT I LEARNT FROM BOOKS: SEVEN FACTORS THAT NEED TO BE MONITORED

There are good books and great books on how to move towards and achieve goals and dreams, I follow that. And I found that there are some other factors too that need to be considered and monitored which make the way easier. There can be many things, but I conclude that following seven factors with wisdom can help to achieve goals and dreams quite easily and can help one live up to one' s full potential. They certainly helped me.

Factors that may need to be monitored on daily basis

1. Your sense of urgency compared to your full potential, as a percentage. Compare the priorities percentage you are working on with your full potential!

2. Compare the percentage of your dream level or vision level that you are working on now with what you are capable of working on!

3. Compare the percentage of your productive time now with your full potential!

4. Compare the percentage of your speed you are working at now with what you can work with!

5. What is the percentage of the true level of your relationship with friends, colleagues and behavior that can be with what it is now! (Words - purpose behind these words, one's Respect, Love and Gratitude behind these words matters.) It's often the relations which multiply our energy which make us perform many tasks at a time.

6. What is the percentage of your wisdom level you will bring to bear on whatever good or great things you do in your life!

For example:

a. The wisdom from worldly matters - hatred, jealousy, laziness, anger, greed.

b. The wisdom from emotional traps - unwanted biases for countries, religion, expectations, opinions.

c. The wisdom from mind traps - knowledge, ego, designations, powers, education, finance.

d. The wisdom from Time traps - past guilt, future worries.

7. And finally, all the important areas of your life you should be working on to lead a balanced life:

- relationships or socializing
- health
- education
- finance
- business
- career
- hobbies

We should be sure to do something every week or on a daily basis on these areas of life.

DID I GET BACK MY ENTIRE LOST WORLD?

I couldn't get back my entire lost world, but it seems I may recover most of my dreams. I may not be able to recover the biggest relationship that I lost, but that pain itself started taking the shape of a classical book I am writing on relationship. I may need some time to complete it.

The treatment in the company hurt me a lot, but that was the only event which reminded me of all my dreams I had as a teenager. Also, it helped rekindle my passion to do something great. That awareness and wake-up call may last till the end of my life.

That awareness will help me to try anything worthwhile that I really love. The event also helped me to form my own company, along with continuing a job for a reputable firm.

IF I COULD SHARE WITH YOU THE BOOKS THAT CHANGED MY LIFE

If I could share with you something of immense importance, then it will be the books listed below. I would love to recommend many more, but space doesn't permit for now. Get them. Read them. Love them. . . and live them!

Also please add some of your own ways and explorations to live your life at your full potential – the life you always dreamed of.

I will wait to hear your long stories!

Recommended readings:

1. *Magic of Thinking Big* - David Schwartz

2. *Maximum Achievement* - Brian Tracy

3. *Secret - The Power* - Ronda Byrne

4. *Albert Einstein* - Ronald Clark

5. *My Einstein* - John Brockman

6. *Network Of Thoughts* - J. Krishnamurti

7. *License To Live* - Priya Kumar

8. *The Power of Your Subconscious Mind* - Joseph Murphy

9. *Blink* - Malcolm Gladwell

10. *The Power of Believing* - Claude Bristol

11. *A Better Way to Live* - Og Mandino

12. *Emotional Intelligence* - Daniel Goleman

About Sonpal

Sonpal Rathod is an engineer and gratuated in mechanical engineering. He owns his own firm which deals in machinery business.

Sonpal helps people through his writings. He writes on core factors in a simple way with a logical mathematical and scientific base. He helps by taking people directly to the core problems and their solutions. He writes on various factors of life to uplift their emotions – including relationships and achiveing their dreams in their hobbies as well as in their businesses.

He started his writing with poetry, lyrics and articles as a teenager, and later progressed to writing on self-help, emotions and relationships in recent years.

Sonpal is very compassionate writer, and his writings go straight to the heart. He has shared the stage with Brian Tracy, Nick Nanton and other similar celebrities. He co-authored the book *Beat The Curve* with Brian Tracy.

Sonpal is writing lyrics for an upcoming Indian fllm, and soon you will see him with lyrics and videos with International songs on online world and music sites. You will also see his landmark book on emotions and relationships soon.

You can connect with Sonpal at:
Sonpal@wordsareworldandbeyond.com

CHAPTER 36

WINNING WITH POSITIVE CHANGE

BY RALPH MASENGILL

Want to be very successful? Here is a simple secret few take advantage of in their personal or business life. You will be a true winner only if you are:

1. Willing to take a calculated risk and endorse positive change on a regular basis.

2. Learning how change affects our emotions and our feelings.

Let's take a short journey together.

What we are talking about is understanding the risk of change. Why is it so important that we know about and understand change? We humans, and there are no exceptions, are constantly involved in change. Change never stops. It is always constantly going on in us and around us. The truly successful men and women of the world have a good understanding of change and how you can manipulate change to your advantage. You cannot stop it, but you can control most change.

Are you in a personal or business rut? In a rut, you have no control where that rut will take you. You have lost your freedom to act. To not change is to lose control of your future. To be in a rut is losing your freedom to control your life, business or both. Laurence J. Peter states that, "A rut is a grave with the ends knocked out." He is talking about life without understanding the importance of the effects that change has on all humans.

Mark Twain put it his way, "Twenty years from now you will be more disappointed by the things you didn't do than by the ones you did do. So, throw off the bowlines. Sail away from the safe harbor." Many good people refuse to accept the risk and uncertainty that change always brings with it. They stay in a self-imposed rut. They force themselves to live in a stagnant prison of their own making. They have part of it right. There can be some security in a prison. I would name that prison Opportunity Lost. When it comes to change we really only have two choices. One is to embrace change with gusto. The second is to stay in a rut by refusing to admit that all change is constant, live in denial and because you made a bad choice, end up losing your freedom to act. The solution is to simply agree to devote time and effort to understanding change and how it makes us feel.

Someone said, "Life isn't about how to survive the storm, but how to dance in the rain." I believe the happiest and most successful people do not necessarily have the best of everything; they just make the best of everything they have. Choose Change. It is the path to true happiness and business success.

You and I are always undergoing continuous change intended or not. The exciting truth is the more we know about change, both positive and negative, the more we can profit from change. If you want a more enjoyable and profitable personal and business life, you must have a solid understanding of what change is and how it makes us and the people we deal with feel. In other words, understanding change and how it makes all people feel will put you in a winning position in your life and your business.

If that is true and it is, what is change and how does it affect all of us on a continuous basis? After 40 years of study and research here is my definition of change:

> *All men and women regard all change both good and bad change with a feeling of loss (examples would be remorse or that pit of the stomach feeling), and that feeling of loss always creates some form of anger, anxiety or fear.*

Understanding how change works can change your life for the better and give you a solid advantage. That is a guarantee. Here are some amazing facts about continuous change.

1. Most of us will not change until the pain of not changing is greater than the pain of changing.

2. You and I often prefer the security of known misery, to the supposed misery of unfamiliar insecurity.

3. Change is consistent, intended or not.

Number one on the list above was true for me in a big way. Until I learned how to handle continuous change and the <u>feelings</u> that change had on my personality, nothing seemed to get better. I seemed to be stuck in a continuous rut. Understanding continuous change turned my humdrum life around. Understanding change is not hard, but you must work at it on a regular basis. Understanding change can be the one thing that can put you in the winner's circle often. It did just that for me.

What do others say about change?

- "They always say time changes things, but you actually have to change them yourself." ~ Andy Warhol

- "Only I can change my life. No one can do it for me." ~ Carol Burnett

- "Change your thoughts and you change your world." ~ Norman Vincent Peale

- "Nothing endures but change." ~ Heraclitus (540BC - 480BC)

- "Nobody can go back and start a new beginning, but anyone can start today and make a new ending if you are willing to change." ~ Maria Robinson

On the Oprah Winfrey Show, I heard an interview where Oprah was sharing with a guest about a dream she had where the children in her dream were asking her, "What can you teach me?" She said what she learned from that was, to look at every event in her life from that perspective. Then I realized as she was sharing, that is exactly what has made the difference in my own life in dealing with <u>change</u>. Now I welcome it knowing it leads to a greater understanding of my purpose on this planet. Dealing with both positive and negative change is a learning process that allows you and I to know what kind of emotions (feelings) continuous change will cause.

No one really likes dealing with change, no one. However, we all like the results of positive change. We are never in pain because of change, only our *resistance* to change can cause us pain. Once you stop resisting what happens in your life and accept it, the sooner you have the opportunity to feel less stress and set your business and your life up for even more success. For me it was one of those amazing "ah-ha" moments where you are never the same after that. To truly be successful in any undertaking you must embrace positive change and the pain that resistance brings willingly and often.

We all take risk every day when we embrace positive change. Do we take a calculated risk or do we sometimes just roll the dice and just hope for the best? The former is not acting on opportunity; it is acting out of ignorance. I admit that in my younger days, I did more rolling of the dice than I want to talk about and I had to pay the price. I paid the price by losing time, money and happiness many times out of my own ignorance about change. One time I almost lost my business. All of us can and should learn from our mistakes. Mistakes can be a teacher. However, it is a very expensive and painful way to learn.

Charles Tremper puts it this way: "The first step in the calculated risk process is to acknowledge the reality of the risk. Denial is a common tactic that substitutes deliberate ignorance for thoughtful planning." Executing a plan will involve change. Being willing to change is always a calculated risk that should be encouraged. For one thing it is where most business and personal success comes from in today's world.

Many successful people have something to say about risk taking. Winston Churchill said, "There is nothing wrong with change, if it is in the right direction." Author and lecturer Earl Nightingale stated, "You can measure opportunity with the same yardstick that measures the risk involved. They go together." I believe it is clear that all positive change requires calculated risk taking. Do your homework and success can be yours.

Is the opposite of risk, security? Some say it is. I believe those people are in error. Here is what Helen Keller had to say about security: "Security is mostly a superstition. It does not exist in nature, nor do the children of men as a whole experience it. Avoiding danger is no safer in the long run than outright exposure. Life is either a daring adventure on nothing." Former President Eisenhower said, "One can find outright security only in a prison. In order to be absolutely secure, you must give up your individual freedoms." Dennis Waitley in one of this lectures said, "Life is inherently risky. To become the success you want to be, there is only one big risk you should avoid at all cost. That is the risk of doing nothing." I personally believe total security is a myth. Understanding how change makes all of us feel makes the task less stressful and more fulfilling.

Without calculated risk and positive change, there would be no United States of America and no free enterprise system. Our free enterprise system is based on planned change that requires risk that then creates an opportunity that can lead to a solid reward. Risk and change are things we should get up with gladly every morning. In order to succeed beyond even our most daring dreams we must be willing to accept calculated risk and change as a way of life.

Imagine two ships going in opposite directions. One is going north and the other is going south. However the wind is blowing east. This can happen because of the set of the sails. The Captain of each vessel has control of how the sails are set. It is always our choice which way we go because we have control of the set of the sails on our ship. It is never necessary to follow the wind. By setting the sails correctly we can choose our direction. We have control.

First make sure you know how the market "winds" are blowing and then and only then set your business "sails" accordingly using positive change and taking the calculated risk that is always part of the package. Do that correctly and you can, with assurance, reach your destination of enhanced sales and profit and/or a better life. You can then taste sweet success.

The first step is to know the direction of the market "winds." Get this wrong and all your other efforts do not matter. Over the years I have been amazed how little time and money many spend on effective market research. Hunches do have their place in the business "sea", but this first step is not one of them. Solid accurate market research is the capstone of any good business arch. You must react to the market. You must change in order to win. Get the market "winds" right and make the correct changes and you will take home the profit trophy.

317

Change is something you must do on a regular basis if you want to be successful in life or business. Resistance to change has always been a part of the human psyche. We must work hard not to resist positive change even though it is not our nature. The solution is simple but not easy. Learn all you can about change and how it makes us all feel and be willing to take a calculated risk. Knowing what to expect when you need to change will help you be all that you want be in this world. Work hard to see positive change as a friend and do not resist this widely misunderstood process. Positive change is just that, a positive. Embrace it and you have a great opportunity to succeed in your personal and business life above your present goals and dreams. Understanding change is well worth the effort required.

About Ralph

Ralph Masengill is an advisor, coach, marketing expert, business consultant and public relations strategist. Many words could be used to describe Ralph Masengill, but he prefers to be called "friend," a title he fully expects to earn.

Ralph is one of the original change agents in the United States. Before the quality movement came into vogue, he and his associates were presenting seminars and papers to senior management across the nation pointing out that until a business, a team, or a person is willing to understand and submit to positive change, effective quality improvement and substantial profit enhancement were not probable. Masengill and his Associates have always worked from the industry or business side of marketing. Masengill has also worked closely with numerous colleges and universities, helping them satisfy their special needs, and he is considered an expert at improving communication between the private "for-profit" sector and academia.

He believes every company has a personality dictated by the personalities of those in charge, and every company should be marketed based on that personality. Only a well-planned, individualized public relations and communications strategy that truly reflects the objectives, needs, and personality of the company and its leaders will be successful in the long run. Anything less is smoke and mirrors, not cost effective, and in most cases is detrimental to the organization and its leaders. The key is to tell the truth very well about the leader and the company he or she leads.

As an entrepreneur, Ralph has the business expertise, knowledge and marketing background to understand how companies work from within. He has the wisdom of one who has made the journey of sustained success himself. And he has an ethics-based philosophy of helping others and the community around him. In short, Ralph is a man whose experience, skills and vision can help anyone develop a longevity-focused program for continued success that allows the leader to more fully enjoy his or her leadership position.

Ralph's life story is one of personal challenge, tragedy, and triumph. His professional career has been defined by great success in both the private and public sectors. He brings to the table forty-plus years of professional business experience. His company Masengill Marketing Associates, has won over 850 national and regional advertising and marketing awards.

He is a dedicated leader who truly enjoys working with people. He is easy to get to know and an excellent listener. Ralph does not understand second place, and he is all about getting clients what they want, when they want it. He will do everything possible to make sure you obtain your goals, and he will make and offer many suggestions that can make reaching your vision a reality.

Ralph and his wife Dianne live near the Great Smoky Mountains in East Tennessee. They have four grown children, two dogs and two cats. Ralph enjoys woodworking, sailing and working with his favorite charities.

CHAPTER 37

FINANCIAL FREEDOM – GUARANTEE YOURSELF A PAYCHECK FOR LIFE

BY RODNEY JONES

Financial freedom is the freedom to make financial decisions for ourselves and our families. With our government eroding our rights and freedoms and exercising more control over our financial lives through regulation, **now is the time to secure your financial future with a guaranteed paycheck for life**. With the recent collapse of financial economies such as Greece, Republic of Cyprus, and Puerto Rico, Americans need to pay attention. The financial instability of the United States' economy is concerning to many. We are experiencing unprecedented levels of debt in the United States. The government is printing money and saturating our economy, and thus weakening the US dollar worldwide. **The time to pay the piper has come and will have an effect on all Americans.**

I have already seen many people that are going to face the real likelihood of outliving their money. Can you imagine never worrying about how to pay your bills or the stress of whether you will outlive your money? By the end of this chapter you will have the tools you need to guarantee yourself a paycheck for your lifetime. You can go to bed at night knowing for certain that you have a guaranteed paycheck for life. I call this "sleep insurance."

Here is how lifetime paycheck works. When you decide to take a more efficient, more effective approach to your financial future, your money will have a parking place in a financial vehicle that gives you the following:

- Immediate Bonus
- 100% Guarantee on your account (you can never lose principal and interest and you keep control)
- Upside growth with no downside losses
- Tax-deferred growth
- Guaranteed paycheck for life that you control and decide when to turn on and off
- Tax-free income with the correct strategy
- No annual management or transactional fees
- Vehicle backed by A++ superior-rated carriers and all states have an Insurance Guaranty association to provide protection to consumers
- At death, your assets pass outside your probate estate
- No risk

Your account is immediately awarded a bonus, yes, a bonus from day one. This bonus ranges from a 4% to 10%. Let's say John moves $400,000 from his 401(k) at work into this "sleep insurance" and immediately his account is $440,000 (with a 10% Bonus). It's like this company just gave me $40,000, just for doing Business with them, Wait! This is not the good news. The good news is this: while John's $440,000 is participating in the market (from day one), as the market has gains, John's money increases and these gains or upside accounts are locked in each and every year. Locking in gains each year is a powerful tool for your money. It gets even better, when the market has a downside or loss, your account value will never go down, therefore you can never lose a dime, and this is guaranteed.

Wait, this is not the best news yet! The best news is the GIR, Guaranteed Income Rider. The GIR is a separate account that you have the option to add to your "sleep insurance" vehicle. This separate account usually has a fixed interest rate between 4% and 10% and grows each and every year until you decide to turn on your Guaranteed Paycheck that you cannot outlive. Notice you have control and decide when to turn your income stream on and off. It is also possible to design a strategy to provide a paycheck that will continue to go a spouse. What is the downside to this GIR? Depending on the fixed rate that you control and decide, a small fee of .05% to 1.5% will be deducted annually from your market account growth.

Let's look at a hypothetical example of how market risk plays out, versus "sleep insurance," a paycheck for your lifetime:

Larry has turned 65 and the market has been good these last ten years. Larry has accumulated $500,000, and is ready to retire. He feels he has a "balanced" portfolio (with 60% stocks, 40% bonds). Even though Larry has a social security benefit each month, he still needs to withdraw $25,000 from his nest egg to support his lifestyle. "Your lifestyle now is directly proportionate to your future lifestyle."

He must also increase his withdrawal each year by 3% to adjust for inflation. In 20 years, the market has 15 upside years and only 5 downside years with an average return of 8.03% during this period. The problem with this is the market does not credit average returns. The market credits actual returns. (This is exactly what happened between 1993-2013.) In this scenario, Larry will be completely out of money at age 83.[1]

The impact of a downturn market can be devastating to your net worth and even more devastating to your future retirement. Market volatility places your money under a tremendous amount of risk each day.

Now let's look at Amy, who saved the same amount as Larry. Amy is turning 65 and is ready to retire. She also has $500,000. She, like Larry, will need $25,000 of income each year for her lifestyle and will be adjusted for inflation.

Amy turns on her "Guaranteed Paycheck for Life" and will receive a guaranteed paycheck in the amount of $38,955.87 each year for the rest of her life.

What happens upon Amy's death? Depending on her selection prior to receiving payments, Amy's beneficiary would receive the remaining balance in her market account, which includes the original principle amount plus all upside (no downside) plus her bonus, minus any payments received. Other available options are to continue the income stream for a loved one or a lump sum payout to a favorite charity.

1. Robbins, Tony; *Money Master the Game.* Simon & Schuster copyright 2014. Pages 410-413.

As you can see, Amy has a much better retirement experience than Larry. This "sleep insurance" with a "Paycheck for Life" rider provides safety, long-term growth, and is guaranteed to protect your retirement nest egg. Eliminating your risk and ensuring that you will not lose money while still experiencing the market gains, provides you with a secure, "worry-free" and happy retirement.

With more than 10,000 Baby Boomers retiring daily and with Americans living longer, this longevity often erodes their sources of income. Economic trends and shifts also add to their financial challenges and increase the risk of retirees running out of income. You can take action to guarantee yourself and your loved ones that you will not outlive your money. You must have a strategy for turning your hard-earned dollars into income that you cannot outlive.

You worked hard for your money, I will work hard to protect it.

~ Rodney Jones

About Rodney

Rodney Jones is a man of faith. Rodney helps his clients to see and achieve their financial goals. He was brought up in a blue collar manufacturing culture where the norm was to graduate from high school and work at the foundry like past generations, but Rodney had greater ambitions. Rodney attended Southern Illinois University and Butler University. In 1990, Rodney earned his designation of Life Underwriter's Training Council and began educating clients and professionals on insurance and finances.

Rodney owns two business entities, RL Jones Insurance Group and RL Jones Financial Group. Both of his successful businesses are centered on the philosophy – "If you have the desire to protect and grow your assets, then I have the desire to show you how."

Rodney has helped several hundred clients to protect their assets and reach their financial goals. Rodney's clientele ranges from executives and small business owners to laborers and their families.

Rodney is a highly sought after speaker and trainer. He was selected as one of America's PremierExperts® and has been on several media outlets including highlighted appearances on ABC, NBC, CBS, and FOX affiliates. He has also been selected to participate on several Advisory Boards of Fortune 500 companies. Rodney became a "best-selling author" in his book *Uncommon*. Rodney balances his time between his clients and educating professionals in his field. Rodney and his wife Amy have four children, and reside in Westfield, Indiana.

You can connect with Rodney as follows:
Via email: rjones@gordonmarketing.com
Via phone at: 317-626-4902 or 1-800-388-8342 Ext.302.
Or visit his website at: www.RLJonesFinancial.com

CHAPTER 38

FRUSTRATION PARENTING

BY LOUIS CERVANTEZ

Frustration: the feeling of anger or annoyance, caused by being unable to do something.

~ Merriam-Webster Dictionary

I could add a few more "colorful metaphors," but my wife whom I will henceforth call "Critter" would get mad at me. (OK, I know you are wondering: On our second date we collected bugs for her biology class – she did not like to be called "Bugs" so I came up with my "Critter" and it stuck. I think it is more endearing than: "my wife.")

Critter and I were almost through getting our daughter through high school. She was a "piece of cake" to raise. My most fond memory in terms of frustration was getting her to clean her room. She was in the second grade? Anyway, after trying different actions, I told her that if she did not clean her room I would clean it for her. I did clean it for her. Things of value I put in our room, toys and stuff on the floor went into the trash. We never, ever had to tell her again! Like her mom, she is a Type A personality, especially in sports and when young, was not afraid of anything. She put a lot of boys to shame. Like I said earlier, "piece of cake"!

Before I go any further I want to set the stage. Critter and I are "Go Getters". She is very much a Type A personality. Always coming up with ideas, which she expects me to implement. I like to evaluate based on my "vast experience," we both like to move now, multitask, get it done now, and we have two businesses. And then came our son!

The purpose of this chapter is not to give you the one magic formula that will transform your challenge child. Nor is it a "How to" chapter. Rather, it is a journal of the adventure of Critter and myself through time, with a trying child that fits the definition with which I started this chapter to the "proverbial" T. (Does anybody really know what that means?) We formally adopted our son on November 18, 2005. Before that, we started with Classes, then Evaluation Torture, then Foster Parent Licensing, then Foster Parenting . . . while being evaluated for parenting! Would that all parents go through this first! Don't get mad, stay with me. That is my only editorialization. . . promise.

It just so happened that our son went to kindergarten at the same school we sent our daughter. We heard from teachers and staff about his "wild as a March Hare" stories. (Their cliché not mine.) Because I have this vast experience I mentioned earlier, I sought and obtained all of the information about his background, State records, everything. We started foster parenting when he was around 4 years, maybe 5 years old. When we got his birth certificate that said he was born to my wife (she does not recall), I tell her that I told the doctors to give her an extra dose of the Epidural . . . he was 6 years of age. Being the thorough guy I am, I started a "log" or "journal" for no other reason than to show the state when they did their monthly/ quarterly visits that we were on top of things and in compliance. After the visits stopped, I kept on going on with the journal/log. In retrospect, I should have started when we first "foster parented." Oh well.

The first year was hard. As I reviewed my log for this chapter I could tell the good years and hard years just by the number of pages in the log for each year. I also kept a "Bankers Box" with a file for all of the activities and actions that occurred during each school year. They corresponded nicely with my log! Imagine that. Ah! . . . you ask, "Why was it so hard?" Well, because he had been used to being here today and somewhere else next week in Child Protective Services, it was actually hard for him to adjust to stability. I counted 25 negative actions that he did from not listening/obeying to emotional bursts that first year.

So, like any normal parents we took him to a psychiatrist, and put him on medication. In addition, I took him for an annual physical every year having stopped the last three years. In case you noticed, I keep saying "I". Critter has been by far the more instrumental, but because of our one business, which is more of a job, she can't just leave because of her patients. I had more mobility and I did the running around. It is much better with two. She softens things up when I blow! Back to the story. Critter did not want a zombie (I did). I was super busy that year and having to put up with him in the middle of the night was not fun especially given that I was up in the middle of the night working. I, again being the meticulous guy I am (have you noticed I haven't used 'father' yet?), read a lot of books, and the Internet (which was not as comprehensive as it is now). I called all sorts of mental health care personnel; they of course, wanted us to take him in.

With psychiatric counseling and low-impact meds and supplements, he had a good 2nd Grade. I did not and chose not to list his bad actions, there were also some good actions; rather, I looked at that year's file and the number of pages in my journal and decided it was a good year. 3rd Grade was a hard year. Some 20 different negative actions, and to be fair, there were some good things. One of which was a quote from the log "he likes to help his dad" . . . (there, it only took three years to start becoming a "dad". (I feel a cliché coming . . . "better late than never!") We added counseling with a psychiatrist and a psychologist who suggested some steps to take. . . from talking in parables to rewards. Ha, my dad never rewarded me! He just grunted. But I could tell from his eyes that he was proud of me. Our son does not even look straight at you, more like straight through you. On or around this time (sounds like an attorney), we took in what I shall refer to as a Nanny.

Two sisters from Georgia went to the same church as we did and one eventually died from cancer. To help the second sister, we took her in as part of the family and all she had to do was pick up our son and have dinner ready! And a few other things. She was mainly our son's tape recorder. Our son was always talking, talking to her. I remember the first psychiatrist telling me that we would never stop that talking all the time. I thought at the time: "Yeah right, you don't know my tenacity!" . . . the Psychiatrist was right. His next year in school was good. Imagine that. How do I know? Nanny and (you got it) my log and files. But as things go, she missed her family in Georgia and got pressure from them to go back. No other real family members here. And the car I bought her conked out. . . not repairable. She did not want to be a burden to us and her family beckoned, so she returned to Georgia. (Second to last cliché: The Lord/Universe works in mysterious ways. . .) I believe she helped our son a lot.

Since 5th Grade, our son has had a lot of difficulty. He stopped his medication for he was made fun of. "You are acting funny better take your meds." He hates that and I can't blame him. It seemed we were now entering into a new phase. In Nevada, the 6th Grade is considered middle school. I believe he had a hard time adjusting to the more demanding school rigors. How could I tell? You got it...the log. By now the frustration level for me is at "critical" point. Critter took the brunt of one year having to work all day then invest all evening until 11:00 p.m. helping him with his homework. Rather interesting was that despite her efforts organizing his work, getting it done, having a special green folder to put in his completed work, he did not turn it in!

So in conjunction with the school, we came up with "Tutoring." This helped for a while, but it started to annoy our son and the tutor got frustrated. Better him than me. Bad, Bad Me. . . though it does remind me of a joke, "don't try to teach a pig how to sing, it annoys the pig and frustrates you!" (There is that frustration thing again.) But it seemed that it helped a little because as I observed incognito, it gave our son an audience and he talked and talked and talked and did some homework. Enough so that he could pass. . . with really low grades. So, in despair, we added more severe punishment. No electronics, we even took the door off his room entryway and used corporal punishment on an 8th grader! In Nevada corporal punishment is allowed as long as the child is not harmed. It initially got his attention, but did not change his behavior. We rarely used it after that. We added outside resources such as Math and Reading classes, etc. No Change.

So you ask, what can I take away from this story? I am glad you asked, but first there is a song I heard some time ago. . . "doom, despair, anxiety on me, deep dark depression, excessive misery, if it weren't for bad luck I'd have no luck at all." The reality is that this song does not apply. I just threw it in to make you think I was going over the edge! (Because of frustration.)

The first point I want to make is that you keep a log or journal. One need not write in it every day. My routine was twofold:

A. I wrote up notes for the psychiatrist or psychologist. Big difference in approach. Only a psychiatrist can write out prescriptions. It was important that he, my Critter and I were on the same page.

B. A psychologist is more into listening, asking as opposed to probing. Looking for a crack. Neither of them found it. But we had to try.

Another point is that you can look back in the log and maybe something that did not work two years ago will now work. And who knows maybe an action I described may be of benefit in your situation. I included around 18 ideas in the story.

Secondly, Read-up! If you are not a reader, get a CD or download info and listen up. Learn as much as you can about what challenges your family member. Even though it may not change a thing you will feel better for it. I think there is a Buddhist saying (I ask forgiveness if I got it wrong): "shoveling, shoveling, shoveling ENLIGHTENMENT, shoveling, shoveling, shoveling." I have read close to 32 books, numerous articles and numerous audio/visual downloads and I still get frustrated . . . and our son's behavior has not changed too much either, although I must say some good stuff is starting to come out of him.

Thirdly, you say: "So if nothing works (well...some things do work) why go to all of this effort?" Because as Winston Churchill once said during a talk in the U.S., during World War II, to a group of University Students, "Never, Never, Never Give Up."

I started out defining frustration as anger and annoyance. At one point I mentioned that I walked away and just let my Critter handle it. (I was a wuss.)

I wrote this chapter so you may know these two opinions:

1. In reading, I discovered that the brain continuously works at trying to get the right and left brain to talk. I believe that is one of my son's challenges. The brain will continue to do so. The study was based on young soldiers returning from war with brain injuries. This connecting action will continue until an average age of 25. He is 15. I believe he will do it! Thus we have another partner!

2. My frustration level has gone down A LOT. Why you ask? Because I have gone through and am going through this challenge, armed with knowledge and history, thus I do not fear it! Critter and I are comfortable knowing that if something doesn't work we can change it. We still get frustrated, but (last cliché) . . . "we keep on keeping on."

About Louis

Louis Cervantez graduated from Utah State University and acquired his Post-Baccalaureate from Oregon State University. He acquired customer and sales skills as an Assistant Vice President and Manager for a bank in Salt Lake City, Utah.

Despite a car accident by a drugged driver, Louis persevered in trying to recover and as time has marched on, the neck and spine have progressively gotten worse. Through his faith and education on the challenge he has worked with the doctors to control and manage the increased pain and functionality.

In Las Vegas, Nevada, Louis and his wife have two businesses. Advanced Sonography Inc. provides Ultrasound Sonographers to Physicians. This allows the physician to see more patients and lessens the physician's overhead by not having to pay for expensive Sonographers, especially if they do not have a lot of Ultrasounds done.

The second business, "Oh Baby Baby" is for entertainment purposes only – "4-D Ultrasound" – and newborn-to-toddler attire boutique at a Mall in Henderson, Nevada. Expectant mothers and families can enjoy "a womb with a view," through an 80-inch monitor. The Ultrasound room is set up like a family living room. Mother-to-be and father and sometimes-whole families including grandparents, uncles, aunts and cousins come to see the baby. The primary question asked. . . what is it? Boy or girl? Others are in the hopper!

Louis has enjoyed politics and Public Speaking and has given a few campaign speeches. He also has a love for law, saying it is sometimes easier to remember statutes as opposed to birthdays. His strong points: Leadership and developing businesses.

Louis can be contacted at:
louiscervantez@gmail.com
www.facebook.com/louiscervantez
LinkedIn:www.linkedin.com/pub/cervantez-louis-a/4b/741/92a